The Salt Companion to Geraldine Mo:

SCOTT THURSTON lectures in English Literature a... ...
University of Salford. He has published articles on linguistically innovative
poetry and interviews with the poets Allen Fisher, Adrian Clarke, John
Wilkinson, Maggie O'Sullivan, Ulli Freer and Ira Lightman. As a poet his most
recent book is *Hold: Poems 1994–2004* (Shearsman, 2006). He edits *The Radiator,*
a little magazine of poetry and poetics.

The Salt Companion to Geraldine Monk

Edited by

SCOTT THURSTON

SALT

CAMBRIDGE

PUBLISHED BY SALT PUBLISHING

PO Box 937, Great Wilbraham PDO, Cambridge CB1 5JX United Kingdom

First published JULY 2007

Printed and bound in the United Kingdom by Lightning Source

Typeset in Swift 10/12

ISBN 978 1 876857 74 5 paperback

Salt Publishing Ltd gratefully acknowledges
the financial assistance of Arts Council England

1 3 5 7 9 8 6 4 2

for
Jeff Nuttall
(1933–2004)

Contents

Foreword

Geraldine Monk is not the type of poet who waits for inspiration. The moment of insight doesn't visit her at its own speed. She is not a talent, like Larkin or Hamilton, from whom we breathlessly await our two or three poems a year.

Rather does she work as artists commonly do in other media. As a painter goes to his studio and puts out his colours, as a saxophonist goes to his rehearsal room and works on his phrasing, so Monk goes to work on her words every day, allows one cluster to set in motion a whole sequence, summoning up gags, puns and sonic felicities to spin her off into the next. Inspiration for her is continuous because her inspiration is the practice of composition itself, an activity in which, through all pitfalls, trajectories, catastrophes and famines of one woman's day-to-day life, she is utterly riveted and professionally dedicated. As a priest devotes himself to his ceremonies, so Monk devotes herself to her words. It's what she does, come what may. Tennyson had the same work pattern, believing that if he was to be honoured with the title laureate he ought not to be idle. Similarly Ken Smith wrote for his statutory daily number of hours whilst Gregory Fellow at Leeds.

Reactionary opinion would possibly say that this was a kind of doodling, a disrespectful demotion of the muse from angel to pastrycook. There is certainly a strong thread of the artisan about the way of working.

The importance, as with so much work over the last century, lies more in the work itself than in what the work is about. The painting is important, not the scene it depicts. Monk's poetry is important, not any great rueful truth she may have to reveal about the mystery or history of life.

Monk's work is panoramic. Each day becomes a landscape marked out in short lines, continuous paragraphs, staccato image-chains

situated across the page as the stuff that feeds them is spaced, spattered
or repeated across the day, one incident cutting in on another, as an
assonance, a pun or suggestion tips us into what follows.

Monk loves puns. Try these. Back and forth from disillusioned Labour
to patriotism in

> Some union Jack. Some bloody union. Remember Jack.
> Flying flags. Pigs might. Flies might.
> No Jack. Not pickets.

From onomatopoeic cricket to relentless time in

> Image and out.
> Clock.
> Tock.
> Cuckoo.

Look at the titles. *Noctivagations*. Vaginal night voyages. Puns seem to be
the way she hits the ignition. The lines thus detonated are the work of a
highly sensitised rhythmic sense. They recall the riffs and rim shots of
great drummers but they are not left as they spontaneously occur.
Anyone who could believe this isn't really listening. They are worked,
tailored, trimmed and polished for maximum effect in performance.

Because she works in a workshop manner Monk works with other
artists. She has written for radio ('Manufractured Moon') and changed
her rhythm so that it sounds like wireless. She has written work put
together as though it were fiction ('Short Sorties'), performed in varied
venues with painters ('Fluvium') and musicians ('Songings'). Her work is
objective and crafted.

Monk had a lot of time for the great Bob Cobbing in most of whose
work the meanings of the words are totally irrelevant. The words are
sounds and the work is music as much as it is literature. Monk is not so
abstract. In her panoramas her clusters feed, as we have seen, from inci-
dents, accidents, half-memories of meals, menu items, timetables, cata-
logues, heartbreaks, a love-life as headlong and bashed-about as
anybody's, eavesdropped dialogue (great snippet from a New York
restaurant), even the ads on passing busses. In the midst of this, from
the city's railway bridges, she catches the pulse of Manchester: 'B.eating.
B.eating. B.eating . . . ' She shares this kind of spaced detail with Maggie
O'Sullivan, Bill Griffiths and other contemporaries.

However, she has ongoing themes that sometimes give her a more coherent content. Monk is concerned with places. Her travelogue is political and informed. In Toledo 'Duende's all the raging' recalls Lorca on flamenco. In Prague she recalls St Vitus and St Agnes. Flying she recalls Davis in *All About Eve*: '"Fasten your seat belts", says Bette.' In the film she continues 'We're in for a bumpy ride.'

But as a Lancastrian, Geraldine Monk does for Greater Manchester what MacSweeney did for Northumberland and Sinclair for East London. Sometimes she is explicit as in her commissioned poem about Manchester and her oblique homage to her father called 'Imagining a Walk Round the Grounds of Church and Oswaldtwistle Cricket Club One Fine Evening in Autumn.'

Sometimes her perceptive hostility to metropolitan attitudes expresses graphically the Lancastrian identity which is always evident when she reads in her rich local vowels. Neither masked nor affected, her tongue gives her performed writing the confirming authenticity great blues singers enjoy through their pronunciation. This is nourishing brain-food.

JEFF NUTTALL, July 2003

Notes on Contributors

David Annwn's latest collection of poetry is entitled *Bella Fawr's Cabaret*. His work 'tabula gratuloria' is to appear with Thomas Ingmire's calligraphy in the San Francisco Harrison Collection.

Sean Bonney was born in Brighton, grew up in the north of England and now lives in London. He has had poetry published in many magazines, including *Quid*, *The Gig* and *The Paper*. His full length productions include *Notes on Heresy* (Writers Forum, 2002), *Poisons, their antidotes* (West House, 2003) and *Blade Pitch Control Unit* (Salt, 2005). A part-time lecturer, he has taught at Birkbeck College, Roehampton, and the University of Southampton.

Chris Goode was for three years the artistic director of Camden People's Theatre, where he curated two editions of the poetry festival Total Writing London. He now works as a freelance theatre maker and writer. As a poet he has published three chapbooks with Barque, most recently *No Son House* (Barque, 2004). He lives in north London with an imperious cat and three experimental musicians.

Bill Griffiths was born in Middlesex in 1948. Not a bad time, he considers, for if the 1950s were a bit static, the 1960s brought an outburst in popular culture: music, football, bikes, pop festivals, that made it an exciting time to be growing up. By 1972, his first poems were published in *Poetry Review* under the editorship of Eric Mottram, and subsequent booklets were published in conjunction with Bob Cobbing's Writers Forum. Over the last decade he has moved gradually from little press booklets to paperback—with most recently *The Mud Fort* (Salt, 2005), collecting his short poems from 1986 on. Other interests include Old English, the piano, North-East dialect (he is currently Visiting Fellow at the Centre for Northern Studies, Northumbria University) and website design. Visit www.billygriff.co.uk

Elizabeth James is a poet and librarian with a research interest in book history. She lives in London and works at the Victoria and Albert Museum in the Word & Image Department. Poetry publications include: *Base to Carry*

(Barque Press, 2004) *Recognition* (Writers Forum, 1999) Two Renga, in *RENGA+* [Collaboration with Peter Manson] (Reality Street, 2002) and *Neither the One nor the Other* [Collaboration with Frances Presley] (Form Books, 1999). Other publications include: 'Poetry and Experimental Typography' [compiler and main author], in James Bettley, ed., *The Art of the Book* (V&A Publications, 2001).

Christine Kennedy is a Sheffield-based artist and writer. Her publications include *Possessions* and a new limited edition of *Twelve Entries from the Encyclopaedia of Natural Sexual Relations* (both The Cherry On The Top Press, 2003). She was a contributor to *RENGA+* (Reality Street, 2002).

David Kennedy lives and writes in Sheffield. His books include *The President of Earth: New & Selected Poems* (Salt, 2002) and *The Roads* (Salt, 2004). Newer works, in collaboration with Christine Kennedy, can be seen at the 'LitTeR' http://www.leafepress.com/litter/ and Ahadada websites. A book on elegy is forthcoming from Routledge.

Geraldine Monk was born in Blackburn, Lancashire in 1952. Via a variety of routes and circumstances she came to Sheffield, South Yorkshire in 1984. She has lived there ever since.

Jeff Nuttall was born in Clitheroe, Lancashire, in 1933 and grew up in Herefordshire. He trained as a painter in the years following the Second World War and began writing poetry in 1962. He published widely with Writers' Forum, Turret Press, Unicorn Press, Fulcrum, Trigram, Pirate Press, Rivelin and Penguin (Modern Poets No. 12). He taught fine art in schools and polytechnics, acted in film and television and was best known for his remarkable book *Bomb Culture* (1968) which formed a manifesto for the internationalist revolutionary counter-culture of the cold war generation. His *Selected Poems* was published by Salt in 2003. He lived in Crickhowell, Wales and died in 2004.

Frances Presley was born in 1952 in Derbyshire, and now lives in London and Somerset. She is a free-lance author and also works at the Poetry Library. She studied modern literature, writing dissertations on Ezra Pound and Guillaume Apollinaire, as well as the contemporary French poet, Yves Bonnefoy. Publications of poems and prose include *The Sex of Art* (North and South, 1988), *Hula Hoop* (Other Press, 1993), *Linocut* (Oasis, 1997); and *Private writings: a Vermont journal* (Maquette, 1998) with drawings by Peterjon Skelt. She has collaborated with the artist Irma Irsara, on a multi-media performance about clothing and the fashion trade, *Automatic Cross Stitch*, (Other Press, 2000); and with the poet Elizabeth James on an email text and performance, *Neither the One nor the Other* (Form Books, 1999). *Somerset Letters* (Oasis, 2002), with drawings by Ian Robinson, explores community and landscape, through a dialogue with other women poets. *Paravane: new and selected poems, 1996–2003* was published by Salt in 2004: the title sequence is a response to 9/11/2001. *Myne: New and Selected Poems and Prose, 1976–2006*, was published by Shearsman in May 2006. She has written various reviews and essays and is on the editorial board of the experimental poetry journal *How2*.

Harriet Tarlo teaches Creative Writing at the University of Leeds. She has published essays on modernist and contemporary British and American poets, including Basil Bunting, H.D., Lorine Niedecker and Rachel Blau DuPlessis. Her poetry appears in little magazines and anthologies such as *FOIL* (Etruscan Books). Her recent books include *NAB* (Etruscan Books, 2005), *Poems 1990–2003* (Shearsman, 2004) and *Love/Land* (REM Press, 2003) and she is currently working on an academic book on contemporary British radical landscape poetry.

Scott Thurston lectures in English Literature and Creative Writing at the University of Salford. He has published articles on linguistically innovative poetry and interviews with the poets Allen Fisher, Adrian Clarke, John Wilkinson, Maggie O'Sullivan, Ulli Freer and Ira Lightman. As a poet his most recent book is *Hold: Poems 1994–2004* (Shearsman, 2006). He edits *The Radiator,* a little magazine of poetry and poetics.

Introduction

Geraldine Monk is one of the most exciting and consistently engaging poets writing in Britain today. Since her first books appeared in the late 1970s she has produced an extraordinarily wide-ranging and innovative poetry with a strong underlying commitment to feminist and other political concerns. Monk has published almost exclusively throughout her career with small presses—including her own Siren Press and Gargoyle imprints as well as other presses run by poet-publishers, such as Bob Cobbing's Writers Forum press, or more recently Alan Halsey's West House Books. The publication of Monk's *Selected Poems* by Salt in 2003 collected a number of earlier works which were either out of print or very rare and gave rise to the possibility of this companion volume: the first critical book on Monk's poetry and designed to be read alongside the *Selected Poems*.

The diversity of Monk's concerns is reflected in the range of approaches and interests of the writers whose work is collected here. Virtually all of Monk's published output is discussed in this collection, with particular attention paid to the impact of her first books in the late seventies and early eighties, to the important long poem *Interregnum* (1994)—considered by many contributors to be amongst her finest work—and to her most recent publications at the time this volume was compiled. The complexity and scale of *Interregnum* itself has permitted three separate considerations which cover themes of difficulty and emotion; place, landscape, nature and women's relationship to nature, and the importance of history. Taken together, these three essays represent the fullest critical account yet of this key poem of the nineties. Other contributors deal with the necessity of reading Monk's work within the crucial contexts of women's writing in general, and of women's experimental writing in particular, whilst acknowledging the

craft, eeriness and political sharpness of her poetry. Further contribu-
tions examine the significance of Monk's practice for the development
of visuality in poetry and also the role of voice and performance in her
presentation of her work. Furthermore, it is a privilege to be able to
include in this volume a recent statement of poetics and accompanying
poem by Geraldine Monk herself which brilliantly illustrate a key theme
of her work: that poetry can be means of collaborating with the dead.

To introduce each contribution in turn, Bill Griffiths opens the
Companion with an account of the context and publication of Monk's
early work: the books *Long Wake* (1979), *Rotations* (1979), *La Quinta del
Sordo* (1980), *Banquet* (1980) and *Spreading the Cards* (1980). Griffiths knew
Monk personally during this time and assisted in the publication of *Long
Wake*. He offers a useful guide to the overall themes and devices of these
works: the memory and dream poems of *Long Wake* with their attendant
awareness of place, the responses to the harrowing work of Goya in *La
Quinta del Sordo*, the seasonal cycle explored in emotions of *Rotations*, the
sensual language explorations of *Banquet* and the wide-ranging explorations of language and event in *Spreading the Cards*. As Griffiths
suggests, this early work shows 'remarkable confidence in generating
subject matter from the immediate and personal'; a facility which is
still present in Monk's mature writing.

The trio of essays which take *Interregnum* as their main focus begins
with Christine Kennedy and David Kennedy's piece, which approaches
Monk's work from the perspective of 'difficulty.' This is a key concept
that has attended the critical reception of innovative poetry like Monk's,
often as a form of objection to such work's challenge to traditional
forms. The authors demonstrate the constructed nature of 'difficulty' as
it relates to innovative poetry but argue that if innovative poetry is
difficult, then it is to do with the kind of experiences that it explores
and the intensity with which it does so, rather than as a function of
purely formal devices. *Interregnum* takes as its focus the deaths of ten
men and women from Pendle, Lancashire accused of witchcraft and
hanged in Lancaster castle in 1612. The poem opens by exploring the
current life and rituals surrounding Pendle Hill before descending into
the maelstrom surrounding the trials within which Monk evokes the
voices of the dead accused. As the authors argue, the difficulty of this
text lies principally in the way in which Monk handles this dark material. She takes the reader fully into an engaged, imaginative reading
without the mediation of any quaint historical devices which might set
up a safe distance between the reader and the events. The emotional

intensity of the poem is thus pitched very high: dominated by the themes of oppression and resistance and how these conflicts are inscribed on the body. The authors therefore conclude that the 'difficulty' and challenge of Monk's poem lies in how it demands that the reader examine his or her own cultural prejudices and assumptions in the act of reading: a demand that can be heard elsewhere in Monk's oeuvre.

Harriet Tarlo focuses on the role of place, landscape and nature in *Interregnum*, making a link with the work of eco-critics such as Kate Soper and Patrick D. Murphy and eco-feminist Annette Kolodny in examining the way that Monk's work challenges simplistic ideologies and seeks a more integrated approach to understanding the relationships between the human and the non-human world. For Tarlo, reading *Interregnum* involves being pushed to consider our 'human investment in nature, how this sits with our sense of the sacred, and our cultural sense of ourselves, be it in terms of gender or nationality.' Tarlo examines these themes in Monk's early poetry before looking at how the first part of *Interregnum* dramatises the relationships between human and nature, human and animal, in the interactions between contemporary users of Pendle Hill. The notion of the patriarchal domination of nature is crucial here, as is the view that this is linked to the domination of women which is central to the main section of the book. Tarlo shows how Monk challenges patriarchal constructions of women's identities and sexuality and explores how women's identification with nature can become a force for liberation and expression. Tarlo concludes her essay by examining how the role of Jennet Device—the nine year old whose testimony at the witch trials was instrumental in the fate of her family—operates as a figure for the precarious and exploited position of the virgin girl in society.

Sean Bonney's account of *Interregnum* places Monk's work in a tradition of radical British writing which includes her contemporaries Maggie O'Sullivan, Barry MacSweeney and Bill Griffiths as well as earlier poets such as Basil Bunting, Gerard Manley Hopkins, William Blake and Abiezer Coppe. As Tarlo, Bonney is concerned with Monk's engagement with place, but takes a more historical perspective. He examines how the opening section of *Interregnum* deals with the present Pendle Hill as a tourist site on which various hill-walkers, day-trippers, Christians and Pagans converge in tension with the local inhabitants. 'Palimpsestus'—the second section of the poem—then acts as a bridge between the present and the past history of Pendle in making the link to the witch trials. Citing Kurt Selligman's argument that the revival of witchcraft in the middle ages was the response of the poor rural population to increasing oppression by Church and State authorities, Bonney reads Monk's portrayal of the witches' defiance of authority as key to the poem. In *Hidden Cities* (1995), Monk's alternative bus tour of Manchester, Bonney identifies Monk's poetic insistence that any reading of history has 'real and active consequences' on the nature of the present, signalled in this text's opposition to the official tourist version of Manchester's history. Bonney concludes therefore that Monk's concern with place is inextricable from her concern with history and that her poetry constitutes a political act in its aim to grasp the 'entirety of history in order to change the present, and the future.'

In a more thematically driven essay, David Annwn explores the history of the meaning of the Scots word *eerie*, inspired by how Monk's poetry often involves 'doubles, mirrors, shadows and guardian spirits.' A key sense is of a state of consciousness aware of 'prevalent mysterious powers', which Annwn, with reference to the French writers associated with *l'ecriture féminine*: Hélène Cixous and Julia Kristeva, contrasts with Freud's *unheimliche*: arguing for the latter as a more static conceptualisation of this kind of awareness. Whilst acknowledging the role of clairvoyance and other related psychic activity in the history of women's writing, Annwn carefully qualifies the risks of designating Monk's poetry as eerie, since it plays into the hands of a common critical trope in regard not only to Monk's work, but also to that of poets such as Maggie O'Sullivan, whereby women's writing becomes othered as an exotic, otherworldly, intuitive practice: a move often tantamount to undermining its intellectual seriousness. Instead Annwn cites the increasing usage of eerie by critics 'to denote that acuity to seeing that which is subtly present, (but not apparent to everyone), and the linking of that faculty to rare skills and formal experimentation.'

Annwn demonstrates this usage in his readings of a wide range of extracts from Monk's work, including specific accounts of *Long Wake*, *Fluvium* (2001) and the pamphlet *Mary Through the Looking Glass* (2002): this last recently republished as part of Monk's *Escafeld Hangings* (2005). In his extensive reading of *Mary Through the Looking Glass* Annwn explores Monk's concern with the confined female figure of Mary Queen of Scots, imprisoned in Monk's adopted home city of Sheffield (and the central figure of *Escafeld Hangings*). Mary's postures before the mirror seem embued with all the eeriness of an encounter with the subconscious, with dreams of freedom and desire, whilst Monk's writing, in its virtuosic punning, shifting of registers and sonic exuberance, constantly reminds one of the crafted nature of this transport. Indeed the key to eeriness lies within this sense of craft at levels of language not usually encountered in the everyday.

Frances Presley discusses Monk's work in the context of debates about women's experimental writing, particularly in relation to what Clair Wills has called a false polarisation between formal experimentation and expressivity, as if such qualities were mutually exclusive and reflected differences between male and female writing. Presley acknowledges how experimental poetry by both men and women can be expressive, but also suggests that a commitment to a socialist framework in male experimental writing often coincides with male critics' apparent discomfort with the feminism of Monk's texts, and how she portrays her female self. Whilst acknowledging the important influence of Bob Cobbing on Monk's poetry, Presley also points out how Monk has developed her practice to take into account the possibilities of concrete and sound poetry as a new form of communication, without withdrawing from an engagement with the debates of current politics and religion informed by gender.

Presley's reading of Monk's fourth poem in *La Quinta del Sordo* acknowledges the political resonances of a depiction of bullying as an allegory of Thatcherism and shows how the poem situates this in the context of children's games, as both preparation for the socialising and controlling games of adulthood and a means for surviving or resisting adulthood; showing how Monk's work was also bitterly aware of women's complicity with cruel and irrational policies during the Thatcher era. Presley explores how the experimental, the expressive and feminism persist and transform in the totality of Monk's oeuvre, taking a tour of *Noctivagations* (2001) before coming full circle with a consideration of 'Mary Through the Looking Glass.' Alert to Monk's interest in 'girls and women in real or imaginary prisons, rather than at play' Presley also makes a powerful connection with the image-theme of girlhood: linking the poem to 'the land of children's games, of grown up nonsense rhymes which might provide a means of escape.'

Elizabeth James undertakes an examination of the role of the visual in Monk's poetry on several fronts. Thematically she explores how the concern with eyes and seeing in Monk's poetry indicates an interest in 'the implications of visibility for the individual', particularly for the female individual. This is connected to the themes of witnessing and the notion of blindedness as a social condition in *Interregnum*, and the making visible of those who are invisible, such as the incarcerated Mary Queen of Scots. Vision in Monk's work is also linked to memory and memorialisation, to prophecy and to human sympathy through weeping. This powerful gathering of concerns extends to a consideration of the visual appearance of the poem on the page itself: the role of layout and typography. As James argues:

> The page as such has cultural valency: 'Centre' and 'margins' are socio-political and cultural categories also. Matters of practical poetics, such as prosody, typography and visual arrangement, can be held to imply and even to activate these categories.

James also includes in her discussion a consideration of the fact that many of Monk's books bear portraits of her, both photographic and graphic. Reading these images as varieties of experimental self-presentation, James points out how Monk once again confounds the false binary of experimentation and expressivity in her interest not only in disjunctive collage poetics but also in more traditional explorations of personae, dramatic or lyric. James concludes her discussion with a detailed account of Monk's book *Sky Scrapers* (1986). This poem-sequence, ostensibly 'about' clouds and the sky, explores the visual in many of the ways outlined above: thematically, James argues, the book rehabilitates the pathetic fallacy by turning clouds and sky, not into pseudo-people, but into sites or screens for the associative projections of language. Layout is used subtly to signal shifts or patterns in tone and argument, and the cover and frontispiece play an important role in placing such visions in an urban context. As James concludes, although Monk is not a practitioner of exclusively visual poetics, her work in this area is an important contribution to the development of visuality in poetry and such an approach is a key part of her commitment as a writer.

Chris Goode takes the importance of performance to Monk as a starting point for a discussion which focuses on the idea of voice: both on the page and in live and recorded performance. For Goode the idea of the 'outward movement' of the voice models the activity of Monk's poetry. Speculating on how the way in which a poem appears on the page can evoke a poet's voice (stylistically or individually), but does not, nevertheless, resemble the experience we have when we hear the poet herself read, Goode argues that the crucial element of performance is how the poet's voice is embodied. Monk's 2003 performance at the Camden People's Theatre (hosted by Goode) also reveals Monk's related concern with dis- or post-embodied voices, in her billing of her reading of other poets' poems as a 'séance.' In Monk's important poetics text 'Insubstantial Thoughts on the Transubstantiation of the Text' (2002) she discusses and perceives continuities between oppositions such as vocalised/unvocalised, private/public and dis/embodied. Through this Goode builds up a picture of a poet engaged with the paradox that finding one's own voice is also to acknowledge the constraints of one's own body and socio-political identity. However, rather than seeing voice as a category to be stabilised, rather like the stylistic voice which can amount to a kind of brand identity, this situation is actually an opportunity.

For Goode, voice can be seen as a performed event rather than a static value: as Monk herself writes: 'To perform is to *in habit* space.' This has important consequences for Monk's practice and Goode explores this principally in relation to Monk's first CD collaboration with electroacoustic composer Martin Archer: *Angel High Wires* (2001), where the treatment of the recorded voice creates all manner of creative opportunities. In relation to Monk's treatment of text on the page, Goode describes how she uses the full range of typographical devices available in modern word-processing packages to make possible on the page what isn't possible in the performed voice. Again, almost paradoxically, this contributes to further individuation of voice when the texts come to be read. Crucially, when the voices that concern Monk are those of others— Gerard Manley Hopkins or Mary Queen of Scots, for example—this complex set of shifting relations opens up imaginative space in which seemingly unbridgeable gaps between the past and present, between self and other suddenly become crossable.

It is this very possibility that is explored by Monk herself in her own contribution 'Collaborations with the Dead.' Working from a model of identity that acknowledges its psychological and physiological limits, Monk nevertheless affirms the human need and desire to overstep 'social, temporal, geographic and individual entrenchments.' Within the context of writing she identifies the means of this enquiry as experimentation with form and content, but argues that this too is ultimately limited, until it comes up with the possibility of disrupting itself via collaboration with an other. Acknowledging the frustrations and tensions of creative collaboration with other writers she also wittily posits an alternative, that is, collaboration with writers who are no longer living. Outlining the role of Gerard Manley Hopkins' poetry in Monk's composition of *Interregnum*, her use of Roman poets in 'Roman Rumourals' and use of Mary Queen of Scots' letters and poems in *Escafeld*

Hangings, Monk reveals a incisive visionary and revisionary practice which, whilst she acknowledges that it is necessarily conducted 'without permission', emerges as a deeply serious and engaged relationship with literary history. Monk's ideas here are also given full illustration by the presentation of her collaboration with John Donne: 'A Nocturnall Upon S. Lucies Day, Being the Shortest Day.'

Monk's poetics of collaboration finds a poignant analogue in the fact that the Companion is dedicated to the memory of the poet, artist, musician, publisher, teacher and actor Jeff Nuttall (1933–2004) who is also the author of the volume's foreword; quite possibly one of the last pieces of writing he completed before his death in January 2004. Remarkably Nuttall was also the first person to ever review a book of Monk's poetry and Monk has acknowledged the importance of Nuttall's influence for her development as a writer, through her contact with him in Leeds in the 1970s. The gesture is a significant one as it also indicates the importance to Monk of her participation in the energetic, constantly-shifting and cross-disciplinary social networks that have attended the production of innovative writing over the past few decades—indeed, many of the contributors to this volume can be said to share in this context as fellow writers and performers as well as critics, musicians, actors, directors and visual artists, to many of whom Nuttall was also an inspirational figure. It is therefore fitting that this critical companion to the work of one of our most adventurous and talented poets should be carried out under the sign of Nuttall, as much as Monk's work itself demonstrates the scope of its own developing importance in the landscape of contemporary British poetry.

Scott Thurston

Editor's Acknowledgements

Geraldine Monk herself deserves a special mention for her support and involvement in this project from the start including granting permissions, making available copies of her books, advising contributors, giving bibliographical advice and offering her own material. Nate Dorward, Robert Sheppard and Gavin Selerie also contributed valuable bibliographical information and advice, for which I am most grateful. I would also like to thank Peter Griffiths for his image-making of the covers of Geraldine's books and for his keen and sympathetic understanding of the project. Thanks are also due to Lawrence Upton and Adrian Clarke for granting permission for the reproduction of the Writers Forum covers and to Peterjon and Yasmin Skelt for the reproduction of the North and South cover. Finally, I would like to thank the contributors themselves for their commitment, patience and dedication in creating this Companion.

Scott Thurston

Geraldine Monk in Staithes

BILL GRIFFITHS

This brief survey looks at Geraldine's early work in print, during the time she was living near Staithes in North-East England.

In 1977 I was working in Germany, and my first contact with Geraldine was by post—I think Allen Fisher 'introduced' us. On returning to England, I was very pleased to be invited up to North Yorkshire to visit. Geraldine shared the stone-built extension to an old farmhouse with Bob Clark, the artist; this was inland from the fishing village of Staithes in a sheltered valley eventually accessible from the coast road. (The farmhouse was built half-way up the east side of the valley; according to geographers, this is the spring line, but if so it had since failed.)

Apart from the distant but unmissable Boulby Potash Mine to the north, the location was isolated and possibly idyllic. You could walk to Staithes, or catch the one-an-hour bus to Whitby (south) or Middlesbrough (north). Not far from the farm was the grand headland of Boulby, identified (inaccurately) in the nineteenth century as Beowulf's resting-place. It was all very bleak in winter—somehow it put Ted Hughes and *Crow* in mind—but warm and flowery in the summer, by which you can tell I was a moderately frequent visitor over the next few years.

We walked much, and must have talked a good deal (literature, art, music), but my impression is the landscape was less an influence on her initial work than the sense of isolation, her household with Bob, and (it may be) memories of Lancashire where she grew up.

In 1979, I encouraged Bob Cobbing of Writers Forum to publish a booklet of her poems. A little extra enthusiasm was needed, as Bob had just published booklets by two London poetesses and felt rather discouraged by the response they had received. Nonetheless, *Long Wake* went ahead, and justified not only its printing but its reprinting soon after. And so we have Geraldine's first 'book' in print.

This was a duplicated production, though the evenness of the type points to WF's 'golf-ball typewriter' stage (in 'Dream Two' there is a slightly emphatic 'a' where a typing error in a stencil has been daubed over and retyped). The cover—by Bob Clark—has titling and transformed visage (Geraldine was his favoured and nearest subject), and was printed, on the duplicator again, in two colours. The whole is side-stapled. (See p. 139 for an image of the cover.)

The title 'Long Wake' suggests the ambiguity of consciousness/oblivion; with memories and dreams forming the main subject matter; the closing poem, 'Lyke Wake', resolves this towards a whiteness of winter with references to the Cleveland poem 'Lyke Wake Dirge' (fifteenth/sixteenth century) and Eskimoesque chant, ending:

> phosphorus   snow ghost
>   passing strangely now
>   feline shivers of
>   violet and blue ignite
>   caress this mute
>   albino.

> (Monk, 2003, p. 9)

Layout and cultural awareness are important in this set of poems, as well as personal observation and effectiveness of word. The farm was remote, but its library was impressive—Bob's art books on van Gogh, Soutine, etc., a set of world music LPs, purchases, presents, a range of literature, little press material . . . (On checking this with Geraldine, she writes: 'Definitely would be reading Stein—I came across her when I was 17 . . . I would have been probably reading Lorca, Georg Trakl, Dylan Thomas (always Thomas!), Hopkins of course and the Beats, oh I was also big-big fan of Emily Dickinson at that time (hence my early love of long dashes!) and also everything that dropped through our letterbox').

The poems typically refer to Geraldine as a youngster in Lancashire, along with references to contemporary Cleveland, and involve impressions of place, family, childhood. The format is often geometrical, benefiting from fixed-space typing, and not so easy to achieve today. But here is the opening of 'Return of Dream One***Pendulum' which uses a more continuous format:

> The fish are / dead / lying open / mouthed / I / walk
> village / streetdown / towards / deathwake / cure I /
> have / biscuits soaked in / lemon / juicesky sea / at

mosphere lem / onjuice / the fish / willwake / willmake /
lively as Scaling / Dam in Spring /

(Monk, 2003, p. 6)

Lugubriousness, language, and the stillness of winter (alert to Spring).

∽

A second book from Writers Forum in 1980 was titled *La Quinta del Sordo* ('The house of the deaf man')—the reference being to the little house Goya lived in outside Madrid 1819–1824. The title poem is followed by 5 poems, each relating to one engraving in Goya's series of 22 'Disparates' (Foolishnesses or Proverbs). These are: 1. *El Caballo Raptor* (the horse abductor—showing a woman falling from a rearing horse) 2. *Disparate Ridiculo* (ridiculous foolishness—showing people nesting on a tree branch) 3. *Disparate Desordenado* (disorderly nightmare—a standing man, joined from head to waist with a woman, gestures at a lunatic—a detail of this etching is used on the booklet's cover—see p. 139 for an image of it) 4. *La Lealtad* (I find this one difficult to interpret; Geraldine kindly supplied this summary: 'A figure sits dead centre with what I find is almost a serene expession (in Goya terms) with a dog cowering under its legs whilst other figures dance round her pointing and taunting (I think it's female—well I read the figure so). I don't like this title at all as it seems to me an utter misreading—I see the central figure as the epitome of passive resistance— quite the opposite of loyalty. The viewpoint of the poem is taken from the taunting figures.') 5. *Disparate de Miedo* (a proverb of terror—a gigantic phantom,—'Whether of war or death or common sense (!) I'm not sure'— looms over tiny human figures—'weeny soldiers (yes they seem to be soldiers)').

A cautionary note at the back explains that these titles are not Goya's and indeed the images have a brooding, gnomic ambiguity—but some description is advisable as the poems take the form of fantasias prompted by the original etchings.

The title poem, 'La Quinta del Sordo', describes the horrors that crowded Goya's imagination at this time—'sweet and sticky leeches of twilight'—exerting unendurable mental pressure: 'How tight grew your creatures of myth | How tight grew the monkey wrench' (Monk, 2003, p. 19).

The first 'print' poem relates to the sense of horse (aligned left on the page) and falling woman (aligned right on the page). The text then changes to a single central column, describing the general impression of an 'airquake' and something of the artistic process:

> unblinking
> the eye of a squid
> devours
> their future shadows
> stretched and melted wax
> frozen

(Monk, 2003, p. 20)

For the second print, the poem opens with an apposite sense of the ludicrous:

> We are gathered here today
> because peacocks are pretty birds
> and perfect monsters of iridescence

(Monk, 2003, p. 21)

The image of people in a tree is seen in terms of imminent disaster ('stumbled and tumbled viciously | off its floating circles' (Monk, 2003, p. 21)), the folly underlined by their un-consciousness of the risk they are in:

> but we will not follow such wandering disasters
> we are too smug and swinging
> happy from this bough and bony thing

(Monk, 2003, p. 21)

The third poem centres on the 'siamese' image of the gesturing figure and its load 'fused in trepidation' (Monk, 2003, p. 22). Before them is an 'obese gutter pressing crowd' while the lunatic seems invoked in the reference to 'black marrow gape' (Monk, 2003, p. 22). The closing lines carry (perhaps) a further reference to the print as print:

> Come now
> Let us beckon
> Let us reckon hard
> with this block vengeance

(Monk, 2003, p. 22)

The fourth opens with an image of rotation—'here we go sound around the one in the middle who we | shall riddle' (Monk, 2003, p. 23). The lines are set continuously in a justified block, extra spacing indicating the performed pause; the tensions and silliness of strained relationships conveyed more by frequent rhyme and word transformation ('choke/spoke', 'blind/find/d eye' (Monk, 2003, p. 23)). As for the ties of loyalty:

> for a while just tow the line and you'll be   perhaps
> and maybe wet with sweet dew if the morning ever   or
> never

> (Monk, 2003, p. 23)

The fifth and last poem climaxes with a narrow centralised column of verse, echoing the fearsome towering phantom of Goya's print, and emphatic with a frequent use of block capitals making the vertical image seem taller and stronger (in the etching, the scale of the phantom is indicated by a comparison with a diminutive tree). Beside the phantom itself, with 'low BELLOWING shroud' are references to war ('blood-rowned', 'DRUM', 'BRITTLE WEAPON') and the sequence ends with a 'SH | OUT' (Monk, 2003, p. 24).

The foolishnesses are seen (I suggest) in terms of human relations and their insane incongruities. Ostensibly an exercise in terror, the etchings are extended here to suggest a range of human frailties and challenging situations that make a very intense literature. A variety of formats is employed, and typically a sense of word sound and word play. The page size is now A4, with in each case a poem taking one page. The text is generated on a fixed-space typewriter, the printing being by photocopier in the second edition of 1990; binding by staples left. This is an awkward format for bookshops, but as Writers Forum distributed almost none of its publications by formal channels, this mattered little, and poem size and shape is allowed to dictate the larger page size.

≈

Slightly earlier than the above is what we might call an 'art book', *Rotations*, published by Geraldine's own Siren Press in 1979. In this case the poems are interleaved with original woodcuts by Robert Clark, in varying coloured inks. The text was set and printed litho and the book assembled by Tony Ward of Arc & Throstle Press, Todmorden, with the usual care I associate with his productions. The size is slightly over A5; the booklet is centre-stapled, with a wrap-around cover litho-printed with a further design by Bob Clark.

Unlike the Goya, the poems do not directly parallel the visual. Bob's woodcuts are figurative (Geraldine transformed), the text is 'pastoral', a cycle of the seasons. These are not strictly 'illustrations' therefore, though the warm red inks of the prints corresponding to Spring and Summer contrast with the blue and black of Autumn and Winter. It is the one publication at this time that seems directly inspired by the natural world of Staithes. Stars figure in each of the four poems (the lack of lighting around the farm made star-gazing a rewarding task; Geraldine won any name-the-constellations contest). Images of insect, plant, and weather abound, though detail is mostly used to support a quasi-astrological 'character' for each of the seasons—vital Spring:

> The brittle morning air
> soaked in vinegar cracked
> with wing
> beats and mating
> cries

> > (Monk, 2003, p. 13)

Static Summer, when:

> moonpull
> juggles electric storms
> and day-trippers
> with a little time

> and time again

> > (Monk, 2003, p. 14)

Decaying Autumn:

> Fungi perfect their spores gorge
> sardonic emulations to the wind

> > (Monk, 2003, p. 15)[1]

---

[1] In the original publication these lines read: 'Fungi perfect their spores/pouring | sardonic emulations to the wind' (Monk, 1979, unp.). See Elizabeth James' article in this volume for another example of Monk's revisions.

Derelict Winter:

> days are coated in tar and fibre-glass
> as lovers roll from warm sheets to desolation
> [. . .]
> Winter stalking
> black wolf pelts rain

> (Monk, 2003, p. 16)

with an overall awareness of 'this | endless circuit' (Monk, 2003, p. 14).

~

Siren Press was the vehicle for two important books of Geraldine's in 1980: *Banquet* and *Spreading the Cards*.

Banquet is A5 landscape, but centre-stapled in a 'calendar' format. The text is generated on a fixed-space typewriter with remarkably even impress, and printed litho. The cover illustration derives from a black-and-white film image of a handsome man reverently kissing (or quietly eating?) the bare shoulder of a lovely lady. Greater use is made here of the width of the page, several poems using 'inset' sections across the field of the page.

The theme is 'this sad banquet' (Monk, 2003, p. 27) though the poems have an abstract quality rather than specific subject matter. The image of the peacock recurs—as male demand?—and reference to the 'beautify-ing horror' (Monk, 2003, p. 27) and 'the infatuation with strangeness' (Monk, 2003, p. 29). The rich language (low on word-play this time) has a lush density of image that ought to convey the erotic: 'succulence on the gentle push | to putrefaction' (Monk, 2003, p. 29) but more usually resolves to the oral and the culinary:

> seismic contraband
> thrown
> PLOSIVE
> from gilded beak

> (Monk, 2003, p. 29)

and

    pick up the threading
    mosses-come-galaxies
    come crunch and spongy

               (Monk, 2003, p. 30)

and 'PEACH so gentle bruised GINGER | flames' (Monk, 2003, p. 30).
    A metaphor of eating for life-processes passes through the eight sepa-
rate (untitled) poems, that close by offering '(small delicacies of bril-
liance)' (Monk, 2003, p. 30).

                        ∼

Spreading the Cards—as a preliminary to fortune-telling?—was also
published by Siren Press, but printed letterpress in a sans-serif type by a
local firm in the North-East. The size is approx quarto (perhaps a little
squarer) and the glossy cover features a glamorous photo portrait of
Geraldine herself. The booklet is centre-stapled. (See p. 139 for an image
of the cover.)
    It is a collection of short individual poems, some located in the
North-East ('Three Poems for the Sun (After the N. Yorks moor fires,
summer 1976)') or Lancashire ('Pendle Hill (Home of the Lancashire
Witches)'), and even a record of a summer working away ('Van Roll in
Sussex') but more usually less specific ('Voyage', 'Edge' etc.). The title
derives from the opening poem 'Spreading the Cards' which plays on
ancestral and modern, burial and sociability:

    calling 'cross
    juke room jamming hot/
    hornet smoke red
    eyesting

               (Monk, 1980, [p. 3])

Layout tends to the cross-page facility of *Banquet*, and there is a mature
certainty in the handling of word material: 'and chink chink of
acrimony'—my favourite line (Monk, 1980, [p. 4]).
    Even the specific titles resolve into poems that give a general or
oblique view of their subject. Thus of 'Pendle Hill':

    You double talk between heaven and clean cut hell
    Two prickly voices and a second sight
    throwing visions from ectoplasmic mists

                        (Monk, 1980, [p. 19])

'Van Roll in Sussex' has a literal set of events set left ('V.W. VAN HITS |
SIDE OF ROAD [. . .] UNINJURED [. . .] ENGINE STILL | RUNNING
KEYS | MISSING [. . .] EXPLOSION IS | IMMINENT [. . .] ESCAPE DOOR— |
JAMMED') while centrally reactions are registered ('words trickle from
roofs of | mouths shock soaked | and pale') and right is set a parallel
with Mayfly history ('FLITTING THROUGH IRIDESCENT SECONDS')
(Monk, 1980, [p. 16]). But generally in the book the conscious account or
description is subordinated to working through words and images, so
that the poem has a unity of feeling and thought rather than of detail.
'Face(ts)'—the brackets are Geraldine's—opens:

> imperfect orb
> lost world
> flat spinning
> to stagnation
> this face does a
> half turn to darker regions
> another version
>   change/changing
>
>   (Monk, 1980, [p. 13])

Glib postures and inferences are avoided, there is nothing didactic
about this verse. Rather, the title poem ends: 'as always | revealing noth-
ing' (Monk, 1980, [p. 3]).

But plenty has been achieved. The poems of this earlier period show
a remarkable confidence in generating subject matter from the immediate and personal; they explore a variety of techniques in using words
and constructing poem and poem sequence; and produce some remarkably effective plays of language.

In 1984, when the owners of the farm proper sold up, Geraldine and
Bob settled to move to Sheffield.

Editor's Note

As the books *Long Wake*, *La Quinta del Sordo*, *Rotations* and *Banquet* are now
available in Monk's *Selected Poems*, it has been decided to refer to these
reprinted forms. However, it should be borne in mind that these works
have undergone considerable transformation from their original book
presentations. As Griffiths suggests, the design of these early books is an
integral part of the meaning of the poems contained within: a point
discussed by several contributors to this volume (see Elizabeth James in
particular but also Christine Kennedy and David Kennedy and Sean
Bonney).

References (including original publications)

Monk, G. 1979. *Long Wake*. London: Writers Forum and Pirate Press
———— 1979. *Rotations*. Staithes: Siren Press
———— 1980. *La Quinta del Sordo*. London: Writers Forum
———— 1980. *Banquet*. Staithes: Siren Press
———— 1980. *Spreading the Cards*. Staithes: Siren Press
———— 2003. *Selected Poems*. Cambridge: Salt Publishing

Poetry, Difficulty and Geraldine Monk's
Interregnum
CHRISTINE KENNEDY & DAVID KENNEDY

Preamble

Plutarch wrote that it is a very difficult matter to trace and find out the truth of anything by history. However, it is a safe bet that a lot of useful matter could be found out by a history of difficulty in modern poetry. A full history of the concept and its construction has yet to be produced but is urgently needed. An Internet search for 'poetry + difficulty' finds thousands of sites—from weblogs to peer-reviewed e-journals, from 'for' to 'against' and everything in between—where the two terms are intimate or synonymous. The prevalence of the concept suggests that we have always already agreed what difficulty is and what it does. Our reading of *Interregnum* will argue that because Geraldine Monk's book-length sequence is concerned with a linguistic sociality outside the dominant order it enables a different focus on difficulty that allows a re-thinking of it and its automatic attachment to certain sorts of writing. Our argument is a simple one: if innovative poetry is difficult this is to do with the type of experiences it explores and the intensity with which it does so.

Difficulty and Contemporary Poetry

In a discussion of the alleged difficulty of much contemporary poetry, the American poet and critic Ron Silliman sketches the following cultural scene:

> Imagine the life experiences of a person relatively unfamiliar with poetry coming to a reading in the United States in 2003. This person lives in a

society in which the Talking Heads had a hit record singing the zaum poetry of Hugo Ball in 1977. The most surreal songs of Bob Dylan were released—and not on any indy label—some 36 years ago. [. . .] The most popular motion picture of the past two years [*Lord of the Rings*] had substantial portions of dialog spoken (with subtitles) in Elvish.

(Silliman, 2003)

Silliman argues that in this cultural scene we are used to decoding a range of complex texts from pop records to signage. Consequently, 'it is the surface of the univocal poem [. . .] that is the deviant experience'; and 'the one-dimensional surface profoundly is the exception to our experience of language, not the rule.' His conclusion is that difficulty exists 'only for readers for whom the definition of poetry has somehow become so constrained that it can only mean certain things' (Silliman, 2003). Difficulty is not natural: it is constructed.

Silliman's argument will be a familiar one to readers of poetries variously termed 'experimental', 'avant-garde', 'linguistically innovative' or 'linguistically investigative' but it raises more questions than it answers. Two things strike one immediately about Silliman's non-poetry examples: first, that language is only one part of the different cultural experiences they offer; and, second, all three take place in genres with well-established channels for the transmission and reception of apparent difficulty. People who bought the Talking Heads record are as likely to have been attracted to its driving dance beat as to its bizarre lyrics. If buyers had been attracted primarily to the lyrics, they would have bought the record for that reason in the wider context of experience of a genre where nonsense titles and lyrics are common. Typical examples are hit records from the 1960s and 1970s such as Manfred Mann's 'Do Wah Diddy Diddy'; Marmalade's 'Ob-La-Di, Ob-La-Da'; and Middle of the Road's 'Chirpy Chirpy Cheep Cheep.' Similarly, regular moviegoers will already be used to subtitles in both foreign language films and in sections of mainstream Hollywood films.

What this suggests is that in many cultural genres apparent difficulty and its reception are, one might say, pre-constructed. This is far from the case in contemporary poetry where the reception of apparent difficulty is barely constructed at all. For example, Shira Wolosky's useful introductory study *The Art of Poetry: How To Read A Poem* considers a range of poetry from Shakespeare onwards and makes detailed readings of around a dozen twentieth century poems by writers such as Yeats, Eliot, Frost, Pound and Stevens. However, only a handful of her chosen poems—Pound's 'In a Station of the Metro', William Carlos Williams'

'Between Walls', H.D.'s 'Eurydice' and Marianne Moore's 'The Paper Nautilus'—can be said to be truly divergent in terms of form, lineation and prosody either from her other examples or from what her readers are likely to have encountered already.

Silliman also argues that the apparent difficulty of much contemporary poetry is not an issue 'for ordinary readers, those who come to the experience with no prior expectation, with no need to automatically toggle between "right" & "wrong", easy & hard' (Silliman, 2003). It is an assertion partly borne out by the experience of teaching a range of innovative poetries from Objectivism to performance writing to undergraduate students and adult learners who had no knowledge of and therefore no preconceptions about them. They were able to respond directly to the words on the page. They sometimes found those words and the relationships between them unexpected but they didn't already have difficulty in place as a kind of filter. However, to approach this from the opposite direction, it would be disingenuous to pretend that readers don't need to develop particular competencies and skills when reading the type of poetry Silliman terms 'univocal' and 'one-dimensional.' It would be wrong to assume that a characteristic of such poetry is that it is always easily reducible to sense. For example, what 'sense' can we really make of the final line in 'The balled | Pulp of your heart | Confronts its small | Mill of silence' from Sylvia Plath's 'Cut' (Plath, 1987, p. 24)? It would perhaps be more accurate to say that our conception of poetry may assume that a characteristic of poems is that they include small areas which are unclear but which perhaps don't matter as long as we can get a general sense of the rest of the poem. Without thinking about it, we scan for a general sense we're happy with. As is the case with a wide range of language uses, we look for fluency not accuracy.

The efficacy of competencies and skills developed through reading, say, Sylvia Plath will be called into question by an encounter with contemporary innovative poetries. This is certainly the case with the opening of Charles Bernstein's 'Motion Sickness'—'The blue pertains | amassed at course return' (Bernstein, 1983, p. 19). It is also certainly the case with the opening of Maxine Chernoff's 'The Case for Day': 'An angle of interest—| too late | for windows' (Chernoff, 2001, p. 33). Silliman is right that 'the one-dimensional surface profoundly is the exception to our experience of language' but it is far from the exception to most people's experience of poetry. The reasons for this are complex and numerous and involve, amongst other things, access to publishing and distribution; literary prizes and visibility; and the economic relation-ship between what is published and what is taught. Indeed, education is the first and last place many people will encounter poetry and this encounter will determine life-long reading competencies. Or, to put this another way, most people will not read contemporary poetry seriously after they leave school; and even those who go on to study literature at university will not be obliged to study it. Peter Barry reports that a 1998 survey by the Council for College and University English (CCUE) of seventy-six U.K. university-level institutions found that 'only nineteen said that contemporary poetry was compulsory for their students—fifty-one said it was optional' (Barry, 2000, p.3). It is also worth noting that literary studies in the UK are currently undergoing one of their periodic internecine methodological disputes. Recent interventions by Catherine Belsey and Jonathan Bate have argued, respectively, for literary studies to follow the model of cultural studies; and for a return to historically based methods such as textual bibliography. In both scenarios, the inter-pretive reading competencies demanded by contemporary poetry will have little place.

We might also note that the Shira Wolosky book referred to earlier is emblematic of the way the received history of twentieth century innov-ative poetry—with the exception of a few isolated figures—generally peters out somewhere between 1950 and 1960. This historical stopping point is instructive because it would seem to represent the point at which it becomes difficult to talk about 'poetry' in an all-inclusive sense. It represents the point at which what have come to be called 'experi-mental' poetries become visibly self-identifying in terms of divergent practices. This means that readers coming to poetry and wanting to explore beyond that point will find little to help them. They may give up completely or just explore the only routes readily open to them, routes to what Peter Middleton has called 'the poetry of mass observation which largely passes for verse these days' (Middleton, 2003, p.9). As inno-vative poetries have increasingly been denied—and, wary of commodification, have often actively rejected—access to the structures of transmission and reception available to so-called 'univocal' poetry, they have increasingly been located, produced in and addressed to distinct but often barely visible socialities. For example, Australian poet Pam Brown's 'new and selected poems' *Dear Deliria* gathers a body of work which often seems to be addressed to specific artistic, poetic and political groupings before any general reader of contemporary poetry. It is an impression borne out by Brown's comments in conversation with

John Kinsella. All these factors, then, contribute to the cultural construction of difficulty in contemporary innovative poetries.

Difficulty and Geraldine Monk

Geraldine Monk is widely renowned as a performer of her poetry. Hearing her read a variety of work in a variety of locations and contexts, it becomes clear that the majority of her texts are only fully activated in performance; and that that activation comes in a large part from the texts' co-extensiveness with other types of language usages and voicings. Monk's voicings can veer from intimate whispers to booming full-throated shouts and cries, from broad Lancastrian to something approaching RP, from Sitwellian articulations to everyday speech. Her language usages include comments about the venue, apologies for not having assembled a clear programme of work, indecisiveness about what to read, greetings to friends in the audience, and remarks to late-comers. In a reading of her work Monk is always doing at least one of the following: speaking, acting, speaking acts, or acting speech.

Such a portrayal might imply that a Geraldine Monk reading is difficult and that the audience is left floundering amongst a bewildering array of references. However, a Geraldine Monk reading is not just a performance of texts: it is equally a performance of Geraldine Monk as a poet and, most importantly, as a communicator. Indeed, it may be that Monk's ability and willingness to communicate with an audience is what makes her unique. A Geraldine Monk reading is not difficult because her compelling performances of her texts articulate an understanding of those texts. Monk's poetry can be characterised by an emphasis on the rawness of data coming through the five senses; an often vertiginous evocation of motion; references to uncontainable female sexuality; explorations of how the authority of representation systems are always compromised; and the confident portrayal of a desiring self in search of the world she wants to have. Monk's performances articulate an understanding because they allow her to act as a kind of intermediary between the rawness of her material and her audience.

It is also worth noting the operatic and musical aspects of Monk's readings. This remark is not intended to evoke the old chestnut that all art aspires to the condition of music. (It is, of course, well known by now that all art actually aspires to the condition of language.) However, in the context of our earlier point about performances articulating an understanding, the written text is a score in the sense that its full articulation is not on the page. As a *lieder* cycle needs the presence and actions of a voice to access the deep emotional and psychological world and time of its individual parts, so a Monk text needs its author's voice to release from language deeper levels of experience than the dictionary or encyclopaedia, levels of meaning to which contemporary poetry is usually confined. It's not surprising that one of Monk's recent works is *Angel High Wires*, an electroacoustic song cycle in collaboration with musician Martin Archer based on Schubert's entire lieder output (see Chris Goode's essay in this volume).

Difficulty and *Interregnum*:
'Nerve Centre'—Oppositions and Exchanges

Interregnum, first published in 1994, is an imaginative exploration of the notorious witch trial of 1612 when ten people from the Pendle area of East Lancashire were hanged as witches in Lancaster. Originally running to nearly 120 pages, *Interregnum* is epic in scale and scope. Reading it is arduous and challenging. Its emotional range and impact are equivalent to an opera cycle and the text is constantly changing in form and voice. Without the intermediation of Monk's performing voice, the reader is dropped into a language world of uncertain bearings. A contrast with opera is again instructive. In the theatre, the *mise en scène* is immediately visible so that when someone speaks or sings complex pieces of language they are located for the audience. Monk's performances of her texts with their combinations of voicings and usages partly provide such a *mise en scène*. Without the intermediation of Monk's performing voice, the arduousness or potential arduousness of the performance for Monk herself is thrown back on to the reader. Similarly, in contrast to conventional re-imaginings of historical events, *Interregnum* deprives readers of the comforts of quaint historical language and trappings. There are no 'ye olde this' or farthingales here. The reader has to confront the material head on. This, then, is one location of difficulty. Another obvious location is in the reader's inability to perceive *Interregnum's* scale and scope because a book's sequential organisation necessarily compresses them.

Interregnum is divided into three parts: 'Nerve Centre', 'Palimpsestus' and 'Interregnum.' 'Nerve Centre' contains eleven poems divided across three subsections: 'The Hill', 'The Hill People' and 'Hill Outriders.' The 'Nerve Centre' section focuses on Pendle Hill where the Pendle witches are believed to have met. Pendle Hill has other supernatural associations because it was there that George Fox, founder of the Quaker movement, allegedly had a visionary experience in 1652: 'From the top of this hill the Lord let me see what places he had a great people to be gathered' (Quakerinfo.com). It is still a place of Quaker pilgrimage today as well as attracting those interested in witchcraft, particularly at Halloween. In the words of one modern local witch:

> It's practically not safe to go out that night! The lanes round Pendle are stiff with traffic. It's traditional to go wild on Pendle Hill that night but [. . .] for reasons of personal safety I wouldn't want to be on the hill. I'm not a person who likes crowds or people out of control on drugs.

> (Pendle.net)

The Ribble Valley Borough Council website confirms that at Halloween local police have to set up a one-way system to control traffic over Pendle Hill. Whether this traffic is earthbound or aerial is not stated.

The preceding paragraph may seem something of a digression but 'Nerve Centre' presents a portmanteau of stories and voices to establish this modern scene orbiting round an ancient place whose intrinsic atmosphere is written deep into the environment. The eleven individual poems of 'Nerve Centre' introduce some of the latter-day groups drawn to Pendle Hill e.g. 'Good Friday Hikers', 'Hallowe'en Bikers', 'Fox Hunt', and 'Flyer' (Monk, 2003, p. 101, p. 102, p. 108, p. 110). The poems make powerful portrayals of the physicality of the people and the materiality of their activities. In fact, the poems are full of disconnected body parts and objects. At first sight, 'Nerve Centre' seems designed only to reflect these varied groups via a disparate collage of techniques: conventional free verse, open field composition, double columned text and centred text. However, 'Nerve Centre' does much more than give a species of 'users' guide' to Pendle Hill: it establishes the concerns that will be worked out in the rest of *Interregnum*. Pendle Hill itself is established as an environment whose components—material and atmospheric—are supremely durable and capable of perpetuation. The wish expressed in 'Good Friday Hikers'—'(will-we-see the Irish sea | beyond Blackpool tower)'—is echoed in 'Fox Trot' where '(IT) the hill (I) | saw sea to top it the hill' (Monk, 2003, p. 101, p. 109) reworks the actual words of George Fox 'When I was come to the top, I saw the sea bordering upon Lancashire' (Quakerinfo.com). The durability of Pendle Hill is capable of surviving even the slaughter perpetrated by the age of the automobile: in the words of the opening poem 'Pendle', 'odd creatures | sometimes

missed sometimes hit | warm runny things | cold unmoving tarmac'
(Monk, 2003, p. 99). This also serves to establish Pendle Hill as a micro-,
multi-verse of oppositional forces: the social versus the natural.

'Nerve Centre' establishes, then, strong senses of geography and landscape and of the body and social and natural spaces. As we read through
Interregnum, it becomes clear that all paths and tracks through the text
go through these areas. 'Fox Hunt', in the voice of a hunted and killed
fox, portrays the consequences of the exercise of the prerogatives of
power that is certainly a theme throughout *Interregnum*. At the end of
the poem, the mutilated dying fox describes itself: 'staggering and bled
| I rose red | a reversed emblem' (Monk, 2003, p. 108). 'Reversed emblem'
does more than commentate punningly on 'rose red': it presents an
image of life as a hanging on between life and death and of such
moments between the two as crucial points. This highlights the way
that 'Nerve Centre' establishes an emotional key for the rest of
Interregnum. It is a key that is pitched extremely high. Like the
transfigured fox, it resonates with agony and ecstasy and currents of
exchange between the two. A between state is, of course, a species of
interregnum.

Difficulty and *Interregnum*: 'Palimpsestus'—Portals

From the beginning of part 2, the exterior world established in 'Nerve
Centre' starts to disappear progressively. As its title suggests
'Palimpsestus' is a fragmentary collection of writings and voicings.
Bracketed commentating statements in bold upper case letters punctu-
ate sections in lower case letters. All sections and statements are introduced and end with three dots signalling their incomplete nature. The
reader immediately begins wondering about the exact nature of the
palimpsest being presented here. A palimpsest can mean either a manuscript where the original text has been effaced to make way for a second
text or a manuscript in which portions of earlier erased writings are
found. There are clearly two texts here but their exact identities—
primary and secondary—remain unclear.

In the original Creation Books edition, 'Palimpsestus' was spread
across thirty-four pages with the commentating statements—
e.g. '. . . (STUMBLING SURVIVAL). . .'—each receiving their own separate
left hand page. In the Salt edition, the whole section is run on which
changes the way the text is read. The layout of the original edition
suggested a number of possible readings. The capitalised commentating

statements could be read as introduction to the lower case text on the right hand pages. They also suggested an antiphonal, call and response structure. Finally, the capitalised commentating statements also signalled a possibility that the section could be read in both directions. The layout of the Salt edition seems to invite only a linear reading.

The different effects of the old and new layouts are worth noting because 'Palimpsestus' replaces what might be called the vox pop of 'Nerve Centre' with a largely mediumistic register. This is made explicit in 'piercing second sight | chucking up visions from | ectoplasmic mists' (Monk, 2003, p. 112). Where 'Nerve Centre' presented descriptions of different lifestyles and external descriptions of geography and place, 'Palimpsestus' articulates life experiences and inner life or lives. What seems to be happening in the section is that we are given a kind of linguistic portal back to the experiences of the Pendle witches which, like Pendle Hill, have always been present. The opening sections of the text refer to '. . . perpetual | dreamdrip-backdrop | pooling centuries' and 'unstopped centuries | seep | unbearable sorrowlove' (Monk, 2003, p. 111, p. 113). The portal opens because the 'unbearable sorrowlove' of the past connects with similar unbearable feelings in the present or very recent past. We get glimpses of an unhappy home life in '. . . Three o clock Good Friday dinner | hits | floral wallpaper' and 'young blood | wetting scrubbed floorboards' (Monk, 2003, p. 114, p. 117). There also seem to be references to what might be termed memoirs of a Catholic girlhood in '. . . Three aves | rise | Rise | RISE' (Monk, 2003, p. 114) although this passage, like the later 'Three biters bitten' (Monk, 2003, p. 116), is also a quote from a charm that Anne Whittle or Chattox admitted she had recited to lift a curse. Finally there is a suggestion of limited opportunities for working-class women:

. . . Three women		Three sisters.
	Three mill workers.	
spin.	wind.	cut.
FATE.	FATE.	FATE.

(Monk, 2003, p. 120)

The opening of the portal between past and present, collective and individual, is at its clearest in the following passage towards the end of 'Palimpsestus':

can't breathe even moan
girl-mind

        hooks on transference
        out-of-body trance
     crawls into cool dreams of
     future
     disconnected bliss

            (Monk, 2003, p. 118)

The portal opens because the collective experiences of the Pendle witches offer both a means of identification and a possibility of escape. In this context, the capitalised commentating statements— e.g. '. . . (LEGIONS OF FRANTIC MISERIES) . . .' (Monk, 2003, p. 113)— almost work as portals themselves because they can be read as descriptions of the past and the modern present or very recent past. They can also be read as doors with the past pushing on one side and the present on the other. In the context of our discussion of 'Nerve Centre' they are sites of currents of exchange.

    Such a reading suggests, if not a clear linear narrative, then at least a drama composed of discrete scenes. However, 'Palimpsestus' works impressionistically with things flickering in and out of focus, voices reverberating distantly or close by. It's usually uncertain who 'owns' the life experiences and inner life or lives being articulated. Individual and collective voices move in and out of each other. Similarly, there is a distinct impression but never a direct portrayal of coven activities. As in 'Nerve Centre' there is a constant exchange between agony and ecstasy—

        . . . meretricious bleedings
              fruit-dew
             body-bunch
             sex-shiver
        fever. fever. fever.

            (Monk, 2003, p. 113)

—but again it's left unclear who is experiencing these states. This derives from the way the whole section is voiced. Where the eleven poems of 'Nerve Centre' were clever and witty impersonations, here there is a powerful sense of the poet seeing as the speaker or speakers. 'Palimpsestus' also performs an important structural function. 'Nerve Centre' established an unchanging natural and to a large extent psychological environment. This is developed in 'Palimpsestus' by the idea of the past being durable and accessible. 'Palimpsestus' introduces speakers who seem to demonstrate militancy and extreme resistance. This not only connects with the unchanging environment of 'Nerve Centre': it also looks forward to *Interregnum's* final section.

Difficulty and *Interregnum*: 'Interregnum'—Descent Into Hell

Interregnum's final part was originally also called 'Interregnum' and was divided into eight subsections. The subsections were originally titled 'The Great Assembly & Feast', 'Chantcasters', 'Annexation', 'Speech-Snatchers', 'Out-Thoughts', 'Wish-Boned', 'Interregnum' and 'Touching the Everywhere.' The Salt edition has no title for the final part and has re-titled some of the subsections while preserving their original order. 'Spread', originally part of 'The Great Assembly & Feast', becomes a new second subsection. 'Wish-Boned' is silently transformed into the 'Out-Thoughts. . .of ALL.' The penultimate 'Interregnum' is now re-titled 'The Replies.' These subsection changes are minor but have the effect of tightening the drama of the work and giving it sharper focus. The decision to drop 'Interregnum' as the overall title of the final part is perhaps less judicious as its absence tends to dilute the important meaning of a period of freedom from customary authority which the Pendle Witches exemplify.

'The Great Assembly & Feast' and 'Spread' are an introduction in the form of a mega-mix of body parts and speech parts, human and animal bodies, poetic re-imaginings and references to the Pendle Witches' confessions at their trial. For example, 'stolen mutton | (done to a turn)' refers to an event described in James Device's confession while 'Tib' and 'Fancy' are names of two of the witches' familiars (Monk, 2003, p. 123, p. 124 / Pendlewitches.co.uk). In the context of difficulty, no perspective is offered here. What seem to be external criticisms of the witches are mixed up with mediumistic recreations of their experiences. Physical horror and emotional exuberance are two sides of the same coin but it's unclear which is the dark side. This makes for a powerful sense of uncertainty about whether the witches are acting or being acted upon by forces they cannot control. The witches' confessions and other historical evidence suggest they lived as beggars and were often close to starvation, a state which swings its sufferers between hallucinatory elation and abjection. Just as 'Palimpsestus' marked a reduction from a geographical space to an often fevered inner life, so 'The Great Assembly & Feast' and 'Spread' mark a further reduction in which the environment of *Interregnum's* actors and speakers is shrunk to their own bodies.

The overall effect of the two sections is to leave unanswered any questions about what the so-called witches actually did. Or to put this another way: if witchcraft is a fantasy then whose fantasy is it?

'Chantcasters' is divided into 'Demdike Sings', 'Chattox Sings' and 'All Sing' which read simultaneously as cries of affirmation and resistance and recognitions of and resignations to fate. Demdike's hymn to the 'sapphire-shot | charged, steep sky' (Monk, 2003, p. 125) suggests that individuality rests in the ability to perceive. Chattox's song is much more of a lament with its recognition that everything that 'seems to us sweet of us, | and swiftly done away with' and its bleak 'So beginning, | be beginning to despair' (Monk, 2003, p. 126, p. 127). The final 'All Sing' is even bleaker with its 'delights buried deep. | Tell us where?' answered by 'In the deathdance in the blood' (Monk, 2003, p. 128).

In strictly narrative terms the four 'gaol songs' of 'Annexation' depict the immediate period of incarceration and the sensory deprivation of prison is powerfully conveyed. Most importantly, the section portrays the law as a discourse. The lines 'plot holes | to fill dynamite | blow bleeding syntactical | structures to smithereens' (Monk, 2003, p. 131) refers to an actual plot to release the witches but 'syntactical structures' emphasises they are confined as much in a world-view as behind 'impenetrable walls' (Monk, 2003, p. 129). This is further emphasised in 'Speech-Snatchers' that depicts the witches' interrogation: 'this space sucks speech-magic' (Monk, 2003, p. 133). The opening lines of 'Blind Talk' sum up the encounter between 'speech-magic' and syntactical structures: 'we only believe | your truth telling | it like we | want to | hear' (Monk, 2003, p. 134).

If the final section of *Interregnum* starts with a mega-mix of languages and bodies, it ends with clearly audible voices of the witches in 'Out-thoughts' and 'The Replies.' 'Out-thoughts' is made up of ten mono-logues and a chorus which can be characterised as inadmissible evidence: clear descriptions by the alleged witches of what actually happened and/or what they thought they were doing. Once Chattox and Demdike were called witches there was no 'syntactical structure' to contain the former's account of her 'unchallengeable leaps to | lucidity' (Monk, 2003, p. 140) or the latter's assertion that the clay models which were alleged to have caused the deaths of local people 'were my art' (Monk, 2003, p. 141). It is notable that the natural world of 'Nerve Centre' returns in many of the 'Out-thoughts' and gives a picture of life as a hanging-on, an in-between, because most of that life is lived out in the open, exposed to the elements. Whatever collective activities the alleged witches were actually engaged in, 'Out-thoughts' makes clear that they were a much-needed albeit temporary escape from such exposure until 'rain spat and scattered us | back to predictability' (Monk, 2003, p. 147).

Where 'Out-thoughts' present evidence inadmissible to authority's 'syntactical structures', 'The Replies' present the alleged witches within the culmination of those structures: their trial. As with many other sections of *Interregnum*, 'The Replies' moves from mediumistic recreations of actual speech to the poet seeing as speakers without necessarily impersonating or inhabiting them. Anne Whittle, Katherine Hewitt and James Device fall into this first category, the Hewitt and Device sections being respectively comic and unbearably moving. Elizabeth Southern falls into this second category:

> Their movement formed
> our position.
> We slid to the edge
> without heaving
> or flutter. Without motion or commotion.
> We hadn't the learning
> to read us right.

(Monk, 2003, p. 154)

Conclusion

The reader closes the book. The book of belated 'raw foresight' answers to the cooked books of official record. The fate of the Pendle witches is an historical fact but what remains in the mind is a powerful impression of a shared triumph in the continuation of existence. This is both what makes *Interregnum* such a remarkable text and makes reading it such an arduous experience. As we have argued throughout this essay, *Interregnum's* difficulty comes not from its mixing of voices, registers and poetic forms but from its emotional pitch. It is a montage of bodily, linguistic, perceptual and temporal transformations which is keyed by one dominant current of transformation: from ecstasy into suffering and back into ecstasy. The suffering of the witches' existence as starving beggars leads them to escape into ecstasies of allegedly transgressive collective behaviours and practices. In turn, these collective behaviours and practices lead them into further suffering at the hands of the authorities. 'Out-thoughts' and 'The Replies' demonstrate the resistance of all concerned and how this transforms suffering into ecstasy in and as an act of defiant will. When Elizabeth Southern says 'We hadn't the food | for big-boned words to | kick mule-like | the wisest fool' (Monk, 2003, p. 154) it is also a reminder that all the accused had were their bodies. Those bodies, their interiors and exteriors, therefore became the sites where the Pendle witches' original suffering and ecstasy were tied together. Those bodies then became sites where suffering and ecstasy were re-tied together because the original suffering and ecstasy took place in social spaces the witches did not control. It was perhaps their mistake to assume that control over their bodies and their perceptions would give them total control over their status as social actors.

Reading poetry that explores such concerns is as difficult as reading, say, an account of the last days of Simone Weil and raises similar questions: at what level can we relate to it? to what levels of personal and social experience does it speak, if any? It is difficult because we cannot answer those questions without inevitably raising others about our own bodies and our own status as social actors. The continuing pertinence of such questions is underlined by the note to the Salt edition advising readers that *Interregnum* draws on the words of 'The Birmingham Six and Stefan Kiszko' (Monk, 2003, p. 235). Finally, it is difficult because, as we argued earlier, there is no mediation or intermediary between the reader, the text and the questions it opens because of the experiences and emotions it transcribes.

The emotional content of the testimonies of the captured, interrogated and tortured characters of *Interregnum* is difficult for the reader. This is because it places the reader, or *can* place the reader, in a relation with the text which is parallel with the relationship of the tortured captive and the interrogator / gaoler. The reader is likely to experience emotional resistance to full imaginative participation in this process. The captive is dependent upon the gaoler for survival, receiving simultaneously life-sustaining nurturing and life-threatening abuse within the same relationship, and the consequent production of emotion within the captive is of an intense ambivalence which can only be understood as a traumatic experience in itself. The agonized and ecstatic emotional currents which simultaneously flow through the text give a form to this trauma, but also point beyond the period of captivity to the outsider and liminal emotional experiences and activities of the witches. In all these dimensions the emotions of the text are likely to be difficult for the reader to access, and difficult to acknowledge.

Whatever expectations the reader brings to the text, such a discomforting experience is probably going to produce an emotional distancing. This might be characterised by a response to the text which avoids discussion of the emotions contained there, and the brutal, abusive basis of the narrative. There is a deeply ingrained assumption that the reader's experience of a text is likely to be nurturing. The reader would probably prefer a text which reassures them of the stability and propriety of the pleasures to be experienced in the text, and the uncomplicated and unchallenging nature of pleasure itself.

The relation between emotion and innovative poetries returns us to our starting point about the nature of difficulty in such poetries. In her review of Monk's 2001 collection *Noctivagations*, Frances Presley notes that the discussion of experimental poetry by women continues to be characterised by a false polarisation between experimental and expressive. Presley comments that,

> It seems to me that a lot of experimental male poetry is intensely expressive, or emotional, but generally within a socialist framework.

> (Presley, 2003)

Presley's comment is an acute one with application beyond male poetry because it points to some of the ways in which experimental poetries differ from what we are obliged to call mainstream poetries: 'expressive, or emotional [. . .] within a socialist framework.' The emotions experimental poetries express are likely to be of a different order than the collections of uniformly elegiac personal anecdotes and social observations that continue to be regularly produced by major poetry publishers. These collections are full of feeling but it is feeling that is commodified, easily consumable and, crucially, largely indistinguishable from the life of feeling obtainable from a range of other cultural products such as films, soap operas, docu-soaps and the weekly Top Twenty of secular spirituals. It is a life of feeling presented as a diversion from the contemplation of the cultural, economic and political roots of feeling. Regular immersion in this diversion version of the life of feeling leaves us ill equipped for feeling that cannot and indeed refuses to be commodified.

References

Archer, M. and Monk, G. 2001. *Angel High Wires*. La Cooka Ratcha LCVP149CD

Barry, P. 2000. *Contemporary British Poetry and the City*. Manchester: Manchester University Press

Bate, J. 2003. 'Navigate the circus of fancy with fact'. *The Times Higher Education Supplement*, August 1st 2003, No. 1,600: 22–23

Belsey, C. 2003. 'Why I think we should end apartheid between English and Cultural Studies'. *The Times Higher Education Supplement*, July 18th 2003, no. 1,598: 16

Bernstein, C. 1983. *Islets / Irritations*. New York: Jordan Davis

Brown, P. 2002. *Dear Deliria: New and Selected Poems*. Cambridge: Salt Publishing

————— 2003. 'In conversation with John Kinsella'. *Jacket* 22 (May 2003). Viewable at: http://jacketmagazine.com/22/brown-kinsel.htm

Chernoff, M. 2001. *World: Poems 1991–2001*. Cambridge: Salt Publishing

Middleton, P. 2003. 'Silent Critique: Tom Raworth's Early Books of Poetry' in Dorward, N. ed., 2003. *Removed for Further Study: The Poetry of Tom Raworth. The Gig*, issue 13/14, May 2003, 7–29

Monk, G. 1994. *Interregnum*. London: Creation Books. Reprinted in Monk, G. 2003. *Selected Poems*. Cambridge: Salt Publishing, pp. 97–164

————— 2001. *Noctivagations*. Sheffield: West House Books

Pendle.Net: http://www.pendle.net/Attractions/pendlewitches.htm. Links to online and print resources about the Pendle Witches.

PendleWitches: http://www.pendlewitches.co.uk. Contains the confessions of Alizon Device, Demdike, Chattox and James Device as recorded by Thomas Potts, the Clerk of the Court at the trial of the Pendle Witches.

Plath, S. 1987. *Ariel*. London: Faber and Faber

Presley, F. 2003. 'Metablethers of Getha' [review of *Noctivagations*]. *How2*, Vol. 2, no. 1 (Spring 2003). Viewable at: http://www.departments.bucknell.edu/stadler_center/how2/ current/alerts/presley.shtm

Quakerinfo.com: http://www.quakerinfo.com/pendle.shtml

Silliman, R. 2003. Weblog entry, Friday March 14th 2003. Archived at: http://www.ronsilliman.blogspot.com

Ribble Valley Borough Council: http://www.ribblevalley.gove.uk/static/ page55.htm

Wolosky, S. 2001. *The Art of Poetry: How to Read a Poem*. London & New York: Oxford University Press

Authors' Note

Some of the material in this essay first appeared in David Kennedy's review of *Noctivagations*, published as 'Writing Larks', *PN Review* 147 (September-October 2002) Volume 29 Number 1: 78–79.

'Home-Hills': Place, Nature and Landscape in the Poetry of Geraldine Monk

Harriet Tarlo

In this essay I shall concentrate on place, specifically landscape and nature, in Geraldine Monk's work, in particular in the long sequence, *Interregnum*. It is common for much criticism of work variously known as experimental, avant-garde, linguistically innovative or postmodern to focus almost exclusively on form and language. This has acted as a corrective to the over-emphasis on subject matter and anecdotalism in more traditional poetry and poetry criticism. It has also however contributed to the divide, especially powerful in the U.K., between experimental and traditional poetry and has led, at its extreme, to a fetishisation of form. Neither of these effects are desirable. We are moving now toward critical approaches which consider writers' work more comprehensively, paying attention to issues as well as to poetics, and above all recognising the symbiotic relationship between the two.

Geraldine Monk's poetry lends itself particularly well to such wider consideration. She is a deeply engaged poet whose work is by no means divorced from its cultural context, but who does not want to simplify or reduce concerns about the wider world. Critics, such as Linda Kinnahan, Frances Presley and Keith Tuma, who have all considered her writing from a feminist viewpoint, have made this clear. As an early manifesto, issued with Maggie O'Sullivan suggests, she is aware that her poetics and politics are best fused and that that is where their radicalism lies:

> Ultimately, the most effective chance any woman poet has of dismantling the fallacy of male creative supremacy is simply by writing poetry of a kind which is liberating by the breadth of its range, risk and innovation.

> (Edwards in Allnutt et al, 1988, p. 269)

'Range, risk and innovation' are indeed present and, most importantly, *integrated* at every level of Monk's work. Above all, she is a writer who delights in language, for its own sake as well as for its meanings. One has only to read her early piece, *Angles Diversions Corners* (Monk, 2003, pp. 31–41) to see her mastery of the tricks of the experimental trade: the use of typography, enjambment of individual words, fragmentation of words, neologisms, compound words, ghost words, puns, homonyms and letters functioning as musical notes. All these, combined with the long, thin line of the poem and the lack of punctuation, trip the reader into a riddling question of how to read and makes a sacred 'sect of | word | playing' (Monk, 2003, p. 33). This is not a sect I intend to ignore in my consideration of a particular theme and to do so would be to mis-read the work, enforcing closed meanings on writing which resists them.

Whilst place is important to Monk's work, I would not wish to claim here that landscape and nature are a major, previously undiscovered, obsession of the writer. Monk is not a 'landscape poet.' What this essay will reveal is that her poetry can shed light on this subject precisely because she does not consider it in isolation. Her work, as is common in experimental poetry, challenges simplistic ideologies, such as those idealising and pastoral tendencies common in 'nature poetry', not least because she always considers 'nature' in its cultural context. As a result, it provides an interesting complement to some of the ideas current in eco-criticism. Just as criticism of postmodern poetry is engaged in broadening its remit, so many eco-critics are realising the need to integrate eco-critical approaches with other concerns and considerations. Patrick D. Murphy and Kate Soper for instance are attempting to develop critical positions which draw on the discourses of green theory, feminism and poststructuralism.[1] They are recognising that the world, and the text, are joined-up places, a reality that poets have always been more conscious of than critics. In Monk's case, in a poem such as *Interregnum*, issues of locality, culture, class and gender are inseparable and are in their turn related to place and landscape.

Experimental poetry, such as Monk's, which rejects the illusion of mimesis as natural, allows greater room for new perceptions of key eco-critical debates, such as the relationship between the human and non-

---

[1] Extracts from both these writers and many more can be found in Laurence Coupe's useful and accessible book, *The Green Studies Reader*.

human world.[2] I begin therefore with a consideration of the human being's relationship to place as portrayed in Monk's early writing. This also allows me to show how certain relevant thematic and technical patterns are established in Monk's work prior to *Interregnum*. Monk has always been seen as a writer who is concerned with the local. As Jeff Nuttall notes in his foreword to this book, her Lancastrian identity feeds into both the sense of place and the all important sonic and performative elements of her work. Place appears in both specific and general terms in Monk's writing, ranging from the great European cities to local Lancastrian scenes, rural and urban, from the specific locale to dislocated, lost, ghostly or mythic spaces. Place is also key to Monk's sense of Englishness. In her sequence, *Latitudes*, she explores various images of Northern and Southern England, in relation to the cultural divide between the two. Here is place as division, border and difference, a demonstration of how land can never be separated from politics and society. Monk names several of the poems 'elegies', suggesting a dying culture, and her manipulation of pastoral images shows her cynicism about the ideology of 'Green nostalgia' (Monk, 2003, p. 93). *Latitudes* ends with strong words drifting into precisely the images of the 'green and pleasant land' previously mocked in earlier poems:

Some union Jack. Some bloody union. Remember Jack.
Flying flags. Pigs might. Flies might. Fists might.
No Jack. Not pickets Jack. Don't talk wet. Don't talk
soft Jack.
Jenny.
Wren.
Cherry.
Cake.
Runny.
Oak.
Cricket.

(Monk, 2003, p. 96)

Here the draw to the old images of England is powerful, even as Monk suggests their decline and fall. Nature still has her pull and the mythol-

---

[2] One of the clearest discussions of this debate is to be found in Kate Soper's *What is Nature?* In her discussion of 'Ecological Discourses of Nature' Soper defines the 'metaphysical' idea of nature as the concept through which humanity defines its difference (Soper, 1995, p. 155). This lies at the basis of the question of humanity's relationship to nature. It is this debate which Monk's work sheds light upon.

ogising and idealising of nature is blended into the seductive sounds of Monk's language in this poem. Four starkly separated lines from 'North Bound: Facing South', an earlier poem in this sequence, encapsulate a warning:

Dumbswept. Vibrant. Earth-hug.

The rich nudge.

The lick of Eden.

Dangerous magic.

(Monk, 2003, p. 90)

It is these dangerous, potent seductions of nature that are considered at great depth in *Interregnum*.

Monk's natural images are frequently bound up with images of Old England in this way and the poetic genres, conventions and allusions of her early poetry interrogate our literary and cultural sense of ourselves. In sequences such as *Rotations* (Monk, 2003, pp. 11–16), four poems entitled after the seasons, and *Sky Scrapers* (Monk, 2003, pp. 51–73), poems springing out of cloud names, we find a double impulse, a tone which is neither simply nostalgic nor mocking, but which reflects our own desires and motivations. There is a sense of delight in nature and an element of description, but this is never simply realist. The 'natural' images constantly shade into human perceptions. In *Sky Scrapers* for instance each cloud poem is paralleled with a deeply human-centred poem that may originate with the sky, but ultimately takes us much further. Nonetheless there is a hint of the sacred in Monk's 'nature poetry', a Hopkinesque quality in terms of language and content. In *Interregnum*'s portrayal of place and nature we shall find all these concerns integrated and played off against each other. As readers, we shall be pushed to consider our human investment in nature, how this sits with our sense of the sacred, and our cultural sense of ourselves, be it in terms of gender or nationality.

The first part of the tripartite poem, *Interregnum* (first published by Creation Books in 1994), takes a relatively sardonic look at the contemporary users of Pendle Hill in Lancashire and the third part enters the time and place of the seventeenth century Pendle Witches, famously hung for witchcraft in 1612. 'Palimpsestus', the second part, provides a

transition between Parts 1 and 3, the contemporary and the early seventeenth century, allowing for reflection on themes germane to the whole.
The sequence is dominated by the final section which is approximately
four times the length of the other two parts.

 Interregnum opens with the following heading, poem title and first
two lines:

Nerve Centre

PENDLE

(brooding dislocation)
limits

(Monk, 2003, p. 99)

In characteristically provocative fashion, Monk immediately presents us
with a conundrum. *Interregnum* might be expected to focus very much
on a particular place, past and present. The title of this poem, 'PENDLE',
confirms this and the title of the section, 'Nerve Centre', implies indeed
that Pendle is the central location, the nexus of emotion and energy, for
the sequence. Yet, this is immediately undercut by the sly parenthetical
line, '(brooding dislocation)', and the word 'limits' which can be read as
a related afterthought. 'Dislocation' suggests an absence of belonging,
of a sense of place. This has implications for the first part of the poem
and the sequence as a whole. It could suggest that the contemporary
people who appear in Part I of *Interregnum* have very little or a rather
superficial sense of place and belonging. It could also act as a warning
that we can never really know the time and place of the Pendle witches
or how they felt about Pendle Hill. Did they have a greater or different
sense of place to us? That is a question we can never really answer.

 There will always be 'limits' to our understanding of place and nature
and, by extension, how strong a sense of connection we ourselves can
feel to nature, to how closely the human and non-human world can
inter-relate. The central picture which dominates this first poem, and
recurs again later in Part 1, confirms the sense of severe limitation to
human empathy with the non-human, in this case, animal, world. It is
the image of animals being seen under headlights and ('sometimes') run
over by cars:

<pre>
            grazing
                                    headlights
        catch
                    odd eye
                                    startles
    hearts
        odd creatures
    sometimes missed   sometimes hit
                    warm runny things
                    cold unmoving tarmac
        (lascivious sprawl   conscious and livid)
</pre>

(Monk, 2003, p. 99)

The spacing of the poem suggests the darting panicked animal, perhaps a rabbit or hedgehog. Yet the gap between human and animal is such here that the species is not in fact known at all, is simply named as an 'odd eye' or 'odd creature', suggesting an alien quality as well as 'odd' in the sense of a casual, random encounter. This creature, when run over, is then perceived perversely as 'lascivious', implying a sexual laying out. This establishes an idea which recurs throughout the first part of *Interregnum*, that of the human use of nature for its own titillation and sexual satisfaction.

The first part of *Interregnum* satirises this rude use and abuse of nature. Most of the titles of the ten poems represent a grouping of humans, reminiscent of a social or anthropological study of various tribes. Under the heading, 'The Hill People', we find 'Good Friday Hikers', 'Hallowe'en Bikers', 'Born Agains', 'Pagans' and 'Drivers' and beneath the heading, 'Hill Outriders', there are 'Shift Workers', 'Jesuit Boy Blues', 'Fox Hunt', 'Fox Trot' and 'Flyer.' Significant groupings of contemporary British people who use the landscape are represented here: hikers, bikers and drivers, those with religious motivations, satanic or pagan, and fox-hunters.

The metaphysical (sacred or profane) motivations of hill-visitors are significant for several of the groups. This will both echo and contrast with the Pendle Witches material to come. It is in this first part of the poem for instance that the recurring image of the crucifix as a sacrificial tree is first introduced. Here Monk implies a watered down, contemporary, somewhat dilettante sense of good and evil in our contemporary world. There is little sense of approbation or disapprobation in this, but there is plenty of satire. 'The Hill People' is particularly scathing about the smug hikers setting out on Good Friday for a hike on the hill. They seem blissfully oblivious to the darker connotations of that day in the Christian calendar, singing their ditty to a wickedly easy rhythm, interspersed with the mock Olde English 'fol di ree' and 'fol di raa.' Their 'knapsacks filled | with snap | emergency kits' suggest a cocooned, protected grouping, indicative of a diluted Christianity, with the demons and darkness removed. Yet the 'Hallowe'en Bikers' who follow have just as little depth of conviction in their demonic stance. Rather than bringing with them the whiff of hellfire, they bring instead the stink of 'sweat', 'piss' and 'patchouli.' Again, Monk belittles through the ditty, this time a well-known children's rhyme:

> studs
> ring a-ring
> a-rosy
> clash a holy
> war with
> water
> air
> earth-back
> firing-up
> turned cruci
> forms

(Monk, 2003, p. 102)

While the mounted bikers might suggest upturned crucifixes, their real war is with the elements, using their fiery bikes to up-turn the water, air and earth of nature. Their real motivation is not to be part of the battle of good and evil, but a sexual frisson of 'sweet | tassel thrills', the final jest of the poem being a witty, scatological reference to their 'leg-spreading | fundamental | engines' (Monk, 2003, p. 102).

The dualistic struggle between good and evil is further undermined by the poem 'Born Agains' which opens with the line 'sinlovers' immediately evoking the obsessive attraction between believers, be they Satanists or Born Agains (Monk, 2003, p. 103). The inter-dependency undermines both and is in contrast with the 'pure woolly | heads of | sheep.' These sheep heads can be read as a mocking image for the Born Agains and/or as purer than believers on both sides of the Christian fence. Either way, the sheep are subject to human projection, be it as symbolic Christian symbols or objects for Satanic ritual. Once again, Monk implies that the underlying motivation for the 'Born Agains' is sexual projection of desires taking the form here of a dream of building a thirty foot 'steel | erection', one assumes a crucifix, on the 'rather very small | Pennine hill' (Monk, 2003, p. 103). By a sleight of a mischievous pen, Pennine now reads with the shadow word, 'penile', hovering in its wake. Unusually, the poet takes a stance here, placing a witch-like curse on these plans: 'a fester on | your dreams' (Monk, 2003, p. 103).

In the following poem, 'Pagans', we move from the penile display fantasy to that of nature as the sexualised mother's body. Again, the pagans are dismissed as childlike and ineffectual:

pure Mother Earth fuck
wet volup of
        Venus
limps off at half-cock
wishy-w
roundandwound
little
circles
pretty patters
clownabout

    (Monk, 2003, p.104)

Both the 'Pagans'' desire to thrust into the hill and the 'Born Agains'' desire to erect their monument upon it are masculine projections of nature as feminine and say much about the patriarchal domination of nature, the sacred sphere and, as later poems will reveal, women. They chime with the ideas of Kate Soper who builds on the work of prominent eco-feminist, Annette Kolodny. Soper argues that the association of nature with the feminine has led to a downgrading of both (Soper, 1995, pp. 102-03). Nature is regarded as either a maternal womb or a virgin terrain to be colonised. Men's conflicting feelings about nature reflect their conflicting feelings about women, in particular their desire to dominate and their desire to be nurtured (Soper, 1995, pp. 103–06). Thus nature becomes their 'archetypal primary landscape' where incestuous desire for the mother can be expressed (Soper, 1995, p. 106).

The overall title of this sub-section of Interregnum, 'The Hill People', suggests natives, people who belong to the hill, yet the '(brooding dislocation)' of the very first poem, 'Pendle', suggests that these groups of humans belong only tangentially or temporarily, if at all. The 'Good Friday Hikers' are not of course people of the hill at all, but are walkers who could be anywhere or from anywhere, their mint cake from Kendal, their sweaters from Arran. Regionality, this poem seems to suggest, is lost to touristic tokenism, taking the easy, indulgent bits from each place and culture. Each group of 'Hill People' however feels they have the hubristic right to claim the hill as their own.

The second section of Part 1 of *Interregnum* is headed 'Hill Outriders' and it is here that we find the 'Shift Workers', ghostly figures recalling Lancashire's past as a centre of the cotton weaving industry. Their presence suggests that, for Monk, the ghosts of the past are not so far away from the people of the present and form part of the mystery of the hill. This will be confirmed by the treatment of the witches in part 3. However, the fact that the shift workers are 'Outriders', as contrasted with 'The Hill People', suggests that they are marginalised figures. They stand apart from those who have claimed the hill for themselves: their poverty, their decline as a group or simply their ghostly status excludes them. Ironically it is the shift workers who were the 'real' natives or 'hill people' of Pendle Hill, the ones born and bred there and fated never to travel far from that place, whereas many of Monk's contemporary groupings of people are those simply using nature for travel, leisure and spiritual entertainment.

It is not just the human inhabitants of the hill who preoccupy Monk in the first part of *Interregnum*. Significantly, the image of the animal road victims of the first poem of 'The Hill People' also dominates the final poem of the section, 'Drivers':

```
spin
     can
tin          chrome
aluminium womb
fine
     tuned in
     to cruise
               on out
     your
               bloody
     MIND
          that ani . . .
                    mal
                         (mal)
                              ((mal))

               (((warm runny thing      cold unmoving tarmac)))

                                        (Monk, 2003, p.105)
```

The inclusion of drivers here is important, for when we go to the coun-tryside now, to places such as Pendle Hill, we tend to travel in cars or pass purposefully through in cars on our way elsewhere. This radically changes our relationship to nature. In 'Drivers' Monk questions this urgent need to travel, using the term, 'unmoving' about the tarmac. This suggests an ultimate lack of destination or purpose, a 'motorway to nowhere', an image from a later poem, 'Flyer' (Monk, 2003, p. 110). 'Pendle' and 'Driver' both de-centre the homocentric view, emphasizing instead the flesh and blood of the living/dying animal in contrast to the 'cold unmoving tarmac.'

The 'aluminium womb' of the car suggests the driver's protection from the outside world, yet ironically is a not dissimilar image to that which nature in her guise of mother earth provides in earlier poems. The poem turns on the word, 'MIND', which is a multi-functioning word, a technique commonly employed by Monk. Drivers, as a clan, cruise out of their minds, until they hear, too late, the warning to 'mind' the animal. Their humanity is questioned: not only are they not using their minds, or being mindless, they seem attuned with the tarmac more than with the run over animal, still unnamed or recog-nised by them. The words, 'cold' and 'unmoving' might just as easily be applied to the 'MIND' of the drivers as to the tarmac. The emphasis on 'mal' suggests pain, wrongdoing, even evil. The ever-growing parenthe-ses imply the gradual exclusion or marginalisation of the animal pres-ence, ultimately in death. The drivers though are not wholly unaffected, the poem implies. The clash with the animal has broken the easy rhythm and smooth assonance of the first part of the poem. The 'mal | (mal) | ((mal))' evokes a car stereo (to which the drivers are 'fine | tuned in | to') becoming stuck or stalled.

The animal as it appears in 'Hill People' then has a double presence: it is both the natural resident of Pendle and the victim of human exploitation and destruction. 'Hill Outriders' however questions this pessimistic view. The final poems of 'Outriders': 'Fox Hunt', 'Fox Trot' and 'Flyer', can all be read as concerned with the non-human world, although more homocentric readings are possible, as I outline below. The fact that these poems are written in the voices of the animals concerned establishes the status of these natural residents of Pendle as 'outriders', whilst also giving them a voice in which to speak. 'Fox Hunt' and 'Fox Trot' are set side by side on facing pages: in the first poem, the fox is mercilessly attacked; in the second, the fox is free to wander. The two poems are vastly different in style and tone: the hunted fox speaks in humanised, rather archaic, language while the structure and tone of 'Fox Trot' attempt to embody the thought processes of an animal. In the latter poem the language is sonically stronger and less elaborate and the structure emphasizes the individual sounds of words, rather than the binding of words into grammatical units. There is a great emphasis on physicality, being in the body:

```
paw      sore
         bluster brain
storm    fit
         shudder limbs
seize    throat
         choke neck-a-neck
         hawk
```

(Monk, 2003, p. 109)

In this poem, the fox ascends the hill and oversees the landscape and seascape from above. The difficulty of the ascent is reflected in multiple parentheses, yet it is made. The two poems together can be read as successive stages of a narrative: the fox rises at the end of 'Fox Hunt' ('then staggering and bled | I rose red | a reversed emblem') (Monk, 2003, p. 108) and appears weakened and 'weary' in 'Fox Trot' (Monk, 2003, p. 109). This reading heightens the sense of the fox as a Christ-like figure rising from persecution, symbolic perhaps of the resurrection of the victim, in this case the non-human world.

'Flyer', which ends the section, suggests an even more liberated animal image and an even higher ascent. The bird-speaker of this poem enjoys a 'feathered kind of freedom' above the human scene:

```
now see the little people-pricks
see their little pinpricking
steeples to truth
and that motorway-to-nowhere's endless
curb crawling
every curve
in the unlit lights
of day and darker
I
fly across uncontrolled
airspace and
forests
```

(Monk, 2003, p. 110)

These 'pin-pricks' suggest humans might be seen by a bird as insignificant minor irritations, in particular the phallically-identified idiots and their idols who dominated 'Hill-People.' This 'nature' is not victimised: the air still provides a free 'uncontrolled' space and the forests stand against the motorway, that trivial reminder of petty, human concerns. The plosive p's in the first two lines quoted here evoke scorn and aggression as opposed to the soaring s's which dominate the last three lines of the extract and the poem. In Monk's animal-poems, we see an example of how imaginative literature, in particular experimental poetry, with its freedom of language and form, might be provocative in its reconsideration of human/non-human worlds, priorities and perceptions and might even try to erode away at the remorselessly homocentric perspective which dominates literature.

It is a mistake however to read Monk's animals *only* in a literal sense. The archaic language of the hunted fox heralds the language of the Pendle witch poems to come. Indeed, the whole fox-hunting theme of the poem can be read as emblematic of the witch hunt, as later recurring images of the Pendle Witches as hunted suggest. We can then see parallels between the scapegoating of foxes and the scapegoating of women as witches. It is only a slip of the tongue between 'foxhunt' and 'witchhunt.' As we have seen, Monk's work revels in such slips and the connections made through them. Just as the fox is blamed for the death of livestock, so the deaths of animals and family members, especially children, were blamed on the Pendle Witches' sorcery. In a much later poem, one of the witches, 'Mouldheels', puts the simple argument that such deaths came naturally among the poverty-stricken inhabitants of the Forest of Pendle:

I swear
folk dropped dead either side
of curse—they have a tendency to—
we didn't invent mortality
death came regardless
but the mind slavers—turns cannibal—
chance is connected—devoured
throats hurt—constrict
the inflamed lump of raw foresight—
swallow and keck
swallow and keck
keck.

(Monk, 2003, p. 143)

Scapegoating, as this poem suggests, gives the pack, the 'mind slavers' the right to hunt down the guilty party or to become cannibals of their own people. In Parts 2 and 3 of *Interregnum*, Monk uses another animal image to suggest the complicity of humanity in such huntings of women as the evil other. The image first occurs at the end of 'Palimpsestus' in the context of reflections on the exploited position of young girls in the sexual economy and mythology:

> . . . blinded
> > we pinned the tail in
> > > the donkey's eye
> > brayed
> > hilt deep
> > mortification

> > > > (Monk, 2003, p. 120)

It recurs in part 3 of the poem at the end of one of the 'Gaol Songs' which reflect on imprisonment and forced confessions:

> > blinded
> we pin the tail
> in the donkey's
> > eye

> > > > (Monk, 2003, p. 132)

The pronoun 'we' used here implies the actions of a group, a pack. The party game referred to, that of pinning the donkey's tail, is a game in which the pack gangs up against a blindfolded individual who cannot defend him or herself. Characteristically, Monk has taken an 'innocent' image from folklore or popular culture and changed minor elements (such as eye for tail) to create a more sinister picture.[3] The effect of the changes made is always to make us consider the obvious in more depth. Here, it is the pack who are blinded, not the donkey, thus indicating mass hysteria and blind justice.

What of the use of animals in Monk then? Firstly, it is never only literal. I am far from suggesting that Monk is writing about the torture

---

3 In her review of Monk's *Noctivagations*, Frances Presley has noted a similar use of a traditional game to more sinister ends in the poem *Manufractured Moon*: she shows how Monk uses references to this game to challenge patriarchal relationships. See also Presley's essay in this volume.

of donkeys here, but I would suggest that her use of animal imagery and language is beyond that of the simply metaphorical. In fact, she more commonly brings to life, even literalises, the human use of the animal in previously deadened uses of animal language, metaphors, fairytales, games or sport (the hunt). The first line of 'Hallowe'en Bikers' for instance, 'blackened cow hides', tracks the leather gear of the bikers back in three words to its literal origins, de-romanticising it in the process. The hunting down of the fox, the cannibalistic consuming of the fellow-being (rather than animal), the pinning of the donkey's eye: all of these are explicitly painful. Her self-conscious, defamiliarising use of language invites us to question our easy use of images from popular language and culture and examine what lies beneath them in terms of what we are saying both about our relationship with the non-human world and each other. It further encourages us to make connections between the two.

The first part of *Interregnum* suggests that Monk acknowledges the human exploitation of nature, whilst also touching on the unknown aspects of the non-human world that cannot be controlled or explained by human language and categorisation. 'Good Friday Hikers' mocks the walkers' amateur naturalism:

we fill our lungs
with fresh and windy air
to warble out our
naming of the
parts
    of nature's
rambling
        incoherence
    Fol di raa

(Monk, 2003, p. 101)

Whatever they think they know, nature remains 'incoherent' and the phrase 'naming of parts' once again evokes a controlling erotic impulse, this time comically euphemised away by the healthy hikers. Throughout the sequence, Nature is not portrayed as comprehensible or containable, by modern or historical characters. To Alizon Device, one of the witches, it is 'indifferent nature' (Monk, 2003, p. 160). However, the third part of *Interregnum* does explore in greater depth, and with more compassion, the beliefs and stories of the Pendle forest and hill dwellers. The tone is less dismissive and satirical, partly because of the tragic fate of the

Pendle Witches, but also because Monk is tracing back the watered down spirituality of the contemporary 'hill-people' to the more deeply held beliefs of earlier times. She is especially interested in those elements of religion, particularly prevalent in paganism, which suggest an erotic experience of nature as the mother's body.

We can make many links between the three parts of *Interregnum*. This works against the idea of history, and indeed poetry, functioning as a linear narrative and in favour of a circular reading of both. The end of the poem invites the reader back to the beginning. The second, transitionary part of the poem, 'Palimpsestus' confirms this feeling. As the title suggests, this piece of writing, which can be read as an individual poem, acts as a palimpsest, an overwriting of present on past, past on present as occurred literally in ancient societies. It also suggests an uncovering of that which has been wiped out. 'Palimpsestus' transports us from the contemporary period to the early seventeenth century and adopts a more sensuous, dreamy, almost unconscious tone and language to do so. It is evocative rather than directive and this impression is heightened by the frequent use of ellipses or trailing dots running between lines. The piece opens:

> . . . perpetual
> dreamdrip-backdrop
> pooling centuries
> deep
> crush and spurt of
> wide-open (or)
> and
> so on
> ting (or)
> jang of nerve chords wend-
> welter.

(Monk, 2003, p. 111)

Here and throughout, 'Palimpsestus' contributes to our sense of circular as opposed to progressive time, accentuating the continuity of emotional feelings and physical urges which lie at the bottom of our 'quiet ravings of. | desires' (Monk, 2003, p. 111) and, indeed our actions.

The chant-like, mystical, qualities of this middle section of three are heightened by the incantation of groups of threes which recur throughout. These begin with three disembodied voices:

```
. . . Three peaks.
  . Three dream-rollers.
  . Three prickly voices.
    piercing second sight
    chucking up visions from
                 ectoplasmic mists
```

(Monk, 2003, p. 112)

As the references to trinities accrete in the poem however, Monk leads us into a more profound understanding of their cultural history and gender and brings them closer to the reality of the poem. We associate three with the Christian trinity, but the twentieth century has seen many writers keen to excavate far older trinities of female goddesses and triads of female figures or archetypes still prevalent in fairytales and folk culture.[4] These often represent the three generations, moons or seasons (excepting Autumn) corresponding to the maid or virgin, mother and crone (sometimes a witch). As ever, this is not a mere abstraction in the poem: the three female generations of the Device family were key protagonists in the story of the Pendle Witches. Monk's second reference to three evokes the Christian inheritance of the number three:

```
              . . . Three aves
                    rise
                    RISE
                    RISE
              (in ascending order)
              hymnal sobtexts gusht
              Fruity Womb and Luv King
                king and queen of
                sacred-obscene-heart
```

(Monk, 2003, p. 114)

Here she is more satirical in tone, appearing to critique the exploitation of the feminine in the Christian ideology. The role of the woman here is to be the womb for the masculine seed. Monk's portrayal of the maiden or virgin of the female trinity in 'Palimpsestus' affirms this. She is

---

[4] Two important figures for the resurrection of the 'triple goddess' are Jane Harrison and Robert Graves. See in particular Harrison's chapter on 'The Making of a Goddess' in the *Prolegomena* and Graves' chapter on 'The Triple Muse' in *The White Goddess*.

constantly subject to sexual exploitation, even rape: 'can't breathe even moan | girl-mind | hooks on transference' (Monk, 2003, p. 118). By the final pages of the poem, the harsh realities of girlhood, as opposed to the romanticised, pagan image of the female trinity are exposed. This prepares us for the actual conditions of life for the Device women:

> . . . Three little shit houses
>   spawned
>   spawned
>   spawned
>   (NEVER ASKED TO BE)
>
>   (Monk, 2003, p. 119)

The girl here is born to be the receptacle of others' shit and to have her identity split into three by others' lascivious desires, rather than her own:

> my
> loin seeds
> my me me me
> divided into three
>   (NEVER ASKED TO BE)
> little shit houses . . .
>
>   (Monk, 2003, p. 119)

The final triad of women in 'Palimpsestus' are the fates:

> . . . Three women   Three sisters.
>   Three mill workers.
> spin.   wind.   cut.
> FATE.   FATE.   FATE.
>
>   (Monk, 2003, p. 120)

The threat of the 'cut' of the traditionally blind sisters, the fates, lurks throughout 'Palimpsestus' and finds its culmination in the hanging of the Pendle Witches, as relayed in the third part of *Interregnum*. The description of the fates as 'mill workers' reconnects us to an actual time and place, the lives women really led on Pendle Hill in Lancashire. Monk goes on however to call the three fates 'dispossessed daughters of Eve' (Monk, 2003, p. 120) and this re-establishes the wider spiritual-historical context. Christianity has displaced earlier images of womanhood which Monk is interested in excavating here. The co-existence of these two elements of Monk's meditation on the female trinity are highly characteristic of her work and add to the richness of the text. She remains interested both in social context but also in the history of spiritual ideas and ideologies. We can read the final lines of 'Palimpsestus' as an invocation to the ghosts of the past to finally awaken:

... (HUNTED HAUNTER) ...

... flesh fall from
words
fade
to ...

... (GHOSTS) ...

(Monk, 2003, p. 121)

Language here is both limitation and magical enabler allowing us access to the imagined, re-created past of the final part of the poem.

Part Three of *Interregnum* consists of two single introductory poems, 'The Great Assembly & Feast' and 'Spread', five sections of groups of poems and an epilogue poem. I shall not pay equal or chronological attention to the whole, but shall focus on those poems most relevant to my themes. Here then is a brief summary of the structure, language and themes of the third part in order to contextualise my discussion. The three poems of 'Chantcasters' act as a ghostly re-emergence of the witches and are spoken in their voices. The four 'Gaol songs' of 'Annexation' focus on the imprisonment of the witches, which took place in Lancaster Castle. The suffering of the witches is further elaborated on in the six poems of 'Speech-snatchers' that dwell on language as used in interrogation and confession. These first three parts of the poem, although drawing on seventeenth century material here, reflect more widely on issues which never disappear: gender battles, imprisonment, mass hysteria, scapegoating and the use and abuse of language in the wider world outside poetry. Monk's inclusion of contemporary language such as 'panic police' and 'public imagination' (Monk, 2003, p. 131) adds to this effect.

However, as befits the general drift backwards in time, the final two parts of the poem employ more antiquated language and incorporate Lancastrian dialect, such as 'thi med it up' (Monk, 2003, p. 153). Both

sets of poems are written in the voices of the witches themselves. In the
ten poems of 'Out-thoughts' each of the accused is introduced by their
nickname; in the nine poems entitled 'The Replies' the characters are
given their formal names, perhaps as the court would have used them.
Hence 'Chattox' becomes 'Anne Whittle' and 'Squintin' Lizzie' becomes
'Elizabeth Device.' Both groups of poems end with a final poem in the
voice of 'ALL.' The 'Out-thoughts' seem to represent the more genuine
thoughts of the speakers outside their interrogations; they reflect most
on the past before prison and are most relevant to my analysis of the
witches' relationship to Pendle Hill. 'The Replies' focus on the experiences of the accused in Lancaster Castle and, as in 'Speech-snatchers',
stress the importance of language in the confessions and trials. The
accusers' language is portrayed by the accused as crafty, class-inflected
and oppressive. The same voices appear in 'Out-thoughts' and 'The
Replies', with one exception. Jennet Device's voice is missing from 'The
Replies.' Jennet was the nine-year old sister of Alizon Device, whose testimony was instrumental in the downfall of the witches and this provides
one reason for her separation from the rest in this final part. Jennet's
poem, 'The Eternal Bewilderment of Jennet Device', appears at the very
end of the sequence, as an epilogue, and my analysis of it forms the
culmination of this essay.

Monk refuses a simple explanation of the Pendle Witches' story or a
moral judgment of their actions, not least because she allows different
characters to express different views in the poem. Even the question of
whether they were engaged or thought they were engaged in working
magic or not remains open to debate in the poem. She does however
identify the witches with the hunted fox and with the crucified Christ.
While, on one level, this implies victimhood, on another it suggests
resurrection. As I have argued, the fox of part 1 of *Interregnum* is a heroic
figure. Throughout the Gaol Songs of part three, the witches are
compared to Christ, perhaps the ultimate hero. Frequent references to
the cross and phrases such as 'barely nailed | hands' (Monk, 2003, p. 130)
and 'disfigured beneath crowns' (Monk, 2003, p. 136) confirm the anal-
ogy. Thus Monk challenges the idea of the witch as evil, while maintaining the notion of the witch as powerful in our collective imagination. As the '. . . (HUNTED HAUNTER) . . .' part of 'Palimpsestus' suggests,
the Pendle Witches are still with us, the true 'hill-people' of Pendle. They
are haunting figures, evoking guilt and anxiety in the reader. Ironically
they have become the threat they once, perhaps mistakenly, seemed.
The 'Out-thoughts' section of the sequence may appear to explain the

secret thoughts of the witches but the final poem of the section, spoken in the voice ' ... *of* ALL ... ', denies us an answer:

Wish-burnt to bone:
To out-think. Out-manoeuvre.
Out-last you.
To move. Shapeshift. Move again.
To conjure your breakdown.
Seizure.
[...]
To turn every key   Learn every combination.
Every take-down. Pinning.
Escape reversal.

(Monk, 2003, p. 151)

Monk's characteristically ambiguous use of pronouns here allows two simultaneous readings of this poem. On the one hand, we can read it as addressed to those who imprisoned and hung the witches. On the other, as is common in poems making use of 'you', the reader is made to feel challenged, as if the poem is addressed to him or her self. This increases our sense of complicity, mentioned before in the context of the foxhunt. We too are the 'closed and peevish' mediocre people who condemned the witches and, as in all cases of scapegoating, fear is the motivation:

We wished out. Just to pass.
Please. We said it nice. But no. Fear showed.
through. Had to. Finally. Run a finger down
your spine. Feathery. Teasing.
You turned. You faced us.
We turned. We faced you.
Your mouth turned up.
Ours turned down.

(Monk, 2003, p. 152)

The language here returns to the basic, colloquial language of the witches and the past tense of the narrative, as opposed to the present tense of the ever-haunting witches. Yet the reader still feels implicated in the fear and pleasure the witches' hunters feel as they refuse to let the women go. This reading also provides a challenge and a warning to the reader or literary critic who may attempt to account for the witches through this or that sociological, sacred or gender theory. They will keep shifting and moving out of any image offered to encapsulate or 'pin' them and yet they will keep haunting too:

> Steal
> up behind you
> tap
> (so gently)
> tap   tap
> your left shoulder
> ghosting   you won't see   standing right
> tap again

(Monk, 2003, p. 151)

Why should 'we', the wider culture, have such fear of witchcraft and, by extension, the poem implies, of deviant women in general? The association of the witch with nature and pagan rituals is part of her power and is explored throughout these poems. The opening lines of the first poem of part 3, 'The Great Assembly & Feast',[5] immediately suggest this:

> Loped & strungalong the calmquake forests of astonished
> branches. Crissed rivers teeming spring. Much upona.
> Clambered hummock and dung and sleeping animal-hill.

(Monk, 2003, p. 122)

The closing lines of the same poem associate this witch-as-nature with a suspicious, masculine view of femininity. The witches here are 'they', the other:

> They glamour. They bleed. Deceive. Imperfect animal. Barely
> once removed from. Come. Snake woman. Wolf woman.
> Whore woman. Witch. Deformed and depraved mother woman.
> Worry-to-death woman. Howl all night under reeds. Girlgrace.
> Blood to nothing. Love seed. Nether smell. Pro terra. Contra
> mundum.

(Monk, 2003, p. 122)

---

5   The title of this poem makes reference to James Device's confession that the witches all met for a Sabbat at the Devices' house, Malkin Tower, on Good Friday 1612 where they enacted a satanic parody of the Christian Good Friday and plotted to blow up Lancaster Castle in order to free the witches already imprisoned there, in particular Alizon Device. Monk sums up this part of the story in the following elliptical line in the poem: 'Ganged Malkin Tower to fest and murder plot. Grow semtex—a likely' (Monk, 2003, p. 122).

The horror at the bodily functions of woman and association of these as animalistic, as well as the Latinate language and classificatory tone of the piece, suggests the classic voice of masculine Western Christianity. They chime again with Soper's arguments discussed above about the downgrading of both women and nature through their common association: woman, Soper argues, is associated with her bodily functions and considered outside culture and history (Soper, 1995, p. 103). In Monk's poem only the 'girlgrace' of a virgin is acceptable in a patriarchal society and this is defiled by her 'fall' into adult sexuality. Hence the cult of the virgin already touched upon in 'Palimpsestus': only the Virgin Mother can escape this corruption into 'Deformed and depraved mother woman.' This logic denies not only women's cultural history, but also their female sexuality, both ideologies which Monk challenges in *Interregnum*.

This is the patriarchal ideology; Monk's portrayal of the women's own relationship to nature, as conveyed through the witches' voices, is very different. In 'Chantcasters', the dry tone and short stabbing sentences of 'The Great Assembly & Feast' are superseded by a flowing song-like voice. The poem, 'Demdike sings', is literally 'down to earth', yet poetic:

Wild air.
world-mothering air,
nestling me everywhere,
that's fairly mixed
with riddles
and is rife
in every least things life
and nursing element

(Welcome in womb and breast
Birth-milk draw like breath)

(Monk, 2003, p. 125)

Throughout the poem, air is the element of mothering and hence, life, which nurtures the 'witch' Demdike. This raises the question of whether the feminine perception of nature as mother might be different from the masculine? Although the witches do associate nature with the feminine, there is less emphasis on this as a spiritual association than on nature as a place for a woman to be free, 'as air.' It is possible to read poems such as Demdike's as revealing women's ideological complicity with masculinist culture, yet when Monk adds into the equation the socio-cultural context of women's lives, this perception of nature can be seen to function as a liberator. Throughout the 'Out-thoughts' poems, we find individual witches extolling the freedom of the elemental space of nature in the midst of a confined life:

> Flapping wildly in
> cloud broods
> move and roost of hill rain
> I never tired of.
>
> [. . .]
>
> Consorting with elements:
> fractious, undesirable,
> contra, alive. The pit
>
> against pit of rootless
> ease. The feed for my ungovernable
> core to help me fight the regime of
> mealtimes and the stifling niceties
> inbetween—
> called 'life'.

(Monk, 2003, p. 142)

Alizon's 'out-thoughts' sustain this view of nature as relief from the 'predictability' of everyday life and portrays the witches as girls indulging in sexual fantasies which, as we have seen, are not easily accessible to them in a society which censors female desire:

> Sure we dreamt charms;
> stared into watery space making
> ripples across the boredom
> and piss-thin broth
>
> and those sometimes dry summers
> sinking head-low and happy in
> grasses and bracken:
> mating with ghosts.

(Monk, 2003, p. 147)

In 'Gaol Song Part 1' imprisonment is portrayed as alienation from the speaker(s)' own place and space in nature:

No physics
can explain
the tortured ball of
mind screwed up and
savaged into dense primordial
blacK
        Holes obliterate
inscape
remembered stars
and home-hills filled
with mists
                seep through
the impenetrable walls

(Monk, 2003, p. 129)

The remembered place here, the 'home-hills' of Pendle, is both absent, obliterated by imprisonment, and yet still powerful, seeping through the prison walls of Lancaster Castle. The spatial and typographical design of the poem allows for this double reading of home, swallowed by the space embodied in the poem after the word 'blacK', yet seeping in, again invisibly, through the space after the word 'mists.'[6] So it is that Monk's use of language is often quite explicit, even simple, as in this poem, and yet, through its innovative forms, embodies greater complexities than at first apparent. The gaol here is also open to multiple readings: it may represent actual prisons, but it may also represent the imprisonment of mental torture. In this case, the significance of nature as home, the remembered place, becomes central to the poem. Chattox's 'out-thoughts' poem takes up this image of the lost hill, beginning with the lines, 'As the hill imperceptibly steepened | and dimmed' (Monk, 2003, p. 139). Again, the increased alienation from the hill, steeper as in harder to access, is a mental state, as much the result of the assault of the 'invisible squadrons' plaguing the 'inner roof of my skull' as the result of imprisonment. In these poems then, Monk explores the double-functioning importance of nature to the human, or perhaps specifically woman, as both home/mother and wilderness and, a literal and a mental space of both freedom and security, the 'home-hills.'

Thus far my discussion of the witches' engagement with nature seems harmless and innocent. However Monk also portrays the witches'

---

[6] The capitalised 'K' here allows for 'blacK' to refer to both dense blackness and black holes, the 'K' acting as a conjunctive across the space.

darker beliefs about nature and it is here that she shows their more sinister or superstitious convictions, depending on one's reading of the poem. In her 'out-thoughts' for instance, Demdike gives a heartless, even matter-of-fact, account of her clay charms created to kill or maim:

> Oh certainly the images cried.
> It is the way of clay.
> Wetness . . . oozing through fingers . . .
> make-believe eyes running . . .
> to the far-off alarm call of birds.
>
> I dried them. Fixed them. Thorn-pricked them.
> Then sat well back and waited for the
> diabolical climate to heighten.
> Obliterate.

(Monk, 2003, p. 141)[7]

Here Demdike regards herself as the artist working with 'dumb foxed earth', rather than nature as *her* tutor in the dark arts. Monk's language is always sceptical, but ambiguous, when her speakers give accounts of their witchcraft. Single words cast shadows of doubt across Demdike's story: is the crying clay simply that of the earth and water with which Demdike works or is the 'clay' of humanity which must always cry? are the 'make-believe' eyes those belonging to the images Demdike has made or those of the people who she wrongly imagines (or makes believe) have become her victims?

While these matters are left unresolved, it is evident that Monk locates spells and witchery within the natural world. We can see this in the way Monk has used original sources, one clear example being that of the 'prayer' of the 'three biters' recorded in the Thomas Potts' account of Chattox's Confession in 1612:

> She the said Examinate saith, That shee was sent for by the wife of John Moore, to helpe drinke that was forspoken or bewitched: at which time shee used this Prayer for the amending of it, viz.
>
> A Charme
> Three biters hast thou bitten,
> The Hart, ill Eye, ill Tonge:

---

7   This account is based on Demdike's own confession recorded in Thomas Potts' *The Wonderful Discoverie of Witches in the Countie of Lancaster* (Pendle Witches website).

Three bitter shall be thy Boote,
Father, Sonne, and Holy Ghost
a gods name.
Five Pater-nosters, five Avies
and a Creede,
In worship of five wounds
of our Lord.

After which time that this Examinate had used these prayers, and
amended her drinke, the said Moores wife did chide this Examinate, and
was grieved at her.

(Pendle Witches website)

In 'Palimpsestus', the 'three biters' appear as yet another alternative
trinity (Monk, 2003, p. 116), but it is in the culminative 'ALL SING' poem
of 'Chantcasters' that they become:

Three biters bitten:
Earth's eye. *Earth's* tongue. *Earth's* heart.
Our counterparts cleaved. Wreathed. Cloven.
This age and era's evil ills
dearly and dangerously sweet
delights buried deep.
Tell us where?
A wild web.
A wondrous robe.

(Monk, 2003, p. 128, my emphasis)

The magic here then is of 'earth', 'a wild web' of connections, and, the
poem implies, that it is in or through the bodies of the witches that it
can be accessed:

Around the beating heart.
In the fine flood.
In the deathdance in the blood.

(Monk, 2003, p. 128)

The witches who see themselves as part of nature are not only portray-
ing nature as access to innocent freedoms then. It is also a seeking of
bodily pleasures through pagan nature, which may lead to stranger still
experiences. In her 'Out-thoughts', we see Anne 'drawn to strange things
in earth' and these change her perceptions of the world:

membranes stranger
squatted—flared viral
—acuity mangled senses—
squatted and smeared through under
growth breathing visibly.   audibly.   ir
regular.   wiped glutinous cells against
naked ankles—nerve contractions—
—revulsion—

(Monk, 2003, p. 144)

Here Anne's physicality draws her into a changed mental state: the animalistic language suggests that she feels herself becoming part of the natural world. Both language and structure here suggest an erotic engagement with the outer world, yet one that is earthy and corporeal, not diaphanous and mystical. The awkwardness of the phraseology and use of enjambment as well as the final word, 'revulsion', suggests that such transformations may be ugly, even satanic. The same is implied at the centre of Alice's poem in the 'Out-thoughts' part of the sequence. While the poem, as quoted above, begins and ends in images of freedom for the girl running through the hill rain, there is a still, sinister centre to the poem comparable to Anne's transformative encounter discussed above:

White. Sightless. Bafflement.
Thickening animal throats
mutating child   man   woman
and the half-faced apparitions
stained sliver of eye
meeting sliver of I in
the glare of mutual suddenness.

(Monk, 2003, p. 142)

These poems point us back to the accounts the witches give in their confessions of encounters with familiars, encounters which often contain an erotic, physical element: Alizon Device confesses to meeting her familiar spirit in the form of a 'Blacke Dogge' who sucks at her breast; Anne Whittle (Chattox) meets the Devil in the shape of a man called 'Fancie' and Elizabeth Southern (Demdike) sells her soul to a spirit in the shape of a boy called Tibb who also appears to her as a brown dog who sucks her blood. Here Pendle forest (nature even) conjures up satanic spirits who transform themselves before the very eyes of the witches, but who, Monk suggests here, are not so much the evil 'other' as the other self. It is the 'sliver of I' that the wanderer meets in the woods.

Nature may seem thus far to be an escape from hard reality but it is also of course a part of that reality, as well as a part of the self. Monk portrays hard 'nature' in her poem in the voice of the Bulcocks (mother and son) travelling through the landscape:

> squeezing through gaps
> of hurt and backbreak
> we travelled for miles—
> pressured by ripeness
> by furious blood
>
> (no genteel tittering lark
> puckering lips to an Ooo-o-o-o)
>
> GREAT GOBBY SPURTS OF WIDE OPEN
>
> nagging at the hill
> and hanging valleys
> daft-mad with root spikes
> & spirits
> piked with
> feeling tangents
>
> TILL WE CRIED

> (Monk, 2003, p. 145)

Here nature is neither elegant nor beautiful for people of the poorer class who do not have time to listen to the larks. The 'root spikes | & spirits' evoke two sources of madness: the food the Bulcocks scrape their survival with and the spirits they encounter, the physical and the mystical. In the light of poems such as this, it is perfectly possible to sustain the view that the witches' mystical ideas about nature are merely the sad and fearful delusions of ill-educated people with hard lives. The stanza immediately following Anne's account of her strange encounter suggests a different kind of transformation from the magical, the transformation starvation works on the human body:

> families starved into strange creatures
> —otherworld animals—
> eyelids sloughed and twitched for comfort
> for food and fire
> for quench

retina burnouts
the scorch of contagious dreamscapes
parallel nightmares
beloved anaesthetic.

(Monk, 2003, p. 144)

The concluding verse of this poem implies that the sight of families starving should not have to be endured by the eye or retina of the watcher and are just as horrific as anything the 'otherworld' can produce. What is the 'beloved anaesthetic' here? Is it perhaps nature or witchcraft or both: the transformation of the 'home-hills' into a magical 'dreamscape' filled with more exciting images of transformation than that offered by starvation?

In the Jennet Device poems, we find a culmination of the sequence as a whole and a demonstration of how these differing but interconnecting views of the relationship between the human and non-human world interact. Jennet Device is prominent in the poem as a whole, the penultimate speaker in the 'Out-thoughts' section of *Interregnum* and the final speaker in the 'Replies' part of the poem, and hence the whole sequence. Her poems have a certain poignancy and pathos in particular the extended references to 'mi mother' in the latter poem. Jennet's testimony, though she was only nine at the time, was instrumental in the fate of many of the witches, including her mother. Her grandmother died awaiting trial and her mother, sister and brother were all hung on 20 August 1612. The title of the final poem of the sequence, 'The Eternal Bewilderment of Jennet Device', and the final lines of the poem imply that she did not really understand the consequences of her testimony:

a turn of consequence unknown
till
slow and sinking in
till
known out loud

alone

OH MA
the word all round
is

TOUCHED

(Monk, 2003, pp. 163–64)

The poem appears under the heading, 'Touching the Everywhere', and the use of the word, 'touch', when set beside 'bewilderment', might suggest that Jennet was a little 'touched', in the colloquial sense of the word. But what 'touched' Jennet Device, what made her into a girl who refers to the 'weirdy world' (Monk, 2003, p. 149) and who begins her final poem, 'I weird sang' (Monk, 2003, p. 163)?

Monk does not explicitly answer this question, but her two poems in the voice of Jennet are important for our reading of nature and gender in the sequence as a whole. The word 'touch', as in so many of Monk's words, carries multiple implications here. In the context of Jennet's story, 'touching the everywhere' has sinister sexual, and hence gender, undertones, especially when read back through James Device's and Jennet's own consecutive 'out-thoughts' poems. James's poem of a 'weary life' portrays the Device siblings as finding consolation through incestuous physicality:

Glowy cold. Starved to each
poriferous bone. Aching warmth. Aching
feet creepin up between Alliz inner thighs screamin
gedoffsob-laughin little Jenny joininin
flailin daft-to-bleedin kicks
six seggy eels scouring dark
for blood heated landings and mother
groanin shudup moanin grow up please
to her self-soft sleep and earth warm dirt
of her dreams—
as thirty little piggies
squealed demented—
in extremis.

(Monk, 2003, p. 148)

The images are ambiguous, but by no means painless and harmless, as the reference to blood and 'gedoffsob-laughin' imply. Jennet Device, the youngest, 'eternally bewildered', must surely be the main victim here, her 'out-thoughts' poem evoking her innocence:

That giggle-game trickled to the brink
we re-formed
            ganged
            crawled on all fours
[. . .]

me and Jamie: seeds alert:
playing at animals again.

(Monk, 2003, pp. 149–50)

The animal reference picks up on the 'piggies' of the previous quotation.
The 'touching [. . .] everywhere' implied by this reading of the poems
suggests some reason, not only for Jennet's bewilderment, but also for
her perhaps unconscious motivation for betrayal of her own family who
have not protected her. It also sends us back to 'Palimpsestus''s
reflections on the precarious and exploited position of the virgin girl in
society, reconnecting us to the wider gendered reading of *Interregnum*.
  Yet we are prevented from too easy an interpretation of these poems.
'Touching the Everywhere' can also suggest a reading of nature and
physical relationships as positively erotic, the rediscovery of female
sexuality which is hinted at throughout the witch poems. This is
confirmed by its first appearance in the sequence, in 'Jesuit Boy Blues'
from the 'Hill Outriders' section of part one of *Interregnum*:

Dear and dogged man. Selfbent, bound;
So tied and turned, brows of such care,
World bare, and none to touch my everywhere
Perfumed, greedy, guilt dreams of long-grass
Love-boys, sea-shells, blue-breeze stings and
Salts my tonguing meaty meatless sins to
Whip the words across and cross my precious
Selfworn, world-torn, aching bodybent. Ah!

(Monk, 2003, p. 107)

This is the closest *Interregnum* comes to a love poem and the fantasies
and affections within it are between equals and within an eroticised
pastoral context. Jennet's poems can also sustain this more positive
reading, though the lover here is nature whose sensual powers reach
out to the physical body of the woman. In Jennet's 'out-thoughts' poem
it is the 'Fish-damp creepy green | weirdy world' that provides sexual
stimulation and threat, inspiration and setting for the siblings' dubious
games:

(the rolling dream-hills
                                murmured to the north)
     masked dancer of night
                                s u n b l e d
     taunter   taunted

flayer of shadows
                    cock-walker

(Monk, 2003, p. 149)

In 'The Eternal Bewilderment of Jennet Device' it is Jennet herself who
is the dancer, nature the context for her own wild games:

I weird sang.   High trilled and skirled.
I led a merry crab-dance.   Bright.
Kookie-mad.
Rhymed thing with thing string . . .
word buntings.   Wildways
across XXXXXXXXXX
For ever acting.   Playing.
        all   out

(Monk, 2003, p. 163)

The sonic elements of the language in this extract indicate a brighter,
lighter, more liberated Jennet stimulated into creative play with
language in an eroticised landscape. This echoes the 'out-thoughts' of
Chattox, who sees herself as a wordsmith, and Demdike, the maker of
clay images, a creator or artist. Although Jennet's final poem is set aside
from those of the other speakers, Monk does not then draw a sharp
divide between Jennet and the other witches. Although they were on
different sides of the law in 1612, all the women are active participants
in the world of Pendle Forest and are also equally victims of what we
may term in feminist shorthand the 'patriarchal system' of their day,
Monk intimates.[8]

The central lines of 'The Eternal Bewilderment of Jennet Device' are
taken up with an extended 'weird song' or semiotic soundplay on the
mother. Julia Kristeva's semiotic chora is a 'rhythmic space' through
which the language of the Father can be disrupted through the body of
the Mother (Kristeva, 1984, p. 26). Kristeva describes this as a 'vocal or
kinetic rhythm' in which the semiotic breaks into the symbolic in
poetic language (Kristeva, 1984, pp. 46–49). The theory seems especially
relevant to a piece of writing which is not only written in language

---

[8] It is perhaps worth mentioning here that the real Jennet Device was herself
accused of witchcraft twenty-one years after the rest of her family and shut up in
Lancaster Castle, a fact Monk does not record here but which provides another
interesting gloss on her role in the story (Pendle Witches article).

focused more on sound than sense, but which also represents a child's voice attempting to re-access the lost mother. Thus, as ever, the historical story is allied to abstract theory in Monk and the Lancashire inflexions add to this impression of Jennet's voice reflecting on her (self-) destructive family, her mother's and her own possible murderous instincts:

> OH MA
> mi maa   mi mother
> mUth   er ing
> muth   rin
> muR   ther   ing ringa
> killything-a   Gran.   Ali. J.
> killyall thing-s bright XXXXXXXXXX
> killymaa
> killykin a killy killy kin
> ever mother mothering (eat yer din dins)

> (Monk, 2003, p. 163)

The phrase 'eat yer din dins' provides welcome humorous release here—a common strategy in Monk's writing when the pathos or horror is building. The next part of the poem extends the 'mothersong' into a more generalised reflection on mother as divine and as of nature, the hill:

> O mother mine
> mother o me
> mother o diva
> mother o prima-diva-donna on
> the hill-sang
> Mother-O Me-o
> O
> that lime lit cherry glow
> moment
> table high and turning
> mi heart content . . . .

> (Monk, 2003, p. 163)

Interestingly, the Lancashire voice recedes here as Monk moves from the specific to the general mother image. We can read this song then both biographically as Jennet's song about her own mother, Elizabeth, and as a more general final song or tribute to the mothering hills of home.

References

Allnutt, G. et al ed., 1988. *The New British Poetry*. London: Paladin

Coupe, L. ed., 2000. *The Green Studies Reader from Romanticism to Ecocriticism*. London: Routledge

Graves, R. 1961. *The White Goddess. A Historical Grammar of Poetic Myth* (1946). London and Boston: Faber and Faber

Harrison, J.E. 1922. *Prolegomena to the Study of Greek Religion* (1903). Cambridge: Cambridge University Press

Kinnahan, L. 1996. 'Experimental Poetics and the Lyric in British Women's Poetry: Geraldine Monk, Wendy Mulford, and Denise Riley'. *Contemporary Literature* 37 (4), 620–670

Kristeva, J. 1984. *Revolution in Poetic Language*. trans. Margaret Waller. New York: Columbia University Press

Kolodny, A. 1975. *The Lay of the Land*. Chapel Hill: University of North Carolina Press

Monk, G. 2003. *Selected Poems*. Cambridge: Salt Publishing

Murphy, P.D. 1995. *Literature, Nature and Other: Ecofeminist Critiques*. Albany, NY: State University of New York Press

Pendle Witches website: http://www.pendlewitches.co.uk.

Pendle Witches article. Viewable at: http://www.lancs.ac.uk/users/history/studpages/lanchistory/pendle.htm

Presley, F. 2003. 'Metablethers of Getha' [review of *Noctivagations*]. *How2*, Vol. 2, no. 1 (Spring 2003). Viewable at: http://www.departments.bucknell.edu/stadler_center/how2/current/alerts/presley.shtm

Soper, K. 1995. *What is Nature? Culture, Politics and the Non-Human*. Oxford and Cambridge USA: Blackwell

Tuma, K. 1998. *Fishing by Obstinate Isles: Modern and Postmodern British Poetry and American Readers*. Evanston, Illinois: Northwestern University Press

What the Tourists Never See:
The Social Poetics of Geraldine Monk
SEAN BONNEY

It is interesting to imagine what a reader of what is still conventionally sold as 'poetry' in this country would think when first faced with the work of Geraldine Monk. Bewilderment and confusion are probably most likely, hopefully to be followed by an excitement—particularly if hearing her read the poems aloud—not usually associated with what is still erroneously known as 'mainstream poetry.' I do not wish to go too far into the public arguments about the nature of poetry that continue to have a knock-on effect on the scene, interested readers are pointed in the direction of cris cheek's excellent note in *The Poetry of Tom Raworth* (Dorward, 2003, pp. 186–87). Having said that, and even though the situation does appear to be changing, Ben Watson's provocative claim in *Art, Class and Cleavage*, that 'mainstream—or "comprehensible"—poetry has evidently become the final citadel of bourgeois good taste to be defended from the barbarian hordes' (Watson, 1998, p. 325), does still ring true. Questions of 'good taste', even of 'barbarian hordes', continue to be pertinent when considering those poets who work must be considered in opposition to the standards of official poetry, and by extension, official society.

Since the late 1970s, when she first began to publish her work, Geraldine Monk has been associated with a group of radical, or even revolutionary, poets operating at a considerable distance from official notions of good taste and official poetry. Far from believing a poem to be merely its dictionary definition of a 'composition of high beauty of thought or language', poets such as Monk, as well as Barry MacSweeney, Bill Griffiths and Maggie O'Sullivan, to name only the first that come to mind, proposed the poem as an intricate mesh of meaning, sound and energy likely to have an explosive effect on the reader or listener. There

is no reason why the experience of reading or hearing a poem cannot
as exciting as leaping about to a good rock n' roll band in a sweaty ba
ment, and there is also no reason why this should preclude the intellectual sophistication necessary for a meaningful engagement.

The irony of its marginalisation is that this radical poetry is actually
part of a tradition in British poetry that can be traced back centuries.
Predecessors of this practice can be found in Bunting, Hopkins, Blake,
Coppe—it can arguably be traced right back to the Welsh bards. It is a
gnarly, difficult poetry characterised by sharp, bright language and an
emphasis on sound. Most importantly of all, it is a poetry that refuses to
look away from the frustrations, contradictions and injustices of life in
this country; a key belief is encapsulated in William Blake's famous
insistence that 'poetry fettered fetters the human race' (Blake, 1989,
p. 633). When we add to this tradition the influences from abroad, the
heritage of a twentieth century avant-garde that mainstream poets
would like to pretend never existed, it becomes clear that we are dealing
with a major, and also critical, art form. As with any radical art form,
this poetry is a breaking of hypnosis.

The first thing that a reader new to this work may notice is a bewilderment of meaning. Meaning runs wild, so that it is not entirely possible to pin down precisely what is being said, and separate readings of
the same work will bring different factors to the surface. There may be
a reading that concentrates on the political content, or on sonic effects,
or simply for the pleasure of getting lost in the tensions and energies
central to the work. Any one or a combination of those readings would
be equally valid. That is, the reader has to forget expectations of what a
particular poem will give, or illusions that the poem is being served up
as an easily digested product, and understand that the idea of 'meaning'
itself should not be taken as fixed, and propose instead a meaning that
is broken into and extended by the poetry itself. Essentially, the work is
opposed to a tamed, domestic version of poetry still current in some
quarters. Here is an example from Monk's *Angles Diversions Corners*:

> about t
> urns cork
> screw a
> gain ca
> tch wind
> ow
> frame re
> flect f
> lick knife

(Monk, 2003, p. 33)

The extreme use of line-breaks and the lack of punctuation give a feeling of excess speed, as if the whole thing were running out of control and the words actually falling apart under the pressure of it all. But the excitement of the poem is located precisely in what happens when words do fall apart, or are sliced open; what happens when authoritarian attitudes of fixed meaning are given the slip. Even before the words break, what is being said is not entirely clear: 'about turns corkscrew again catch window frame reflect flick knife.' As with the long poems of Tom Raworth, perceptions are rushing past too fast to settle into any one particular meaning or statement. The eye swings from a bottle of wine being opened to the view of the window, and finally to a flick knife. Perhaps this is a still life, or a domestic scene. The flick knife (not just any knife but one used specifically as a weapon, one criminalised in this country) troubles the perception, and turns the attention back to the corkscrew. We wonder if that too is being used as a weapon. The assumptions begin to break up.

When attention is paid to the line breaks—actually word breaks—it goes further; the violence that *may* be hinted at becomes an actual component of the physical being of the poem; 'urns cork', 'screw a', 'gain ca', 'tch wind', 'ow', 'frame re', 'flect f', 'lick knife.' It becomes sound poetry, as the noises that make up the words are pushed to prominence. And further meanings arise in the breakage; an erotic scene comes into view behind the violence that is itself only hinted at—'screw a', 'lick knife.'

This unsettling has been a continual characteristic of Monk's work; essentially an improvisatory, musical use of language incorporating words broken down into their sound elements thus damaging and extending meaning. There is consistently a sense of danger, and also of play. All in all, a practice a long way from the protected zones of official poetry.

This is not an argument for a nihilist refusal of meaning, however. Content continues to be a concern, and much of the power of Monk's work comes from what an unstable meaning does to the possibilities of content within the work. Here, I will concentrate for the most part on the most dominant content within her work, which she has described on the British Electronic Poetry Centre website as her engagement with 'the emotional geography of place.' This engagement has been evident from her very earliest works, such as *Long Wake* published by Writers Forum through to the travelogues included in her recent collection *Noctivagations*. The most important of these works, though, is her long

1993 sequence *Interregnum*. This work, as well as the shorter sequence *Hidden Cities*, are two of her most explicit engagements with place. Crucially, they are the ones that most explicitly deal with the social and historical issues that have to be raised by any serious engagement with immediate surroundings. As such, they show the essentially political role that this poetry plays.

～

Interregnum is one of the major works of late twentieth century poetry, regardless of genre or nationality. It focuses on the infamous events of 1612 in Pendle, Lancashire, when ten local women were hung as witches. The sequence actually culminates in a stunning set of poems where Monk speaks in the voices of the women as they are being hung. But the poem is not simply about a particularly shameful historic incident; Monk seeks to speak within, rather than about the incident. She achieves this through an intense and emotional engagement with the contemporary space of Pendle, and it is this engagement that I want to speak about here.

The sequence opens with a section called 'Nerve Centre', which notices and engages with the contemporary inhabitants of the tourist zone still known as Pendle Hill. 'Nerve Centre' is an apt title, as it brings to mind the mesh of physical and linguistic energies that Monk brings into play in order to access the past. The first words in the sequence are 'brooding dislocation' (Monk, 2003, p. 99). From the beginning the proposed comfort of the tourist attraction is actually uncertain—it is a windswept place of reflection rather than a joyous hopscotch for holiday makers (the photographs on Pendle's tourist web site emphasise this, with their references to a characteristically bleak day). The inhabitants of Monk's 'Nerve Centre' are named as 'Good Friday Hikers', 'Hallowe'en Bikers', 'Born Agains', 'Pagans', 'Drivers', 'Shiftworkers', as well as foxes and birds. Taken together—each one is given a separate short poem— they provide a mesh of meanings and energies through which the final evocation of the historic act of violence that defines Pendle can be activated.

The appearance of 'Good Friday Hikers' before the others, emphasises the appearance of tourism within the contemporary scene. They certainly appear long before the Shift Workers who actually create the economy of the place:

We love to go a-wandering
across this hillside track
with knapsacks filled
with snap
        emergency kits
        Kendal mint cake
on our backs

(Monk, 2003, p. 101)

They are presented with a naivety and simplicity that is fitting, and that also works as a deceptively naive opening to the sequence, as if lulling the reader into the expectation of a simple dealing with surface materials, before rushing them into the violence and even horror that is a component part of any real engagement with any place that includes history. In particular the first two lines mimic the English ballad tradition, both in terms of rhythm and vocabulary. As this rhythm breaks, the naivety seems to increase, as if an (imagined) connection with the countryside was being contested by the reality of tourism.

Monk is not judgmental or contemptuous, and there is no reason for her to be. The poem captures the wide-eyed excitement of day-trippers, joyful about their escape from routine via a stroll on the hills:

Will we see varieties
of heather
recognise cloud formations
insect bites
bird song

(Monk, 2003, p. 101)

They will. They may even name them, but the fact remains that they can do nothing but skim across the surface. Their naming will never be more than a labelling, and they will be long gone by nightfall. Then other occupants will appear, with a more intimate knowledge of their locale.

The next two presences in this procession of inhabitants are 'Hallowe'en Bikers' and 'Born Agains.' These two would normally be considered to be opposites, Hells Angels and Christians. Both groups, however, have a similar awareness of the fecund energies of place. The bikers are astride their 'leg-spreading | fundamental | engines' (Monk, 2003, p. 102), while the Christians wish for 'a fester on | your dreams | of thirty | foot | of | stainless steel | erection' (Monk, 2003, p. 103). Like the Good Friday hikers, these groups are unlikely to list the given names of the life of the countryside, but consciously or not, they have a closer connection to their realities. Both groups are still of the world of the tourists, however. The Christians are involved in a petty condemnation of the bikers, who in their turn simply want to get drunk, have sex and ride around on their bikes.

Things might be expected to change when the Pagans arrive on the scene, but it becomes clear fairly quickly that they are just another form of tourist. The Pagans here are probably of that variety who choose from the smorgasbord of New Age remedies in search of asserting some kind of identity. Monk points out their shortcomings quite bluntly:

>   alignment of baubles
> primordial crud
> cheapo jewels
> seed-stones
> planetary pulses
> cosmic stew

> (Monk, 2003, p. 104)

With their 'baubles', their 'crud' and 'cheapo jewels', these pagans are no such thing. But still, and more so than the bikers and the Christians, they are at least going some way towards an awareness of the rhythms of the natural world, its 'planetary pulses', most usually expressed via sexuality:

> pure Mother Earth fuck
> wet volup of
>   Venus
> limps off at half-cock

> (Monk, 2003, p. 104)

They may be going at it half-cocked, but these pseudo-pagans are still consciously or not awakening within the poem a sense of rhythms and realities larger than the human:

> bead-smear
> bloodclots
> blossom

> (Monk, 2003, p. 104)

The language has by this point moved far away from the ballad formations of 'Good Friday Hikers', is less easily located, closer to incantation.
There is still mockery—'bloodclots' may be a use of the common Rasta
insult—but the shortening lines and heavy alliteration take the poem
into the hypnotic areas of ritual.

Incantation may in fact be the central point of the entire sequence,
and fittingly so given its overriding subject matter. In an example of her
characteristic fluidity of meaning, when Monk turns her attentions to
the drivers who speed around the hill, incantation becomes buried
inside her noticing of the cars themselves:

> spin
>   can
> tin

(Monk, 2003, p. 105)

Monk here is using the occult technique of saying one thing, and
containing within it something more, and so a jokey description of a car
as a tin can is actually Monk secretly saying what she's doing: in–can–
tin; spinning an incantation.

Class realities are also present, as 'Shift Workers' appropriates the
voices of those who actually live and work around the area. It is an
acknowledgement that it was primarily working class women who were
executed as witches on Pendle Hill, rather than New Age wannabes.
They are the inhabitants of the area surrounding Pendle who come closest to incantation themselves, as they hang around on street corners.
Their chat is described by Monk as:

> weaving through
>   thought
>   warping
>   speech

(Monk, 2003, p. 106)

Individuals stand on street corners, distanced from the tourist activities
of the hill, and their speech patterns are a key part of the place. An
understanding of a place has to include the people who live in it, which
is something that the hikers, pagans, bikers and Christians who visit the
hill may have missed. By moving from ballad to incantation, Monk
forces a consideration of what language, song and spell might mean,

and how they are all linked. This is tied together by attention to local speech, the basic understanding that a place is known by how it is spoken of. Monk's mesh of meaning, through naivety, sexuality, antago- nism, and finally local speech and class realities, attempts a multidi- mensional view of the locale that must be completed by the addition of historical material.

~

It is by 'weaving' and 'warping' local speech through delirium and history that Monk moves into the next section of the sequence, 'Palimpsestus.' This central section of the work is a giddy and ferocious spiral that links the procession of contemporary inhabitants with the procession of accused witches that closes the sequence. As the title suggests, it is made up of two poems running simultaneously; a major text, and an accompaniment that works as a series of markers or guides. When *Interregnum* was originally published by Creation Books, 'Palimpsestus' was split into sections, with the counter poem that runs through it appearing alone on the facing page. This is a rare case of a collected version actually being an improvement, as the Salt Selected version reprints it without page breaks, thus emphasising how it works as a single poem.

Immediately, it gives an impression of takeoff from Pendle Hill, a sudden switch into hyper-drive. It isn't much of an exaggeration to say that the poem works as a time travel device; and rather than giving an account of the delirium of real or imagined readers, it actually seeks to instil that delirium in the reader:

> . . . perpetual
> dreamdrip-backdrop
> pooling centuries
> deep
> crush and spurt of
> wide-open (or)
> and
> so on
> ting (or)
> jang of nerve chords wend-
> welter.

(Monk, 2003, p. 111)

The obvious shift from the 'Nerve Centre' poems is that the poem has entered a visionary space. Monk's 'perpetual | dream-drip backdrop' is the same as what Blake meant by 'eternity.' However, by calling it a 'backdrop', she is careful to link the sense of a 'perpetual' visionary space to the physical world. Indeed, a chief characteristic of 'Palimpsestus' is its physical imagery; thus time itself is here a 'pooling century.' That is, the centuries are pooled in a visionary moment, but also the centuries become a pool that can be swum in. The language begins to 'crush and spurt', and so it seems to lose immediate sense ('wide-open (or) | and | so on | ting (or)') as pressure is put on, but the 'crush' of pressure forces the unexpected to 'spurt' out. And, of course, 'spurt' also hints at an erotic charge which is relevant when one considers the likelihood that witch-hunts were instigated by a Christian fear of female sexuality.

Orgasm can make the body feel as if it is dissolving, which seems to happen in the poem: 'jang of nerve-chords' suggests a body realigned as a musical instrument, or as music itself. The body and language fall into a 'wend | welter', a giddy and erotic turning where sense is almost lost. The incantations and songs of the first part of the sequence have become a spinning vortex, which as it continues throws up ghosts, figures, energies. It seems as if even the poet has lost control, when she says that she is

> . . . giddy with
>   it
> sharp
> stumb
> hotmolten

(Monk, 2003, p. 111)

She's bluffing. This rush of giddy language play has always been a major characteristic of Monk's poetry—it *is* Monk's poetry, in fact, as she understands that a hidden purpose of the poetic (hidden, at least, from the followers of Larkin) is just this sense of bewilderment, this unleashing of language. The work here is, as she has it, 'sharp.' 'Stumb' is, from one direction, a breakdown of 'stumble', as if the poem is moving too fast to even complete its words. But buried within it is the more obscure 'stum', to 'fume with burning sulphur', according to Chambers. Which is fitting to the poem, which begins to throb with the terror—and sheer white knuckle excitement—of a quick trip to hell. Figures take shape, or almost do, and just as quickly disappear:

... lewd and magical suggestions of
form
archways of limbs
full
fungus breathings ...

(Monk, 2003, p. 112)

The imagery here is that of a nightmare, as if the reader and poet have
been sucked down into the earth of Pendle Hill, like the victims in a
splatter movie, and are now forced to breathe in the earth's mould
whilst just barely able to make out horrifically twisted persons. Or, like
Rimbaud in his own trip to hell, have swallowed 'une fameuse gorgee de
poison' (Rimbaud, 1966, p. 182) and are now in the middle of a particularly heavy trip. I have no idea whether psychedelic mushrooms grow on
Pendle Hill—but 'fungus breathings' suggest they do. The mood shifts,
the quick switches from terror to hilarity have the sense of a psychedelic
experience:

chucking up visions from
ectoplasmic mists
unstopped centuries
seep
unbearable sorrowlove
gag
upon hysterical gag punch
whole side-splitting
guts
get funny-a
get rot

(Monk, 2003, pp. 112–13)

The 'unbearable' intensity is making the poet 'gag'—she wants to puke—
but that awareness opens up the alternative meaning of the word, as a
joke, and all of a sudden laughter takes over. Only for a second though,
as the 'get funny-a' spins round into the merciless 'get rot.' The laughing
face sudden freezes into cruelty, the side-splitting laughter is suddenly
a split side, spilling guts all over the floor. On one level, this is the most
accurate account of a mushroom overdose I've ever seen. Such a reading
is not out of place, as it is supposed that witches would use a hallucinogenic ointment of belladonna in their rituals. It is possible to interpret
'Palimpsestus' as just such a hallucinogenic transportation, from the
contemporary Pendle of 'Nerve Centre' into the seventeenth century
witch-hunt.

As the poem continues, as nonsense syllables ('taa taa taffa-teffy' (Monk, 2003, p. 114)) break the language down further, and as it spins again from hilarity to terror, figures begin to form. At times they are characters from a half-remembered folklore, like 'Fruity Womb and Luv King' (Monk, 2003, p. 114), who seem to have more to do with the realities of a pagan mythology than the prancing new-agers from earlier in the poem. Other figures appear, 'Roaring Jack Shirt Ripper' (Monk, 2003, p. 115), who later becomes 'Jack Nazarene' (Monk, 2003, p. 124), showing the two faces of the generalised male oppressor; Jack the Ripper, or Jesus Christ. And finally, the accused witches begin to appear:

> . . . Three little shit-houses
>   spawned
>   spawned
>   spawned

> (Monk, 2003, p. 119)

Here are actual persons, who never wanted to be the 'shit-houses' that class society describes them as, and tries to make them be. So as the phantasms begin to clear, a real sense of the casual inhumanity that allows atrocities like witch-hunts to take place is stated. These are not 'shit-houses', they are women who, within the poem, are aware of the inevitability of their condemnation before it has even happened. Aware, but also defiant; it is notable in the later sections of *Interregnum* that they refuse to deny the accusations thrown at them:

> I dried them. Fixed them. Thorn-pricked them.
> Then sat well back and waited for the
> diabolical climate to heighten.
> Obliterate.

> (Monk, 2003, p. 141)

The nature of witchcraft has been the subject of voluminous study, but the most compelling argument is still the one given by the Surrealist painter Kurt Seligmann in his long study from the 1940s, *The Mirror of Magic*. In this long history of what may be called the counter-tradition, Seligmann locates the emergence of the pan-European witch-revival of the middle ages as a consequence of the position of the peasantry who had been 'driven to despair by the increasing disorder and growing oppression which dominated Europe' (Seligmann, 1948, p. 257).

Seligmann argued that 'one uprising after another had been suppressed bloodily by the united secular and temporal authorities', and so the peasant had taken 'refuge in dreams' and the 'old deities' (Seligmann, 1948, p. 257). Witchcraft existed as a result of the human urge to revolt against oppression, diverted by defeat into a religious system that offered refuge against injustice, and also a mental landscape different to that of the rulers, be they secular or not. Seligmann insists that the witch existed because there were 'nonconformist people in Europe' (Seligmann, 1948, p. 260). Witch-hunts were essentially the suppression of nonconformity, the suppression of a heretical current that runs through the history of human activity and fights against oppression and servitude. Gary Snyder famously recruited the tradition of poetry into this current in his 1960s mapping of what he called the 'great subculture' which runs 'without break from Paleo-Siberian shamanism [. . .] through megaliths and Mysteries, astronomers, ritualists, alchemists [. . .] Gnostics and vagantes, right down to Golden Gate Park' (Snyder, 1969, pp. 105–15).

This 'great subculture' would be more accurately called the heretical tradition, and it manifests as social struggle as often as it does in Snyder's religious and mystical currents. The Movement of the Free Spirit used religious metaphors, but its essential manifestation was a struggle for a definition of the terms and conditions of social reality (Cohn, 1970, pp. 148–62). It also manifests in Blake, in Rimbaud, in Marx and Lautréamont, Surrealism, the Situationist International. And in *Interregnum,* Monk has the witches spell out quite specifically that it is the unwillingness to bow down to society's norms and categories that was ultimately being punished:

> The feed for my ungovernable
> core to help me fight the regime of
> mealtimes and the stifling niceties
> inbetween —
> called 'life'.

(Monk, 2003, p. 142)

This is central to the poem, and is one of the central purposes of poetry of the level of Monk's, to fight the incomparably boring sheen put on everyday life by official 'niceties.' The poetry is itself a part of the historical heretical current, opposed to the official version of reality. Jeff Nuttall pointed out that radical writing is *by its nature* political

(Dorward, 2003, p. 45). He was talking about Tom Raworth, but it can just as well be applied to Monk. The refusal for the writing to be too easily put down—its wild-meaning—is a refusal of the inevitability of reality as it has been described to us.

I don't know how seriously Monk takes ideas of language as magic. She described a recent performance, at the London Total Writing festival as a 'seance', but her writing always has a seam of humour that prevents such metaphors from seeming too earnest. But it is fitting to *Interregnum*. Finally, it is as if she has invoked the witches, and they are seen as contemporary forces that still haunt the land; an unfinished business that still lingers.

But more important than these occult traces is an explicit fury at injustice. This social anger, merely present in *Interregnum*, is an explicit concern in the sequence *Hidden Cities*, a performance text published in *Noctivagations* in 2001. This work was commissioned as one of a series of alternative bus tours around a number of British cities, and so highlights another of Monk's concerns—the performance of the text. Unfortunately, there is not room here to go into concerns of performance; readers interested in Monk's take on it are referred to her *Insubstantial Thoughts on the Transubstantiation of the Text* in the *Selected Poems*.

In the context of *Hidden Cities* the attention to performance and the fact that it was taken out of the context of a conventional poetry reading underlies its political meaning. By being designed to be heard as the listener looks at the actual geography that provoked it, the poem explicitly engages with the fate of the contemporary inner city, and so it seems more immediate and less occulted than *Interregnum*. The introduction, however, emphasises that what in the context of the subject matter may have seemed an exercise in occultism, is an exoteric attempt to imagine the totality of the time continuum:

> Welcome all of you . . . involuntary ghosts of tomorrow . . . scoring future imprints down the roads and junctions of unmarked time . . . welcome to the imperceptible slice between now and now . . . the progression of idle nanoseconds.
>   Welcome to Manchester . . . Funchester . . . Gunchester . . . Madchester . . . Journey with me now and regain a return to where we almost started . . . journey through the making of each suspended sentence . . . spectral word . . . half breathed comma . . . shifting metropolis . . . through these unofficial urban arteries of time-ticking creatures . . . glossed out histories . . . contrived artefacts . . . accidental spaces.

(Monk, 2001, p. 63)

The inhabitants of the present are the 'ghosts of tomorrow', and their footsteps will eventually be the eerie 'imprints down the road' to be tracked by those not yet born, themselves present within 'unmarked time.' As in *Interregnum,* the immediacy of present time is expanded to include the past, and in this case also the future. The listeners are made to understand the importance of considering the past by first being forced to contemplate their own temporary nature, and the fact that in the future they will be as hidden as the ghosts of the past are now.

Having startled her listeners in this way, Monk still insists that we are here in present time, and that the pasts and futures she invokes are also present here. She is careful to locate her poem, and the listeners, within a context of present day Manchester; the 'Gunchester' of inner city breakdown, and the 'Madchester' of the Hacienda club, ecstasy and the band Happy Mondays. This emphasises the fact that any consideration of a past has to take place within the context of the present day, and that any reading of history has real and active consequences on the nature of that present. The past is accessible through speech, 'through the making of each suspended sentence.' It is through the word itself that 'glossed out histories' are uncovered, and 'accidental spaces' are found. This is not mysticism, but realism. Neither is it the Derridean claim that all that exists is the text itself. Monk uses language to uncover what has been hidden, and also to pour scorn on what is officially served up as knowledge and history:

> Looping the central containers of information, controlled culture, civic control: central library, art galleries, tourist info-bureaux, town hall concert halls, halls of illusion, delusion, doctored knowledge, half truths, half imaginings, other worlds. Obligatory bastions of external good taste hiding internal broodings, oblique questions, spider-runs, furry rodents. Civic pride beaming bright-eyed.

> (Monk, 2001, p. 64)

Contemporary cities are heritage centres, with whole zones given over for tourists to explore a sanitised version of their past. The depositories of history and knowledge in any city: the library, gallery, concert hall and tourist information office, work together to give an illusory idea of the past and also the present. For Monk, this 'doctored knowledge' gives rise not only to 'half truths' but more desperately, 'half imaginings.' When the entirety of the truth is hidden, and only the sanitised, abridged version is on offer, then the ability to fully imagine possibilities is severely compromised. Official outlets of art, literature and music are as much to blame for this as any others. A literary world that refuses to acknowledge the existence of poetry such as Monk's in the name of some external notion of 'good taste' must take its share of the blame for a culture where certain 'oblique questions' not only go unasked, but unimagined.

~

The best of Monk's poetry involves an intense and hallucinatory engagement with the energies of place. This differs from classic Debordian psychogeography in that Monk seems almost to attempt a tapping into the energies of the place by occult means. The intense strength of the poetry, however, means that there is a world of a difference between Monk seeing a reading as a 'seance', and a spiritualist in the suburbs bringing bland messages from the dear departed. Iain Sinclair puts it well in his 1987 novel *White Chappell, Scarlet Tracings*:

> The writers were mediums; they articulated, they gave a shape to some pattern of energy that was already present. They got in on the curve of time, so that by writing, by holding off the inhibiting reflex of the rational mind, they were able to propose a text that was prophetic.

(Sinclair, 1987, p. 129)

Prophecy here is not to be taken in its degraded sense of predicting the future, sniffing about in people's tea leaves. Its dictionary definition is of speaking in an inspired voice; the poet scopes a geography and is attentive to its energies.

If the occult metaphors are stripped away, then we are left with the kernel of the heretical tradition, which remains class struggle. In the 'Theses on the Philosophy of History', Walter Benjamin used the term *monad* to refer to points in history 'where thinking suddenly stops in a configuration pregnant with tensions, it gives that configuration a shock, by which it crystallises into a monad' (Benjamin, 1970, p. 254). These configurations are the points in history where the urge for freedom manifests. The unrealised energies of any unresolved moment in history, whether an antiwar revolt or (in its negative manifestation), a witch-hunt, continue to exist. Benjamin argues that a historian must see in this monad a 'revolutionary chance in the fight for the oppressed past', and that the historian 'takes cognizance of it in order to blast a specific era out of the homogeneous course of history' (Benjamin, 1970, p. 254). This position insists on the real consequences of an active and imaginative engagement with history. How this is to be done is still being worked out; poetry such as Monk's is a contribution to this process. It is a poetry that knows that 'until we can remake the past, go into it, change what is now, cut out those cancers—we are helpless' (Sinclair, 1987, p. 113). Benjamin knew that the consequences of this attitude were unavoidably revolutionary:

> In reality, there is not one moment that does not carry *its own* revolutionary opportunity in itself. [. . .] The particular revolutionary opportunity of each historical moment is confirmed for the revolutionary thinker by the political situation. But it is no less confirmed for him by the power this moment has to open a very particular, heretofore closed chamber of the past. Entry into this chamber coincides exactly with political action.

> (Benjamin, 1999, p. 944)

Unresolved tensions in the past, then, are not merely to be opened in the interests of meeting ghosts, or even in the interests of making poems to be served up as entertainment, but as a political action that grasps the entirety of history in order to change the present, and the future. The poet is socially active through the exploration of these energies, not through writing protest poems, as a minor adjunct to journalism. Poetry that is worth the name actually makes a reality, one that exists outside of the surveillance cameras and media metaphysics that make up the experience of living in a modern city. It is an active art form, continually opening up possibilities for new ways of interpreting the world, and so changing it. And it is absolutely necessary. Meanwhile, as Monk puts it so strongly in *Hidden Cities*: 'crushed human nature lies bleeding in fragments all over the face of society' (Monk, 2001, p. 64).

References

Benjamin, W. 1970. *Illuminations*. London: Jonathan Cape
Benjamin, W. 1999. *The Arcades Project*. Cambridge Mass.: Belknap / Harvard
Blake, W. 1989. *The Complete Poems: Second Edition*. ed. W.H. Stevenson, London: Longman
Cohn, N. 1970. *The Pursuit of the Millennium*. London: Paladin
Dorward, N. ed., 2003. *Removed for Further Study: The Poetry of Tom Raworth*. *The Gig*, issue 13/14, May 2003

Monk, G. 2001. *Noctivagations*. Sheffield: West House
—— 2003. *Selected Poems*. Cambridge: Salt Publishing
Rimbaud, A. 1966. *Complete Works*, ed. Wallace Fowlie. Chicago: University
    of Chicago
Seligmann, K. 1948. *The Mirror of Magic*. New York: Pantheon
Sinclair, I. 1987. *White Chappell, Scarlet Tracings*. London: Vintage
Snyder, G. 1969. *Earth House Hold*. New York: New Directions
Watson, B. 1998. *Art, Class and Cleavage*. London: Quartet

Geraldine Monk's Eerie *Revealing*
DAVID ANNWN

In his famous essay on the *uncanny*, Freud mentions how Otto Rank dealt with the theme of the 'double':

> He has gone into the connections which the 'double' has with reflections in mirrors, with shadows, with guardian spirits, with the belief in the soul and with the fear of death. [. . .] Such ideas, however, have sprung from the soil of unbounded self-love, from the primary narcissism which dominates the mind of the child and of primitive man. But when this stage has been surmounted, the 'double' reverses its aspect. From having been an assurance of immortality, it becomes the uncanny harbinger of death.

> (Freud, 1953, p. 250)

These reverses, as described, are in themselves uncanny. By the time of *Webster's New Collegiate Dictionary,* quite fundamental variations are being made between words like uncanny and, for example, *eerie* which, by now, not only refers to that which is fearful, uneasy or fear-inspiring, but also to the consciousness itself of prevalent mysterious powers. *Webster's* groups three words but also attempts to discern daylight between them:

> *Weird, eerie, uncanny* mean mysteriously strange or fantastic. *Weird,* in stricter use, often implies an unearthly or preternatural mysteriousness; *eerie,* a vague consciousness that unearthly or mysterious and, often, malign powers or influences are at work; *uncanny,* in its prevailing but looser sense, unpleasant mysteriousness or strangeness, as of persons, places, sensations.

> (Merriam-Webster)

Geraldine Monk's poetry also involves doubles, mirrors, shadows and guardian spirits but the multiple identities in her work aren't circumscribed by a Freudian sense of the uncanny. They never seek to offset the reality of death only in order then, in turn, to become its unsuspected 'harbingers.' Instead, they confront and question death throughout:

> And that is
> that?
>> Pup-a-luv—
>> that is that
>
> *Then paste this question mark to the centre of the sun*

(Monk, 2001, p. 15)

The insufficiency of *Webster's* 'vague consciousness' is nonetheless a step in the right direction in that *eerie*, as I'll discuss below, is moving into the position of agency rather than just passive receptor. Freud and that writer of uncanny tales, E.T.A. Hoffman, don't describe subjects who actively *use* their sense of the eerie; their senses of the *unheimliche* are distinctly foreclosed options, evocative of a reflexive and ineluctable double-bind.

If Freud takes his cue from Hoffman in this regard, Monk takes hers', (especially in her most recent poetry), from Lewis Carroll. In Carroll's *Sylvie and Bruno* we read:

> The first rule is, that it must be a *very* hot day—that we may consider as settled: and you must be just a *little* sleepy—but not too sleepy to keep your eyes open, mind. Well, and you ought to feel a little—what one may call 'fairyish'—the Scotch call it 'eerie.'

(Carroll, 1889, p. 253)

Derek Hudson writes:

> The element of experiment in the construction of the book has its place in literary history. Dodgson introduced his 'fairies' into human situations and postulated that man may go through three stages in relation to the supernatural—the ordinary state of 'no consciousness'; the mixed or 'eerie' state, in which he is conscious both of his own surroundings and of supernatural presences; and a form of trance or dream-state [. . .] perhaps the work of Dorothy Richardson, James Joyce and Virginia Woolf sometimes suggests the same line of experiment.

(Hudson, 2003, p. 6)

Though the mentioned subject is a man, a 'he', it is important again that an active consciousness is involved here as well as 'supernatural presences.' In these statements, *eerie* is also linked to Modernist experimentation, making this radically different from Freud's static sense of the *uncanny*.

$\sim$

'(espial)', the opening section of *Fluvium*, starts with the instatement of interior wars, conflicts of the 'Drifting cells', in comparison with which the 'Abandoned moon buggies' of space-racing super-powers already seem completely obsolescent (Monk, 2001, p. 85). The challenge in one sense is to realise how haunted and potent the clustering powers of lives on this planet are, the fact of now:

> Breathe fey cloud.
> Wreathe ectoplasm
> Seethe.
> It.

(Monk, 2001, p. 85)

Writing is a form of divination: its unerring stops and starts, its prescience and intuitive tinglings, its premonitory pre-lingual urges. It is tricksy and erratic and risky. Nothing can be pre-judged or guaranteed; no garment cut from this cloth is bespoke. Yet anything, even and especially life's trivia and detritus, can be a sign into *now*, into the poet's way to go:

> It was a *very very very*
> curled up
> beer mat.
> Singular. Stiff.
> It
> r~o~c~k~k~k~kt

(Monk, 2001, p. 87)

Sometimes the simplest, the lexes we call *primary* are the first and best to come. Even tiny rhythms mean metamorphosis:

> ~and~then~
> ~and~then~
> it stopt.
> Blotted out

and wotted
not what to do~
transmogrified.

(Monk, 2001, p. 87)

That switch from the rocking mat to 'wotted' in its old Saxon sense is the cue for revelation. This scrying, the sensing out of forces composing this instant, is the opposite of espial because, in this process, the writer is *seen* as much as all she sees. This séance of the moment is no mere observation. In *Interregnum* we read: 'Words birthed. Made flesh' (Monk, 2003, p. 124). For Monk, this is a long-term association and the same line resurfaces eight years later in 'Vocalised (private)' (Monk, 2003, p. 217). If words and their forms are births, an attentive care and patience, a desire to take in the converging forms of the present are crucial.

Clairvoyance has been no secret in the writings and visuals of Hannah Weiner, Nicole Brossard, Helen Adam and Christine Kennedy. Krispen Mapel-Bloomberg in 'Modernism and the Occult' also mentions Sarah Orne Jewet's and Radclyffe Hall's Spiritualism, Alice Dunbar-Nelson's interest in Obeah, Edith Wharton's 'intense Celtic sense of the super-natural', and Djuna Barnes' relationship with her grandmother's mediumship:

> The rise of Spiritualism paralleled that of the Woman's Rights movement after its inception in 1848, and the two movements intertwined continually as they spread throughout the country.

(Mapel-Bloomberg, 2003)

Emily Dickinson voiced her powerful acuity towards our multiple, haunted selves:

> One need not be a Chamber—to be Haunted —
> One need not be a House —
> The Brain has Corridors—surpassing
> Material Place—
> [...]
>
> Ourself behind Ourself, concealed —
> Should startle most

(Dickinson, 1970, p. 332)

For Monk, presences are implicit in air, in breathing, in our myriad-thronged and flexing identities, in the scapes around us. Her sequences teem with as many waking visions as Oursler's *The Influence Machine* or Fellini's *Giulietta degli spiriti*.

In her Preface to *Out of Everywhere*, Maggie O'Sullivan writes:

> Rather than perpetuating prevalent notions of writing poems 'about' something, the poets here, to my mind, have each in their own imaginative way committed themselves to excavating *language* in all its multiple voices and tongues, known and unknown.

(O'Sullivan, 1996, pp. 9–10)

These terms are true of Monk's work where the speakers often grapple, stammer and cry out to sound the unsayable. Existence is larger, more bristling and polysemous than we can see; we are all part of a process which our conscious minds habitually flow over rather than through. In Monk's *Mary Through the Looking Glass*, Mary flows *through* life/language/memory/prescience not *over*.

The fourth section of *Fluvium*: '(floresce)', shows how a night search for a father can become a new '*aching*' quest, each instant registering its fear and uncertainties freshly:

slike . . .

light?

slike . . .

slike eye-light

(Monk, 2001, p. 89)

The fifth section is entitled '(ghast)', which means to frighten or the condition of being scared, (Monk knows that words listed as obs. in the dictionary can re-emerge from their fourteenth century matrices to pull our readings in new ways). The section opens with the apparent shutting of: 'They closed the shocker' (Monk, 2001, p. 89). But unquiet questions of disease and mortality flit in. When the open sonic 'roosh' comes, the question and sensation which it embodies are *eerie*:

Dart the light-lack room.
Dart the light-back
    death moths
daft and after us
be-by

```
        gone
ar-tificial
            day
made claggy
dreamery
        flicker
germ pods
parti . . . c . . . parti . . c
exits skid

at breakneck
reel the roosh
it came
O
pen M
    Outhed

Yip!
Eerie
question scar-scary
whaaaaaaaaaat
```

(Monk, 2001, p. 89)

As spirits depart so some births can be break-neck: after fishing oblivion, the speaker reels the 'roosh', (excited working-class Lancastrian); of course O spells the open-ness, the freeing and merges, in shape, pelvis, vagina, child's and mother's mouth. Read downwards, M O takes us part-way to a recognition of the mothering of words; mum, ma, mam, mom, those first-utterances.

It is also clear that 'roosh' and the startlement are funny, full of uproarious comic frisson, the ten *a*'s of the question making the reader jump. In conversation over the years, the writer has often said to me that many critics miss the humour and unruly laughter of her work. This is especially hard to believe if one has seen her perform. Journalistic newspeak and chicanery are mocked in Monk's sequences; hers are high octane spirits: skittish conceits and verbal zest. Her comic spectrum runs from cunning and slapstick punning, gleeful yells and mocks, through parody and the bruised black and blues of satire and an *iron pyrites* irony to downright gallows humour.

It is at source in this poem that *Eerie* emerges as a question between the '*Yip!*' (affirmative and animalian yelp) and stuttering 'sca-scary', for the surrounding forces of cognition and inspiration are unavoidable. In performing this poem on *fluvium*, a CD recording by Monk, Martin Archer and Julie Tippetts, the poet breaks from the high fragmented sonarities of the preceding lines here and utters *eerie* in a low, husky tone, stretching the liquid second vowel in a manner highly redolent of Scots. The extended surprising outcry of '*whaaaaaaaaaat*' leads to:

> Whichever way yis eyes.
> *Whichever way yis eyes*
> *wwwwwatter.*

(Monk, 2001, p. 89)

The mutable watery sonics of the w's take over; '*Yip!*' has become the repeated 'yis eyes' (yes-eyes, his eyes). A neo-Coleridgean presence survey-ing fluvia perhaps, but I read this as the birth-fluid of words and water of origins. It reminds me of a line by a very different poet, Jeremy Hooker's 'small sunny boy', who runs beside 'the great wet novelty shouting *wasser, wasser*' (Hooker, 1978, p. 9).

To state the primacy of *eerie* is not to claim Monk's poetry for exotic other-wordliness; quite otherwise, for this world which some call *ordi-nary* or *normal* is a gathering of mysteries. As I've written with regard to three Irish innovative poets: 'the world' is realised as a 'nexus of complex relativities' (Annwn, 2002, p. 22). All landscapes are charged: 'spirits submerged form frantic quivers' (Monk, 2003, p. 7).

This line and the questions that follow it from 'The Three Tremblers—The Coming of the Dawn':

> Are you three hills
>   three days without moon

and

> Have you upturned relics and grey matter centres

(Monk, 2003, p. 7)

reveal that the ideo-linguistic scapes of Geraldine Monk's poetic sequences are as haunted by presences as tradition claims for the uplands of northern Britain. Perhaps it is no accident at this point that my eye falls on a description of John Harvey's *Apparitions of Spirits in Wales* where we find:

> Testimonies to many witnesses to supernatural encounters in seven-teenth and eighteenth century Wales, from abductions by fairies, and appearances of ghosts, devils and witches, to poltergeist activity. [. . .] The

stories here evoke a spiritually dark landscape in which the malevolent dead and damned wander.

(University of Wales, 2003, p. 11)

In Monk's 'The Gathering':

Spirits crowd closer.
Branded collaborators.
The circle grews.
You (you) You (you) You (you)

(Monk, 2001, p. 11)

Eerie then is registration of the pitch and care of Monk's art towards a universe of wonders and wondering.

Of course, writers have used the word about Monk's art before. In *Object Permanence*, the reviewer describes: 'Eerie, violent [. . .] an exhilarating flux of human-animal-alien corporealities approximated in language' (Monk, 2001, p. 122). And it is a sense I keep coming back to in reading her work: 'But, after all: *eerie* is the warp and woof of *Noctivagations*: these wild wanderings and intimate challenges to our sense of private and public language are exciting, frightening and gleeful' (Annwn, 2003, p. 135). I totally agree with Frances Presley in her words about the danger of overstressing wildness in this poetry at the expense of the responsibility and care (Presley, 2003, p. 4); to be a poetic transmitter for the eerie or *other* in our environment takes a rare combination of abandon and continuous craft. Eerieness does of course involve rational *and* non-rational, intuitive thought and feeling; for some writers such approaches to irrationality do, of course, risk an inherent danger:

> Feminine irrationality courts the seductive danger of appearing to be subversive while in fact satisfying all sorts of time-hallowed prejudices about femaleness, and, if valorised within an implicitly male subject, can easily become again a category which leads to the exclusion of dissenting or strong female voices.

(Croggon, 2002)

Monk's voices are not excluded from anywhere.

∼

As David Jones might write: the roots of *eerie* are a particular matter of the linguistic strata of these Isles. The third edition of the *O.E.D.* seems to present us with Monkesque sonic variora:

> **Eerie, eery** (7·ri), a. Forms: 4 eri, hery,
>   4–6 ery, 6 erie, 9 eirie, -y (Anglo-Irish **airy**),
>   8-eery, -ie. [M.E. *eri*, ?var. erz of ARGH]

(The Oxford English Dictionary, 1978, p. 47)

The first meaning implies fear, a notion of superstitious uneasiness. This word occurs in the northern *not the Midland* version of the *Cursor Mundi*. It is still regarded as properly 'Scotch.'

The second meaning is 'Fear-inspiring; gloomy. Strange, weird' and Burns is quoted from 1792: 'be thou a bogle by the eerie side of an auld thorn' (OED, 1978, p. 47). Interestingly, Tannahill, in his *Poems* (1848) links it to the noctivagant: 'The watch dogs howling [. . .] makes the nightly wanderer eerie' (OED, 1978, p. 47). Eerie is, of course, a word particularly associated with both the neo-Gothic of Ann Radcliffe's day and Postmodern Gothicism; it is a quality which has been noticed, particularly recently, in the writing of women poets, from Emily Dickinson to Sylvia Plath, from H.D. to Hazel Smith. Far from accepting any marginalisation of the term into an uncomplicated denotation of the otherworldly or indulgently bizarre in literature, critics, (and women critics in particular), are increasingly using *eerie* to denote that acuity to seeing that which is subtly present, (but not apparent to everyone), and the linking of that faculty to rare skills and formal experimentation. Heather Downey writes:

> 'I am HER, HER, HER,' H.D. writes, 'Names are in people; people are in names. God is in a word. God is in HER.' The depth of Hermione's painful self-reflection is beautifully transcribed in this eerie interior monologue.

(Downey, n.d.)

Sarah Kerr writes of Gertrude Stein's *Three Lives*:

> 'In friendship, power always has its downward curve,' she writes. [. . .] Readers have been conditioned to study this groundbreaking work for its pioneering technique—still beautifully readable, but eerie and fractured.

(Kerr, 1998)

Sonia Mycak writes that Hazel Smith's *The Riting of the Runda*

> is an extraordinary piece-not the least because it is pleasurable, disturb-
> ing, eerie, melodious, sensuous, and a mind-game all at the same time
> challenging, fascinating and engaging.

(Mycak, n.d.)

Maria Damon writes:

> Hannah Weiner's work—her written records of clairvoyant experience—is
> symptomatic of these kinds of creatively transformative traumatic utter-
> ances—and it has the same eerie sort of disembodied mechanical effect as
> tap[dance], in which fragments of inadmissable history orbit in perfor-
> mative play.

(Damon, n.d.)

~

Moving from roots to branches: how is that which we might call the *eerie*
find registration in Monk's work? Why does this quality impinge itself so
often and strongly on her readers and listeners?

There are of course her materials which, as well as involving trips to
Portugal, the U.S., Spain, pub-encounters, Sheffield, everyday curses and
erotic medley also deal with ghosts, spirits, trances, the Golem, riddles,
chants and nursery-rhymes, the Tarot and the Kabbalah, rites, mock-
rites and anti-rites, the Pendle witches, Charon, séances, Cabinet readings, and, perhaps most importantly, the living presences of those
people we call dead, and sometimes the deathliness of those we call
living.

The eerie, to misquote Mary Queen of Scots and that poet whom
Conrad Aiken called the *Tsetse*, is there in her beginnings as well as her
later work. Identity as perceived in the North of England is particularly
fascinating for this poet. After conversations and an interview regarding
my paper on women poets and Basil Bunting (1999), Monk wrote:

> I am a poet from the north who often utilises its language and cultural
> legacy. [. . .] Being from the north inevitably leads to a state of ambiguity
> and ambivalence about the whole geographic psyche-shaping of self. [. . .
>] The north of England has qualities of such historical and geographical
> vividness that it has forged an identity and has had an identity forced
> upon it. That identity is both true and false.

(Annwn, 2000, p. 138)

Long Wake starts with 'Beacon Hill—The Coming of the Night' and the importance of 'instinctive navigations' but on this procession the prospect is 'final' and the proliferation of Polaris and Cruise missiles and surveillance in England in the late 1970s and 80s instils these lines. The proximity of threats to ancient human communities by that which are called 'super-powers' seem about to dispel our lives with a casual flick. Place-words like Hograh, Baysdale though are still relished and more difficult to supplant, the reminders of the potency of older kinds of resistance, that of word-casters and namers. That central quintet:

> HOGRAH   SILPHO
> STUDFAST HILL
> JUGGER HOW   SCALING DAM

(Monk, 2003, p. 3)

both reminds us of that which literally stands fast against global aggression, that gets in its way, and the technologies, like hydro-electricity and nuclear power which can lead like the steps of a dam-race from Laskill to Lastkill and Ladkill. The named Jugger How rises in the precarious terrain of Fylingdale (see p. 128 for a reproduction of the original page layout). Songs of native Americans and chants appear here alongside border ballads: 'The hooded hawk' and then 'Dream One*** Missiles' cuts into the side of these tensions, its sharp sections starting up different, less mediated phases, like dream fluttering under R.E.M.:

> stranded fish . . . . camouflagedfoliage . . . . no . . . . sense of . . . .
> occasion . . . . creeping . . . . taking them away . . . . stranded fish . . . .

(Monk, 2003, p. 4)

Flowing from within come the strands of corded, fearful; the eidetic links previously disconnected and partitioned here are re-engaged and fused in ways that so-called political objectivity can't undermine.

In the fourth section Stump Cross standing stone near Mere Clough, Burnley, is a bronze age monument, ('tired pinnacle?') and it stands close to Mosley Height stone circle in one of the most extensive clusters of these circles in Britain. With the awareness of great reaches of time, and escalating militarism of patriarchal cultures, there is the temptation of Schopenhauerean pessimism. But there are other traditions and possibilities: a child will not let a term like 'the Dead' off the hook, especially when it involves a loved person, a grandmother:

She was bone china eggshell
lying amongst candles and flowers
She was wild cold bryonies
I smiled
She was only beautiful.

(Monk, 2003, p. 5)

There is the child's merging of times: will her mother too be placed *after that mode*, be kept in context, alive in memory with the place-name and monuments of Worm Syke Rigg? The dreams return:

cave . . . crack . . . protrusion . . . appears . . .
hideous . . . haggaback . . . . fatlipped . . . . Leviathan . . . .

(Monk, 2003, p. 8)

Haggaback is also a place-name from Castleton, Yorkshire but its sonic thrust takes us further. 'Lyke Wake—The Coming of the Snow' evokes the slaughter of Sioux families at Wounded Knee and Dee Brown's famous book in relation to the Lyke Wake Dirge. There are many different regional and dialectical versions of this dirge. The belief among the common people in Yorkshire and the North-East was that, after death, the soul of the deceased had to pass over the moorland covered in thorns. The final and most difficult part of the soul's passage was the crossing of the Brig o' Dread described as being 'so narrow and treacherous that only the good can cross it safely' (Meriton, 2003).

The physical status of Monk's books and pamphlets also make them rich fields for paratextual attention: by this, I mean Gerard Genette's approach to the book, both as the text and those textual elements which 'surround it and extend it, precisely in order to *present it*': cover, title-page, preface etc. (Genette, 1997, p. 1). (See also Elizabeth James and Bill Griffiths' essays in this volume.) In the case of Robert Clark's cover of the stapled first edition of *Long Wake*, (1979, see p. 139), this centrally shows a sepia-washed head-and-shoulders view of a long-haired woman closed within an oval cameo. As if influenced by Picasso's *Demoiselles*, her left-hand features are energetically defined as if she is changing to something else. On either side of this motif are totemic shapes, a bird, (crow?) turned towards the woman and a crudely-executed human head; both seem to be mounted on sticks. The central female's eyes are down-turned as if in trance. On the rear cover, the sepia cartouche has turned to an inky black, and the face, even more elemental now but eyes still down-turned, is swathed in a dark panel in a way that reminds of the prints of Munch. These are fine extensions of the ideas of dreaming in a time of fearful threat, visual registration of eerie properties.

In this early sequence as elsewhere, the flexing between dream and conscious worlds, the complex registration of different modes of consciousness in varied forms, the continuous awareness of the experiences, *topoi* and namings of the deceased impinging on our own in experience, fearfulness wedded to verbal play, the sensing out of the hidden, can best be described as eerie.

～

Bob Cobbing's famous statement about a sonic poetry which goes beyond language is worth citing; he writes that he is

> attempting to use a new means of communication which I believe is an old method re-established, which is more natural more direct and more honest than, for example, the present day voice of politics and religion. [. . .] Gone is the word as the word, though the word may still be used as sound or shape. Poetry now resides in other elements.

(Cobbing, 1978)

Monk too has always been interested in experimentation, pure and fractured sonorities and the ranges of sound between inchoate scream to highly complex arabesques of aural irony. I have previously made links between the thematic interests of Geraldine Monk, Maggie O'Sullivan and those of Modernists like David Jones and Basil Bunting. Jones' reverence for words, (and that *Logos* which they embody), was always coupled with an intense care and attention for the vital differences inherent in things; as Hopkins would cite Duns Scotus: the *haecceitas*, the particularities.

Yet, such Logocentrism can, of course, be construed in other ways; in describing French Feminist thought, Elaine Marks writes:

> Logocentrism is [. . .] a sign of nostalgia, of longing for a coherent centre. In order to satisfy this longing absence, difference and death are repressed; presence, identity, and life are given a privileged role. For Luce Irigaray and Hélène Cixous it signifies that women have always been on the side of the term that has been repressed.

(Yorke, 1991, pp. 113–14)

This has given rise to attempts to write 'woman' back into language, to restore to life, voice, presence—in her own terms. As Liz Yorke writes: '*L'ecriture féminine* may be seen as the inscription of the specificity of the female body and female difference' (Yorke, 1991, p. 114). Monk's and O'Sullivan's work bridges those innovative poetries which try to redeem and those which break free of connotation in language. O'Sullivan speaks of the constant 'pull inside' between recording the experience of her female ancestors and vanished histories on one hand and 'freeing myself of the need to contextualise' on the other (Annwn, 2002, p. 10).

Language as a repository of ideas, utterances and meanings for those that have lived before us is supremely important for Monk's work, as is the will not to be confined by those minds or meanings. Indeed, in 'Speech-Snatchers', Monk has given her own vision of the 'Strip Search' of lexes:

> Stripping off the signifieds.   Metaphors.
> The mumbo jumbo dance from sound to seemingness.
> Confined. Inturn the words. Boxed. In.
> This space sucks speech-magic. Interns.
> Usurps control. Cuts.   The Arch and Gaffing
> Lords misrule and twist

> (Monk, 2003, p. 133)

This 'strip', when followed through exclusively, leads to a space of confinement. The implied play between 'Inturn' and 'Interns' is threatening and it reveals the dangers of all linguistic autocracies, however innovative. The aeration of speech and metaphor, the 'mumbo jumbo dance' is with us all, is needed even if that recension to pure, unmediated sound is part of the process of making. Yet Monk's sounding critique goes further than this; because she realises that all human efforts to connote with language are illusory, mere stabs in the dark, a 'seemingness.' A healthy scepticism is shown both ways: towards logocentric authority and to any party line of sheer sonic dominance. To rule out the 'dance from sound to seemingness' and such free-flowing word-play, would be to outlaw the powers of 'Gaff' and misrule. It would confine that which I have called the eerie, and its proclivity to spin awry and widdershins.

∾

Of course, there is the danger of parody, *pace* the Horror and New Age sections in bookshop chains, the materialism of scientific elites, media trivialisation of any consciousness dubbed the paranormal outside the fear- and envy-driven consumer mind-set. As online debates of Near-Death experiences reveal, even the most basic problems of existence are not so neatly resolved. It is no surprise that after William Burroughs' interest in Raudive experiments, I.T. itself *seems* haunted:

> There are anecdotal accounts here and there of people receiving mysterious messages through their computer screens and printers (just as people were noticing strange voices on their audio tapes long before anyone examined it as a 'phenomenon'), largely only EVP researchers *seeking* such contact have bothered to record their accounts.

> (http://muse.jhu.edu/journals/leonardo_music_journal011/11)

Gullibility aside, even the confirmed rationalist James A. Haught notes the boundaries of his conceptualisation:

> Even the packed neutrons in a pulsar are not basic material. They, too, are empty and compressible. If the remains of a collapsing star are 3.2 times larger than our sun, the gravity is too strong to be checked at the pulsar level. The collapse continues until it passes the point of no return—the Schwarzchild Radius. [...] If planet Earth were squeezed to its Schwarzchild Radius, it would be the size of a pearl. Can anyone imagine the matter of the entire Earth being reduced to fingernail size—but retaining all its weight—and continuing to shrink beyond that point? This isn't Captain Marvel comics. Pulsars are real. So are black holes, the astrophysicists say. If they are actuality, then what is our everyday world?

> (Haught, 1993)

One reality which Nate Dorward has perceptively noted in relation to Monk's *séances* is her unerring ability to use those sources which embarrass those who build postmodern canons:

> Her own work is at once haunted and zesty, and a welcome foe to decorousness; the other poets she voiced might to varying degrees be described as perpetual embarrassments to the guardians of the canon: too close to parlour verse (Harold Monro), too vulgarly oratorical (Dylan Thomas, Edith Sitwell), too darn out-there (Gertrude Stein, Bob Cobbing, Thomas Lovell Beddoes).

> (Dorward, 2003)

Indeed, Monk lambastes patronising Stanley Holloway-isms and Alan Bennett-esque versions of Northern vernacular, revels in music hall innuendo, ribs away at that she has called the 'Northern School of Misery' in poetry and gleefully privileges the asides and turns of phrase of the folk living around her over any academic propriety (Annwn, 2000, p. 138). Proprieties of all kinds are up for grabs. Religious dogma and orthodox ceremony is keenly subverted:

> Oh! sacred heart in underground shelters
>   stained with whisperers
>   tell lies
>   chanting priests and dogs
>   eat meat pies
>   Oh! the crisis of Isis in the bulrush

>   (Monk, 1980, [p. 19.])

The spirit of G.M. Hopkins is invoked in *Interregnum*: challenged, admired and pitied (see Monk's own contribution to this volume). There are dramatic echoes from the most unexpected places: from, for example John Berryman's 'Homage to Mistress Bradstreet', with its own Hopkinsesque: 'I am sifting', its dialect: 'Folkmoots, & blether, blether' and archaic festivity: 'Cantabanks & mummers' (Berryman, 1972, p. 54).

This is also apparent in Monk's 2002 Gargoyle edition, titled blue on cream as:

> *Mary Through*
> *the*
> *Looking Glass*

This fourteen-poem sequence is as small in the hand as a compact mirror. In lieu of a title-page, the first page is wordless and features a small blue mirror, (globe?) with ornamental winged swags. It is remarkably similar to the circular mirror on a stand from Corrozet's *Blasons domestiques* (1539). Each section is headed in blue (riverine) italics with the volume's title, like continually reflected phrases recurring on each page. The rear cover features a triple-faced folding mirror in an Art Nouveau version of Gothic style. It is a truism that from the age of Medieval queens, princes and mystics onwards, books have been seen as folding *mirrours*. Encyclopaedias were often called *specula*.

The Marys of *Mary Through the Looking Glass* are legion: Virgin Mary, Contrary Mary and Queen Mary but there is a different Mary linked to looking-glasses in urban legend. Jan Harold Brunvand identifies Mary Worth as the 'Bloody Mary' who appears in young women's mirrors after they say her name three times. Folklorist Janet Langlois inter-viewed Catholic school students from Indiana about the mirrored spirit they called Mary Whales (Norder, 1999).

Yet Mary Queen of Scots is the most obvious presence here, champion of the Old Religion. It is worth remembering in relation to this Mary and Marian devotion in particular, that Monk attended Mass with her mother and family till she was 17. She still recalls the attraction of the Latin response: 'Et cum spiritu tuo!' and this consciousness of the reso-nance and power of ancient formulae pervades her linguistic sense throughout her work.

So there is a natural affinity sensed with the Scottish Mary here: that Mary rumoured to have swum in the spa at Buxton, speaking of 'Bess' in Scottish dialect, ('Ma breath almost barred ma' (Monk, 2002, [p. 4])) and Latin, Saxonisms: ('Woos and ogles' (Monk, 2002, [p. 14])). The reflection-tropes multiply with irony. 'Ma' mirrors and blocks out 'ma', just as breath makes the looking-glass' recessive depths into a foggy, occluding wall. The two 'm' and 'br' sonic panels of the line hinge on 'almost', just as Mary's 'ma' for 'my' hinges on the key and signature-letter of 'm' in al<u>m</u>ost.

This Mary is a figure consonant with those others called upon by Monk: Edith Sitwell, the Pendle witches, the Sheela-na-Gig, Hopkins and Emily Dickinson: all eloquent, all potent and all, either voluntarily or forcibly, tucked, folded away.

We remember Kipling's 'The Looking-Glass':

Queen Bess was Harry's daughter. Now hand your partners all!

The Queen was in her chamber, a-combing of her hair.
There came Queen Mary's spirit and It stood behind her chair,
Singing 'Backwards and forwards and sideways may you pass,
But I will stand behind you till you face the looking-glass.
The cruel looking-glass that will never show a lass

As lovely or unlucky or as lonely as I was!'

(Kipling, n.d., p. 610)

Mary was connected with many other places in and around Monk's North: the Old Hall at Wingfield and Sheffield Castle among them. It is no accident that *Mary Through the Looking Glass* conjures up thoughts of

Lewis Carroll. Carroll, and Lear, under the cover of what others called
'nonsense verse', kept alive that freedom of linguistic play and experimentation, also glimpsed tantalisingly in Hopkins' poetry but which
would only come to a flowering again in English with Joyce, ee
cummings and Stein.

At the outset all kinds of looking-glass gazing are summoned up:

> Mmm-wrens sin sweetie.
> Bugaboo ma lugs hear it
> Map my eyes in you.
> Arrest.
> Toe-holds.   Carpe diem.
> Grrr-masques.
> The long~n the short~n the tall.
> Bless
> O
> Bess
> ma curfew out this mirror flew through.

                                                    (Monk, 2002, [p. 2])

The first two lazy syllables in the murmur of 'Mmm-wrens' reminds us
of 'mirror' and puns on *reines* or queens. Using a mirror to scry or divine,
(catoptromancy), is, of course, an ancient practice but a modern guide
states: 'a "cloud of mist" forming first. The mist could dissipate or
morph into the images. The images could be symbols of the subconscious' (Fisler, 2003). 'Mmm-wrens sin sweetie' and the lines that follow
introduce ideas both of warm sexual desire and female captivity. The
wren, a bird of royalty and augury, was hunted and killed on St
Stephen's Day throughout the British Isles. In a fertility ritual, a band of
boys carrying the wren's body sang: 'The Wren, the Wren, the King of all
birds, | On St. Stephen's Day was caught in the furze | [. . .] I pray you,
good dame, do give us a treat', with no little innuendo implied in the
last line (NOBLE). The wren is an epiphany of the Celtic god of healing,
magic and the otherworld and was seen as the robin's annual feminine
counterpart. As an old Lancashire rhyme has it: 'The robin and the wren
| Are God's cock and hen.' The disapproving 'Grrr-masques' is counter-
point to 'Mmm-wrens', (contrasting reactions perhaps to viewing one's
mirror-image), the succeeding lines mixing the wartime lyrics of Irving
Berlin's 'Bless them all', a world of potential suitors and the prospect of
the English monarch, her Mary's old coeval and adversary.

In both a straight and a darkly ironic sense, Mary Queen of Scots and
Bloody Mary (Queen Mary Tudor of England), had reason to 'Bless | O |

Bess.' Mary Stuart addressed two poems to Elizabeth and had often requested to meet the English Queen. Here the looking glass O, ('the gasping | mouth of mirror is endless' (Monk, 2002, [p. 4])) reminds us that Mary Stuart was often seen as a reflection, the very mirror of Elizabeth.

In the lines 'Bess | ma curfew out this mirror flew through' the five English vowels ripple in these 10 syllables. The two variations of e- and u-sounds, reflecting i's, the internal reflexive mirroring of 'curfew' 'flew' and 'through', the contrasting ou's, and the play of f's and th's reveal an exceptional attention to what words can do. It is as rich a moment of verbal relish as the Gallic and Latin scrollwork of: 'Diversions of exorbitant unicorns' (Monk, 2002, [p. 14]) and that fine moment when Scrooge and Dennis the Menace meet up with the miffed Franco-bourgeois of: 'Bah spoof! | Magnum of champers none!' (Monk, 2002, [p. 11]).

The sexuality of the sequence is emphatic throughout:

Wiregrass cuts a barb
Greeters far—I mean nooky-aye
it's a tear before bed every neet
terse up-river through yr
veer   o soot-sheen
gat a cool clear.

(Monk, 2002, [p. 3])

There is a staunchness about the 'Wiregrass' image in that natural determination can cut through the barb of restriction. In Scottish vernacular, the play between 'tear' (both as eye-water and rip) 'before bed' spreads to 'terse' (abrupt and still tearing), develops to a sense of coition as an act of seeking out the pure source, 'up-river' of the 'soot-sheen.' The erotic sensuousness of: 'Greeters far—I mean nooky-aye' reminds us that in the Medieval Christian world, mirrors were seen as emblems of vanity, sloth, Eve's deceit and the 'false beauty' of women. Sabine Melchior-Bonnet writes that the medical advisor to Duke Albert III recounted the mirror's bewitching power as a mediator of desire:

'I have seen masters who claim to prepare mirrors in such a way that anybody, man or woman, might see in them what he desires.' Once an emblem of supernatural forces, the mirror now reflected an image of interior demons and of *a threatening otherness that blurred identity*. [my italics]

(Melchior-Bonnet, 2001, p. 188)

The associations registered here and my reception of poetry are predicated on these facts. I read Monk's work in the way I listen to jazz and
singing, even singing in another language. I read her work for the same
reason that Robert Duncan says he wrote: 'To exercise my faculties at
large.' Ear, larynx and mind, teeth, cochlea and palate. Whitman's line
on those who are so proud to establish meanings seems apt—who would
try and explain a sax solo or a dance or children's pleasure in raw
sound? All the way from basic delight in *street-gibber* to Joyce's 'Bronze by
gold heard the hoofirons', from John Lennon's 'crabberlocker fishwife'
to Coltrane's phrasing on 'Pursuance.' (Monk hails from Blackburn,
Lancashire, the subject of the finding of enough holes to fill the Albert
Hall in 'A Day in the Life.')

It is notable that Mary of Scotland was a poet and linguist, her first
language being French but she could also speak English, Old Scottish,
Latin and Greek. Thus here we find 'Oui', 'Carpe diem', the Elizabethan
flourish of 'bed heirs' and 'ayeman.' We mustn't forget either that, if
Frances Presley rightly has written, 'Getha' is one pseudonym for Monk
herself in the poems, so is Mary. In *Marian Hangings* the link is clinched
as we move closer to the speaker in three stages: '*Mary-Marie Me*' (Monk,
2002a, [p. 2]). *Marie* can be made straightforwardly from Geraldine
Monk: 'motto immersed in anagram' (Monk, 2002a, [p. 2]). Or *Mary-Marry
Me*? The Mary-Marie of L. Frank Baum's tale is a fledgling witch and we
also might recall Tom Verlaine's Mary Marie who takes leave turning
mirrors to the wall. The identification with the Scottish queen's isolation continues:

> play before dark stately
> homes in caging octagon
> needled crown thralls
> t'thistle'd ownd

> (Monk, 2002a, [p. 2])

And Mary Queen of Scots' own motto finishes the sequence making the
association even stronger.

In the context of her age Mary was a sexually assertive woman, fully
aware of the power of conjugal alliance, choosing her own consorts and
deeply-attached to men like Francis and Bothwell. The lines and sounds
here are both as exuberant and as carefully scored as Niedecker's or
Loy's work. There is also tragedy. It is said that when the executioner

held up Mary's severed head wrapped in a kerchief, the head that rolled away from his hand was almost bald: 'almost bald as a billiard' (Monk, 2002, [p. 9]). Mary's years in prison had seriously damaged her health and beauty. Of course, we remember too that Elizabeth was bald; the two women mirroring each other to the end.

As the sequence develops, images of beheading cluster: 'here comes gruel to snap me out' (Monk, 2002, [p. 14]) puns on 'Here comes a chopper to chop off your head.' The northern injunction to use 'your loaf', (where *loaf* = head), is given a new Carrollesque twist as: 'Ginger queen of subtraction | takes loaf by knife' (Monk, 2002, [p. 15]) and 'Appearances bleed to edginess' (Monk, 2002, [p. 15]). 'Loaf by knife' grimly harks us back to 'Nil-be-mouth-breath' (Monk, 2002, [p. 9]), her food is her fate; as the Scots might say, she must *dree her weird*. As Sophie-Melchior Bonnet writes: 'Death also lurked behind the Devil's mirror' (Melchior-Bonnet, 2001, p. 188).

But Mary is not penitent. We remember Burns' 'Lament of Mary, Queen of Scots':

> But as for thee, thou false woman,
> My sister and my fae,
> Grim Vengeance yet shall whet a sword
> That thro' thy soul shall gae;
> The weeping blood in woman's breast
> Was never known to thee.

> (Burns, 1990, pp. 235–36)

We're left with: 'I will not a tuckle look | even through the glass' (Monk, 2002, [p. 15]). *Tuckle*, (the terminal *kle* reversing *look*), means *a mess* in Lancastrian dialect. It probably derives from '*tuck: Broken refuse of hay, straw, & c.*' (Wright, 1905, p. 258). The sonic charge of the lines is all proud defiance and resistance, a refusal to be demeaned. At her execution, Mary stepped free of her usual black robes to reveal a red dress underneath.

Hélène Cixous and Julia Kristeva have both written inspired critiques of Freud's essay on the uncanny, showing that it is replete with characteristically perceptive yet limited insights. But *unheimlich* doesn't give us a true sense of the Scottish *eerie*, a sense spanning the writings of northern balladeers, Burns, Radcliffe, Carroll, Monk and many more. Other German lexical alternatives don't do much better: *Furchterregend, schauerlich, schaurig*. To adapt a common form of neo-Freudian logic: if postmodern perspectives have led to a return of the repressed, a sense of the *eerie* now takes us far beyond this. It comes as no surprise then that when Wil McCarthy writes of that

> older vision system built into our brains [. . . [which bypasses not only the conscious mind, but also the visual cortex, the 'limbic system' or primitive mammalian brain, the hindbrain or reptilian brain and even the cerebellum. [. . .] There are pathways—very ancient but still functional—that connect our eyes directly to that most primitive bit of neurological tissue: the brain stem. And the brain stem [. . .] is really fast.

> (McCarthy, n.d.)

He calls this thought *eerie*.

Far from relegating the writing of contemporary women poets exclusively to that much-abused sense: the *intuitive*, the term *eerie* now refers us forwards to advanced, exhilarating craft, a honed and an exacting sounding of languages. Where but in Monk's loaded art would we find so splendidly figured, a playful aside to a children's story, (Carroll's Knight saying 'It'll come in handy if we find any plum-cake'), arcing swiftly to sexual domination, militarism and a power that 'scores' a territory 'fleshed' with time? Like McCarthy, she finds the human mind eerie, as crazy at times as her voluptuous Mary might have found monastic deprivations in the Abbeys she visited. (The average lifespan of the British population in the sixteenth century was about 35 years, but that of a Cistercian monk was barely 28 (Edkins, 2003).) This is worth bearing in mind in reading the lines below. So are Monk's vocative skill, her tumultuous humour, her power, her eerie:

> Goosier ma steps through
> looking you. The queen of plum cakes
> ruckles my corsets
> a weaponry beyond exocets
> scoring time fleshed territory.
> Misericord men nibble mean
> leaves
> the craziest paved path
> engraved in grey matter.

> (Monk, 2002, [p. 13])

References

American Association of Electronic Voice Phenomena Publishing. 2003. http://book.aaevp.com/

Annwn, D. 2003. Review of *Noctivagations*, *The David Jones Journal*. Winter 2002 / Spring 2003, 133–136

────── 2002. *Arcs Through, The Poetry of Randolph Healy, Billy Mills & Maurice Scully*. Dublin: Wild Honey Press

────── 2002. 'Tutelar, Or Her Truth's Teller? Myth, Women poets and David Jones' 'The Tutelar of the Place''. Unpublished essay.

────── 2000. 'Her Pulse Their Pace, Women Poets and Basil Bunting' in McGonigal, J. and Price, R. eds., 2000. *The Star You Steer By*. Amsterdam & Atlanta: Rodopi Editions, pp. 123–48

Berryman, J. 1972. *Selected Poems 1938–1968*. London: Faber and Faber

Burns, R. 1990. *The Complete Illustrated Poems, Songs & Ballads*. London: Lomond Books

Carroll, L. 1889. *Sylvie and Bruno* in 1982. *The Complete Illustrated Works of Lewis Carroll*. London: The Bath Press

Cobbing, B. 1978. 'Some Statements on Sound Poetry'. *UBUWEB*. Viewable at: http://www.ubu.com/papers/cobbing.html

Croggon, A. 2002. 'Specula: Mirrors from the Middle Ages'. Viewable at: http://www.thedrunkenboat.com/specula.html

Damon, M. n.d. 'Beginnings: Introductions, Explanations, Forewords'. *The East Village.Com*. Viewable at: http://www.fauxpress.com/t8/damon/p4.htm

Dorward, N. 2003. 'Camden People's Theatre Total Writing London, 27–29 June'. *Paris Transatlantic*. Viewable at: http://www.paristransatlantic.com/magazine/monthly2003/09sep_text.html

Downey, H. n.d. Amazon book review. Viewable at: http: //www.queertheory.com/histories/h/h_d_hilda_doolittle.htm

Edkins, R. 1997. 'Dundrennan Abbey—A Personal Tour'. Viewable at: http://freespace.virgin.net/richard.wordsmith/duntour.htm

Fisler. G.W. 2003. 'Scrying Procedures'. Viewable at:http://astralthyme.com/scryingprocedure.html

Freud, S. 1953. 'The Uncanny', in *The Standard Edition of the Complete Psychological Works of Sigmund Freud*, ed. & trs. James Strachey, vol. XVII. London: Hogarth

Genette, G. 1997. *Paratexts*. Cambridge: Cambridge University Press

Haught, J.A. 1993. 'The Dreams of which Stuff is Made, Pondering the mysteries of matter; Solidity is an electrical illusion'. Sunday Gazette Mail

Hooker, J. 1978. *Solent Shore*. Manchester: Carcanet

Hudson, D. n.d. *Lewis Carroll*. Viewable at: www.ourcivlisation.com/smartboard/shop/hudsond/carroll/chap6.htm

Johnson, T.H. ed. 1970. *Emily Dickinson: The Complete Poems*. London: Faber and Faber

Kerr, S. 1998. 'What We Have Here Is A Failure To Communicate: Gertrude Stein's Fascinating Mistakes'. Viewable at: http://slate.msn.com/id/3056/

Kipling, R. n.d. *The Definitive Edition of Rudyard Kipling's Verse*. London: Hodder and Stoughton

Mapel-Bloomberg, K. 2003. 'Modernism and the Occult'. Viewable at: www .geocities.com/Wellesley/7327/modernism2.html

McCarthy, W. n.d. 'Blindsight'. Viewable at: http://www.scifi.com/sfw/issue303/labnotes.html

Melchior-Bonnet, S. 2001. *The Mirror: a History*. London: Routledge

Meriton, G. n.d. 'A Yorkshire Dialogue, Texts of the 19th Century and Earlier'. Viewable at: http://www.yorksj.ac.uk/dialect/Old_texts.htm

Merriam-Webster. http://www.m-w.com/cgi-bin/dictionary

Monk, G. 1979. *Long Wake*. London: Writers Forum and Pirate Press
——— 1980. *Spreading the Cards*. Staithes: Siren Press
——— 2001. *Noctivagations*. Sheffield: West House Books
——— 2002. *Mary Through the Looking Glass*. Sheffield: Gargoyle Edition
——— 2002a. *Marian Hangings*. Sheffield: Gargoyle Edition
——— 2003. *Selected Poems*. Cambridge: Salt Publishing

Mycack, S. n.d. Viewable at: http://www.australysis.com/newreles.html

NOBLE. (North of Boston Library Exchange.) 'St Stephen's Day.' Viewable at: http://www.noblenet.org/year/ststephen.htm

Norder, D. 1999. 'Looking at Bloody Mary, Mary Worth and Other Variants of a Modern Legend'. Viewable at: http://www.mythology.com/bloodymary.html

O'Sullivan, M. ed., 1996. *Out of Everywhere, Linguistically Innovative Poetry by Women in North America & the UK*. London and Suffolk: Reality Street Editions

Oxford English Dictionary. 1978. Oxford: Clarendon Press

Presley, F. 2003. 'Metablethers of Getha' [review of *Noctivagations*]. *How2*, Vol. 2, no. 1 (Spring 2003). Viewable at: http://www.departments. bucknell.edu/stadler_center/how2/current/alerts/presley.shtm

University of Wales Press Catalogue. 2003. Cardiff: University of Wales Press

Wright, J. 1905. *The English Dialect Dictionary*. Oxford: Henry Frowde

'Ring a-ring a-rosy':
Girls' Games in the Poetry of Geraldine Monk

FRANCES PRESLEY

With the publication of Geraldine Monk's *Selected Poems* from Salt, the totality of her work can be assessed more fully. It combines much of what was previously available in three books: *Noctivagations* (2001), *Interregnum* (1994) and *The Sway of Precious Demons* (1992). For the complete works much research into ephemeral and valuable small press publications would still be required. It is important to stress the totality of her work, which is sometimes overlooked in reviews, especially as this partiality is often experienced by women writers.[1] With the *Selected Poems* we can also see her recent work in the context of the earlier writing, of which it is both development and reprise.

One example is her recent playful return to the work of the Spanish artist Goya in 'La Tormenta', reminding us of one of her most influential early sequences *La Quinta del Sordo*.[2]

> We cannot believe
> our very-eyes oh yes our
> very-eyes we cannot believe
> *Sopa Goyesca   La quinta*
> *creps del sordo*
> *vegetal in season*

(Monk, 2003, p. 170)

---

[1] As highlighted by Christine Battersby: 'The work of women writers and artists has to be constructed into individual oeuvres and situated in traditions of female creativity' (Battersby, 1989, p. 10).

[2] *La Quinta del Sordo* is in *Selected Poems*, pp. 19–24. It was originally published by Writers Forum in 1980.

If Goya is on the menu, he is also the heartbeat of the poem, in the repeated sound of 'chin-chin', recalling his name for the bourgeois: 'chinchilla.' *La Quinta del Sordo* was the sequence that really drew me in to Monk's work, as much for her performance of it, as by a later reading of the text. I will analyse in detail one of the poems in this work and how it reinvents the language and ritual of childhood games as a model for much wider political and feminist concerns. I will then consider some of Monk's later works, mainly from *Noctivagations*, to see how these concerns are developed and expanded.

First though, I want to discuss briefly how Monk's work is positioned in contemporary poetry, and how she positions herself: this includes the debate about women experimental poets and 'expressive' modes of writing. Clair Wills defined it, in a much-quoted essay, as a false polarisation of formal experimentation and expressive elements, and also of the private and public spheres:

> Thus it is not that 'expressive' poetry naively falls back on a stable individuality, and experimental work explores the radical absence of subjectivity. Both are responses to the reconfiguring of the relationship between public and private spheres which makes the 'private' lyric impossible, and in effect opens it out towards rhetoric.

> (Wills, 1994, p. 39)

Wills also analyses how the 'expressive' female self is still present in the work of experimental women poets. It seems to me that a lot of experimental male poetry is intensely expressive, or emotional, but generally within a socialist framework. As a result male reviewers can appear more comfortable with Monk's ghettoblaster sequences than with her female self or selves. The problem with 'expressiveness' in female experimental poetry often has more to do with feminism than any form of rhetoric.

An interesting aspect of *Noctivagations* is the promotional blurb on the back cover: one quote is from an experimental poetry magazine, *Object Permanence*: 'Eerie, violent . . . an exhilarating flux of human-animal-alien corporealities approximated in language', and the other is from the *Yorkshire Post*: 'genuine word magic . . . a wonderful poet: revelatory, intense, ever surprising.' By choosing these extremely diverse admirers of her work, Monk seems to be making the statement that she wants her work to cast as wide a spell as possible: for it to be enjoyed both by the avant-garde and by a much wider audience. She wants to break out of the marginalisation of the experimental, not into the mainstream of

British poetry, who will continue to marginalise her work, but directly to anyone who may hear or read her.

There are those in the avant-garde too who will regard this as impossible, or who might declare with Keith Tuma that Monk's poetry must be 'expressive' rather than 'difficult':

> And the first thing to be said about Monk's poetry is that while it does not use the 'dominant modes' of expression, neither is it difficult. Playful, rhetorical, feminist, it can also be as 'expressive' as an insult.

> (Tuma, 1998, p. 232)

Yet Monk's poetry is both expressive and difficult, in the sense of experimental and abstract. It is as expressive as a Goya, as J.K. Huysmans describes:

> Le Goya: un ecrasis de rouge, de bleu et de jaune, des virgules de couleur blanche, des pates de tons vifs, plaques, pele-mele, mastiques au couteau. [. . .] C'est le vacarme le plus effrene qui ait jamais ete jete sur une toile.

> (Eluard, 1952, pp. 70–71)[3]

One of the major contemporary influences on Monk's work was concrete sound poetry, as defined in Bob Cobbing's 1978 manifesto *Concerning Concrete Poetry*. In an important challenge to the dominant trends in English poetry, Cobbing emphasised the return to the primitive, and to incantation and ritual, through music and poetry. There is in Monk's work a similar emphasis on the physical substance of language, which is also in part a recapturing of a more 'primitive' form of language, common to modern art and poetry. Take for example Cobbing's statement: 'The moment an O becomes larger and fatter or an S more rhythmically snake-like, at that moment does drama enter into the score' (Cobbing, 1978, p. 44). Sometimes it seems as if all Monk's work is a dramatic expansion of the letter O.

However, I think there are important differences between what Monk is doing and concrete or sound poetry. One of those differences is the issue of gender which is of no concern in Cobbing's manifesto. Even if we stay within the terms of concrete and sound poetry it seems to me that too much is expected of what Cobbing calls 'a new means of

---

3 'Goya: a crushing of red, blue and yellow, commas of white, paste of hot colours, layered, jumbled, slapped on with a knife. [. . .] It's the most frantic din that's ever been thrown on a canvas.'

communication [. . .] which is more natural more direct and more honest than, for example, the present day voice of politics and religion' (Cobbing, 1978, p. 43). This is to set two very different means of communication in opposition, without fully taking account of all the alternatives. There is also a risk of placing too much reliance on an abstracted ritual for its own sake.[4] I am interested in how Monk travels with and takes the physical substance of language and her chosen rituals into a fully formed assault on the present day voices of politics and religion.

Alison Croggon recently gave a very interesting paper on the writings of women mystics in mediaeval England, direct antecedents (if we need any) of Geraldine Monk:

> These texts suggest intriguing ways of looking at contemporary practices. They are most subversive in how they assert their rational basis within contemporary orthodoxies, which permits them to clear a space for a largely unheard female vocabulary which then becomes its own authority. Mere emotion is not enough; mere intellectuality would not satisfy their desires nor permit a language for female expressiveness.

> (Croggon, 2002)

La Quinta del Sordo: girls' play

I still have the A4 1980 Writers Forum edition with the blurry close ups of grotesque characters from Goya's etchings on front and back covers. I'll quote from the beginning of the fourth text, based on Goya's 'La Lealtad', though I can't reproduce the original typeface, or that cheap typewriter effect of the period. For the same reason I've also had problems with the justification of the lines:

> Here we go sound around the one in the middle who we
> shall riddle   the bulbous head pearing away we're
> laughing at you   clenched fists may pray and black
> out night to fight the   heardings AMPLIFICATIONS
> go sound around and   jutters through shutters and   B
> rained stained cellars   now you are the queen who'll
> never be seen you're   one on your own so far   from
> home a pig in a choke/spoke more kindly of/a spoke   in

---

4 Cobbing gives an example of a concrete sound poem: 'SAY "soma haoma". Dull. Say it, dwelling on the quality of the sounds. Better. Let it say itself through you. [. . .] Bodies join in song and movement. A ritual ensues.' A footnote tells us that 'soma-haoma' is 'the sacred mushroom which, acting on the body, gives spiritual health' (Cobbing, 1978, p. 45).

the eye/s ticks bent will flick and pick up the pieces
of shadows we form for your   ultimate   annoyance

(Monk, 2003, p. 23)

Although *La Quinta del Sordo* was written at the dawn of the Thatcher era, when I first heard it we were close to the nadir of Thatcherism. I had not heard anything that so perfectly expressed the forces at work at that time: jeering had been given full licence, and the bullies were in charge. At a time when language was devalued, and political debate replaced by fear and menaces, this text provided a way out, a subversion, an opposition. It was a time when I too had become fascinated by games and the rhythm of games, both the kind that were organised in the workplace to control an increasingly oppressed workforce and the games of survival, including ones we had learnt as children.[5]

Its use of childhood playground rhyme is a recurring device in Monk's work, and one that has particular resonance for girls. Girlhood is a time of freedom and even a certain power which is threatened by adolescence. Girls can also be bullies of course, as Thatcher went on to demonstrate. This text is both an exposé of bullying and in its form and performance a magic spell, a protection against it.

The playground rhyme is mimicked in the strong use of internal rhyming words, building up an excess of rhyme which gives a dark edge to the form: 'middle' and 'riddle', for example, suggest a firing squad— also the subject of a famous Goya painting. The physical rhythm of the poem and its utterance are inseparable from the text. Here the circling movement of those taunting the one in the middle is enacted in performance and in the poem. It may be a rectangle on the page, but the words' sense and their justification, make us see and hear it as a circle. There is a rhythm in this text which gathers speed before it collapses in exhaustion and negation.

The movement also represented the circular nature of (Thatcherite) politics, an illusion in which it was impossible to get at the truth,

---

[5] My own dialogue with this text became the more overtly political 'Natural Reaction' in *Hula Hoop* (Presley, 1993, p. 9). It's also interesting that we were both children of the 1950s, the era encapsulated in Iona and Peter Opie's standard work *The Lore and Language of Schoolchildren*. In their words: 'through these quaint ready-made formulas the ridiculousness of life is underlined, the absurdity of the adult world and their teachers proclaimed, danger and death mocked, and the curiosity of language itself is savoured' (Opie, 1959, p. 18). They also include a chapter on 'Guile' which covers the 'whole anatomy of personal humiliation.'

because so many lies were being told, and the language of debate itself had changed. The victim can know that information is being withheld but not know how much or the full extent of the conspiracy. In this situation nearly everyone is a victim, even the bourgeois, the chinchillas, who are satirised but also to be pitied. Women were increasingly complicit, and it seemed to me that Monk was also aware of women's role as executrixes of cruel and irrational policies: 'now you are the queen who'll | never be seen [. . .] a pig in a choke' (Monk, 2003, p. 23). Another queen is calling the shots, and she is not the Queen of the May. The victim at the centre knows what game she's in, and would like to play the queen but knows too much to retreat safely into that fantasy.

Another key element of this text is its humour — I've already talked about the jeering and bullying, but in this tone or climate it is as if humour itself has been co-opted. In order for the status quo to continue there has to be an element of acceptance by the oppressed and that can work equally well through shared humour or black comedy. In fact some of the language sounds like the menacingly good humoured phraseology of organisational politics: 'its only some fun so don't run | for a while just tow the line' (Monk, 2003, p. 23). This 'towing' of the line, also takes us back to the type of movement, both physical and textual which is being enacted: a 'toeing' of the line which is organised and regimented bullying, a square dance for the circle. The text ends with insinuation, of hinted at worse possibilities, which are more disturbing than overt physical violence: 'and you'll be perhaps | and maybe wet with sweet dew if the morning ever or | never' (Monk, 2003, p. 23).

In the context of its performance, however, it was a rhythm which could only gather speed, in which Monk was swaying on her feet so much that she had to take off her shoes, and then could move faster and faster, free of their hobbling and cobbling: a freedom which extends to the limitless line. The toes and feet are an important element of Monk's own manifesto, *Insubstantial Thoughts on the Transubstantiation of the Text,* and the emphasis on public, or pubic, performance in this section entitled 'Voca-visu (orientation)':

Toes in perpetual isometric desperation
clinging for balance:

a body hanging by its feet.
.t.t.t.t.

(Monk, 2003, p. 223)

And her movement represents a whirling out, also a key to the poet H.D.'s work and a strong motif in the novel *Her*. Hermione in *Her* escapes from the claustrophobic circles of family and science by spinning into the wilderness 'which preserves Her' (Doolittle, 1984, p. 56). It is a movement which requires a certain degree of madness or wildness, something Monk said on that occasion: 'You have to go mad like us.' It is not just escape, however, because, as Monk also writes in her manifesto:

> Performance is aggressive occupation of
> Place. Convolvulaceous.

> (Monk, 2003, p. 222)

And that is a rediscovery of the place of girl play and to use the contemporary cliché, girl power: one which survives the worst of adult power games.

2

I propose in this section to examine the development of the experimental, the expressive and feminism in Monk's more recent work, mainly from *Noctivagations*, ending with another recent celebration of circular rhythms and girls' play: *Mary Through the Looking Glass*.

Noctivagations

Noctivagations is divided into nine sections: *The Transparent Ones*; *Trilogy*; *Songings & Strangerlings*; *Dream Drover*; *Hidden Cities*; *Two Dramatics*; *Fluvium*; *Three Short Sorties*; and *Nine Little Ones*, some of which appeared previously in small press editions.

 Dream Drover is an especially humorous ride, with the (woman) poet as driver initially unsure of the controls. The front cover shows a VW Beetle looking very insect like, and the poem begins with some reworked clichés of the driving lesson:

> don't grip the lip
> crossed arms breed a twisted

> (Monk, 2001, p. 57)

The left hand margin of the poems weaves in and out like an erratically steered vehicle which barely negotiates hair pin bends, until there is a final straight drop to the end of the poem. We are a long way from the machine precision of Fordville, and these are the errant roads of 'pure Peak scree' (Monk, 2001, p. 57). There are echoes of Gerard Manley Hopkins, one of Monk's favourite poets, both in rhythm and word play, including the use of compound words. As the poem progresses, the driver or drover achieves the control of Hopkins' windhover, and the movement of the margin is also like a wing:

> as the crosswinds
>> blow-out stretches at a-glancing
>>> and you needn't hold back

(Monk, 2001, p. 58)

Monk frequently breaks words across lines, often to comic effect, as in the Hollywood screen star fantasy stanza:

>> A'm doing dream time-big
>> As tra-laa partial star sashays
>> its hexy little bott
>> om down the mountill

(Monk, 2001, p. 58)

Notice also the odd use of A'm, which evokes a dialect version of I, but is also a way of escaping 'I' into this fluid fantasy. In the same stanza she resurrects the Brontës via Liz Taylor! This juxtaposition is not as strange as it might seem, since in the 1943 film of *Jane Eyre* Liz Taylor acts the schoolgirl who dies of her punishment at Lowood school:

> scheming dreams
>> of young Liz
>>> Taylor shimmying into
>>> Bronte skin
>>> !woah!

(Monk, 2001, p. 58)

In Monk's version she is far from the passive victim, but a shimmy dancer who knows how to belt it out.

The Transparent Ones was originally a performance work called *Metablethers of Getha*. The change in title is a more accurate description of these texts, as the first version could be applied to all of Monk's work. 'Metablethers' is a wonderful neologism which also appears in *Fluvium*— some of the most experimental work in *Noctivagations*. It combines the old English/Scots word 'blether' or 'blather', meaning to talk loquacious nonsense, with the multi-purpose Greek prefix 'meta.' It combines her use of sound and nonsense poetry with a very rooted use of dialect. She is both in the locale, the dialect, and rising above it, transmuting and experimenting with it. The name Getha is evidently one of Monk's pseudonyms, and is used as such in the radio drama *Manufractured Moon*. It begins with the first two letters of her Christian name, but ends in something suggestive of the East, and other spirits. This is not invalid even if we realise that Getha has a very specific meaning for computer users: Get Hardware Address. One of the developments in Monk's work has been her use of electronic technology and terminology, for her own subversive purposes.

The Transparent Ones are the poems written out of her time as a writer in residence at a hospice for terminally ill people. If I like it so much, I think it is partly because Monk is often depicted as a wild woman of experimental poetry, whereas these poems show her capacity for a deep attachment to the people she works with, and her essential humanism. Sean Bonney wrote: 'Geraldine Monk is part of a quite easily identified unofficial tendency in contemporary British poetry. A wild streak [. . .] shared with comparable poets like Bill Griffiths and Maggie O'Sullivan' (Bonney, 2002, p. 58). This is 'wild-poetry', to use Bonney's phrase, and as indeed the title of the collection which features *The Transparent Ones* — *Noctivagations*—suggests, but it is also profoundly responsible and responsive poetry.

The first poem is 'The Gathering', which begins as if with stage instructions, and the staccato phrasing is also used to powerful effect in prose poem sections such as *Hidden Cities* and *Three Short Sorties*:

> (High noon. Mid summer. Terrace. Round table. High Peaks in the distance. Round robin of low sleepless talk. The Transparent Ones)

(Monk, 2003, p. 197)

The reference to 'High Noon' is a deliberate one, and it is typical of Monk's work that she introduces filmic, popular culture references. These are both comic and serious. The struggle with death at the hospice is as intense as any Western gun battle. It is also one of the ways in which we attempt to talk about death.

The Transparent Ones raises questions about life and death which are unanswerable, but she plays in deadly seriousness with those questions:

your natter-flack
questions creating
ineffable Q systems &
split infinities

(Monk, 2003, p. 202)

Her irreverence towards established religion and Catholicism is probably most clearly reflected by one of her subjects in 'Keltic Twilight', who
expresses his 'apostasy' in vivid dialect, which Monk captures: 't-poep-sa-
nutter' (Monk, 2003, p. 206). There are almost unbearable descriptions
and word play on dying flesh, but she never allows the poem to acquire
too much solemnity. Nor does she hide the pain of the last agony, and
the panic:

Skin Panics.
even my words are ridd ~ ~ led.
Sense disappears at every touch.
[. . .]
In the grip of rising panic
we watch the solitary unleaf furl ~ ~
There are moments of relief
in every fiction

(Monk, 2003, p. 211)

Here punctuation, specifically the tilde, is used to express the breakage
or concealment of words and sense, and then becomes visually expressive of new growth. We have also become familiar, perhaps uncon-
sciously so, with the tilde on our computer screen where it can be shorthand for a hidden extended document title. There may be an echo of the
Spanish diacritical mark, used to represent the sound 'ny', where the
missing letter is 'y.' Perhaps also the ghost of Manley Hopkins is here
again, as it is similar to the twirl he used to indicate reversed or coun-
terpointed rhythm.

I particularly like 'Across Your Dreams in Pale Battalions Go',[6] in
which Monk reworks the myth of Persephone, and features another
strong female subject. It includes one of the technical devices she uses
frequently in *The Transparent Ones*, but also occurs elsewhere in her

---

[6] This title is a quotation from the First World War poet Charles Sorley, and the
powerful sonnet 'When you see millions of the mouthless dead.' It was a very
popular poem which would have had a wide audience, but it is also formally
interesting in its staccato, broken lines: an effect echoed in Monk's writing.

writing. There are lines or verses in italics at the left hand margin, and then a verse which is inset in ordinary type. Sometimes the lines in italics seem to act as commentary on the central verse, but at other times they act more as a dialogue or antiphon. As the woman (M) reads the 'childs | Persephone', the language of the poem becomes simultaneously child-like and Miltonic in its desolation. These are lines written from Eve and Persephone's perspective:

> *M shivers.*
> *Shifts unease.*
> > flowers wept
> > crops stopt
> > leaves turned
> > raged-red
> > and shed
> > everything
> > shed

> (Monk, 2003, p. 200)

The female subject, Getha, in *Manufractured Moon*, is the poet's persona, with all her various attributes. *Manufractured Moon* is a drama for radio written in the style of a series of emails from Getha to some other person, an unknown friend. I like the urgent, present tense nervy email style, which plays with, amongst other things, the often violent urban and rural aspects of her locale late at night. The first email subject is 'Fox barks', and must also make a sly reference to the Ted Hughes poem: 'Sat upright and owl-eyed for hours so thoughts got to pellets & droppings of words but to longhand e-mail or fax foxes' (Monk, 2003, p. 187).

Manufractured Moon is also the most overtly feminist of the texts in *Noctivagations*.[7] This is manifest in a partial retelling of a child's street or playground game about wanting to cross the golden river. The children have to ask the farmer's permission, and in Monk's version the farmer (father) becomes a sinister figure: 'Farmer Dark-Force may we par take our father's boiled dinner as it is in heaven?' (Monk, 2003, p. 188). The female self is also evident in her dig at organised religion. She describes a 'Last Supper of 2000' hanging in her room, which shows Christ with a 'heart shaped cob' and all the male apostles (Monk, 2003, p. 187). Later

---

7   Other than the wonderful Sheila-na-gig in 'Found Church Guide', part of *Nine Little Ones*: 'Her glappy lips span worlds | warming cockles to guffaw away | the damned devil' (Monk, 2001, p. 111).

she becomes convinced that one of the apostles isn't male at all, transforms him into Joan of Arc, and finally (he) sashays around like Gilda, a star of the silver screen. Monk makes her own divinity in 'Falling Outs':

> The blind even quivered at the iddy girl tungsten thin and burning bright fell out with all gods in a big way such as only youngage can with starry id.

(Monk, 2003, p. 189)

There is real menace in this urban night, particularly in the figure of a threatening male stranger 'flickering under the leaning street-lamp' (Monk, 2003, p. 191). There is fear and horror, and an edge of madness in the penultimate email: 'Walls grin wetly. And HE's there again', and she signs off, or trails off, as 'Get . . . ' (Monk, 2003, p. 192). In the final email, however, he has been returned to the lower case, and she is simply G. again, 'Back on Track' (Monk, 2003, pp. 193–94).

Mary Through the Looking Glass

Girls and women in real or imaginary prisons, rather than at play, is another important theme in Monk's work, both in *Interregnum* and in the recent short sequence *Mary Through the Looking Glass*.[8] The Mary in question is Mary Queen of Scots, who was imprisoned for some years in Sheffield, Monk's home town. Her identity is not immediately apparent from the title, and clues are hidden in the text: she is subject to as many transformations as Lewis Carroll's Alice. The historical Mary was also fascinated by anagrams, codes and secret messages:

> Bless
> O
> Bess
> ma curfew out this mirror flew through.

(Monk, 2002, [p. 2])

Bess could be Bess of Chatsworth, Elizabeth Shrewsbury, although she could also be another gaoler, Elizabeth Regina. In *Mary Through the*

---

[8] Now re-published as part of *Escafeld Hangings* (Sheffield: West House Books, 2005), a book which concentrates mainly on the figure of Mary Queen of Scots and which includes an audio CD recording of Monk and Ligia Roque performing *Mary Through the Looking Glass*.

Looking Glass we are still in the land of children's games, of grown up nonsense rhymes which might provide a means of escape. Mary's own development has been cut short by her imprisonment, but there are also references to other more contemporary and crueller incarcerations: 'Do we not lobotomise worrisome fruit?' (Monk, 2002, [p. 5]).

This sequence is, above all, a sinister circling game, rather like the fourth text of *La Quinta del Sordo*, or the latter day pagans in *Interregnum*.[9] The text revolves around the letter O which might permit escape, especially through the O of the looking glass. It is a shape and letter that can liquefy and flow, and allow the subject to become the fish and swim away:

> Beware m-e-mirror look out.
> Minnow quicksilver down the
> poisonous poisson

> (Monk, 2002, [p. 8])

There are puns on French—Mary's childhood language—in the play of 'poison' and 'poisson.' I once heard a small child called 'un vrai poisson' and thought at first it was a description of his sweet wriggling fish-like nature.

One of the few periods of relative freedom for Mary Queen of Scots was being allowed to bathe at Buxton Spa. This love of water and swimming is a point of connection for Monk, and also a tribute to her mother, expressed in the early poem 'For My Mother.'[10] When Mary left Buxton for the last time she wrote a farewell verse in Latin on the window pane with her diamond ring.

At times the words become a new and unfamiliar pattern of letters or stitches, which in their strangeness could provide a key to unlock the prison gate: the words 'woos and ogles' (Monk, 2002, [p. 14]) placed together lose their common meaning and become a new aperture.

Another very ironic 'O' is Mary's balding head, and the loss of hair that accompanies the ageing process, but also illness and despair: 'me could murder | alopecia', and 'am almost bald as a billiard' (Monk, 2002, [p. 9]). When Mary was beheaded onlookers were shocked when a

---

[9] 'roundandwound | little | circles | pretty patters | clownabout' (Monk, 2003, p. 104).

[10] 'she gathered | armfuls of | turquoise | effortless | swam | silent as the | orange | black tiger | lilies | they gave her' (Monk, 1992, p. 23).

wig fell from her head to reveal her close-cropped pate. The reference to billiards could also refer to the cover of the billiard table in which her corpse was unceremoniously wrapped.

The text is littered with escaping subverbal fillers, which often feature the letter 'o', whether they are exclamations or soul music: 'whooooa whooooaaa' (Monk, 2002, [p. 8])—a gutsy pop idiom that might have saved Mary had she been educated to be other than a certain kind of queen. One who is no more Tennyson's Lady of Shalott, 'half sick of shadows' (Blunden, 1969, p. 34)[11] in her mirror, and fated to float down river to Sir Lancelot than she is that other symbol of self-absorbed purity, Mallarmé's Hérodiade.[12] This is not a queen who's never been seen.

References

Battersby, C. 1989. *Gender and Genius: towards a feminist aesthetics.* London: Women's Press

Bonney, S. 2002. 'Review of *Noctivagations*'. *Poetry Salzburg Review* 3, Autumn 2002, 58–61

Blunden, E. ed. 1969. *Selected Poems of Tennyson.* London: Heinemann

Cobbing, B and Mayer, P. eds., 1978. *Concerning Concrete Poetry.* London: Writers Forum

Croggon, A. 2002. 'Specula: Mirrors from the Middle Ages'. Viewable at: http://www.thedrunkenboat.com/specula.html

Doolittle, H. 1984. *Her.* London: Virago

Eluard, P. 1952. *Les freres voyants: anthologie des ecrits sur l'art.* Paris: Gonthier

Mallarmé, S. 1945. *Oeuvres Completes.* Paris: Gallimard

Monk, G. 1980. *La Quinta del Sordo.* London: Writers Forum

———— 1992. *The Sway of Precious Demons: Selected Poems.* Twickenham and Wakefield: North and South

———— 2001. *Noctivagations.* Sheffield: West House Books

———— 2002. *Mary Through the Looking Glass.* Sheffield: Gargoyle Edition

———— 2003. *Selected Poems.* Cambridge: Salt Publishing

---

[11] I was forced to recite 'The Lady of Shalott' with rounded vowel sounds instead of the pure Northern vowel sounds, at grammar school in Lincolnshire.

[12] For example: 'Ô miroir! Eau froide par l'ennui dans ton cadre gelée' [Oh mirror! Cold water frozen in your frame through ennui] (Mallarmé, 1945, p. 45).

Opie, I. and Opie, P. 1959. *The Lore and Language of Schoolchildren*. Oxford: Oxford University Press

Presley, F. 1993. *Hula Hoop*. London: Other Press

Tuma, K. *Fishing by Obstinate Isles*. Northwestern University Press, 1998

Wills, C. (1994). 'Contemporary Women's Poetry: Experimentalism and the Expressive Voice', *Critical Quarterly*, 36 (3), 34–52

Author's Note

This essay draws on my reviews of *Noctivagations* and *Dream Drover* published in *How2*.

'Eye-spy': Geraldine Monk and the Visible[1]

ELIZABETH JAMES

I

Asked in an interview about her 'relationship to the visual', Geraldine Monk explained that, having left school very early and later returned to college,

> one of my primary routes into poetry came not via the staid teaching of English lit in schools [. . .] but through my growing interest in the visual arts.

(Monk, 2002c, pp. 176–77)

Several of Monk's peers and elders combine, in varying degrees, poetry with visual art practice, for instance Allen Fisher, Brian Catling, Tom Raworth, and among her closer associates, Maggie O'Sullivan and the late Jeff Nuttall. However her own path remained on the verbal side, as she points out in the interview quoted: 'despite the fact that I have a very strong visual sense I do not work with visuals per se' (Monk, 2002c, p. 177).

This essay sets out to discern and evaluate the importance of the visual in Monk's poetry. It aims to be suggestive rather than definitive, leaving plenty of scope for other readers to test and contest its approaches to Monk's work, or indeed to that of other contemporary poets. We begin by noticing thematic support in Monk's work for this approach, before considering the visual and material poetics implicit in the way Monk designs her poems on the page and in the book. Venturing into the paratextual realm, we look at the images of the poet herself that have been published in contiguity with her writing. Finally,

[1] 'eye-spy' ('The Physical Letters'), *Noctivagations* (Monk, 2001, p. 114).

a more extended consideration of a single sequence is intended to draw attention to the potential of poetry's visual aspects alongside the other resources from which rewarding readings are produced.

II

What will look like will look.

(Monk, 2001, p. 52)

Mentions of eyes and aspects of seeing are recurrent in Monk's oeuvre. From early on, they implied an awareness of the inevitable mutual reflexivity, the mirror-exchange between seer and seen. The 'eyes' on the tail of a peacock in *Banquet* (Monk, 2003, p. 21) are an image for this apprehension, while the 'irridescence' of this bird's plumage in *La Quinta del Sordo* (Monk, 2003, p. 28) exemplifies the instability of appearances, the way phenomena are partly subjective and characterise the experiencing consciousness as much as the external fact. Parting lovers in winter are 'stale-eyed as the sun' in *Rotations* (Monk, 2003, p. 16).

The implications of visibility for the individual in Monk's work are variable and even contradictory. There is the threat of exposure to a 'voyeur' (Monk, 2003, p. 13) or some 'beady-eyed interrogation team' (Monk, 1980a, [p. 8]). Both of these early instances refer to the stars, suggesting the persistence of an atavistic, scrutineering God located in the sky. 'Beady' later becomes even more voyeuristic: 'all spies with bidet eyes' (Monk, 2003, p. 77): revised from 'little eyes' in the original version (Monk, 1986a, [p. 6]). The anxiety persists, in a memory of certain 1950s linoleum designs, in the abstract patterns of which forms were discerned: 'Faces on kitchen floor. | Spectral eyes could not be scrubbed' (Monk, 2001, p. 51).

In the major mature book *Interregnum* whose primary concern is the trials of the Lancashire witches, while catastrophe is primarily activated in language, the victims are exposed by ignorant or wilful witnesses who are probably projecting the error they identify. 'Witnessing', properly, is telling what you have seen, not 'Blind Talk':

BLIND TALK

we only believe
your truth telling
it like we
want to
hear what we
don't is

(Monk, 2003, p. 134)

'Blind Talk' as a whole is laid out on the page somewhat like a face, with the word 'lying' on either side asymmetrically—like the non-matching eyes of 'Squintin' Lizzie', who knowingly flings back the 'aesthetic fear' that motivates those who demonise her, into 'the twisted face of such poppycock' (Monk, 2003, p. 146).

Not that all the supposed witches are safely rationalistic. Demdike confesses to fashioning effigies, 'my art'; however it is not quite certain whether she intends to, or imagines she can, literally 'make or take a life' (Monk, 2003, p. 141). Only her deep and strange absorption in the material process is certain: 'Wetness . . . oozing through fingers . . . | make-believe eyes running . . . ' (Monk, 2003, p. 141).

Meanwhile in present-day Pendle it is suggested the heretical imaginary is still associated with an ophthalmic fixation:

> in the pure woolly
> heads of sheep
> eyes
> slit
> a fester on
> your dreams

(Monk, 2003, p. 103)

and,

> Hail sulphuric eyes
> matter-caked orbs
> alignment of baubles
> primordial crud

(Monk, 2003, p. 104)

Twice Monk includes a reference to a parlour game:

> blinded
> we pin the tail
> in the donkey's
> eye

(Monk, 2003, p. 132)[2]

In the game the donkey is only a picture but in conjunction with 'blinded' (rather than, more normally, blind*folded*), the pierced eye is

---

[2] This reprises Monk, 2003, p. 120.

traumatic. The instrumental implication of 'blind*ed*' takes the figure far beyond a simplistic (and insensitive) metaphor for ignorance or poor understanding. Those whose seeing is deliberately impeded can blunderingly damage the same faculty in others. Though visibility carries the risk of exposure, *Interregnum* shows that if blind*ed*ness is a social condition, 'we' (a different 'we' in the two contexts of 'Palimpsestus' and 'Gaol Song')—are already damaged and can be destroyed.

Another strand in Monk's work associates vision positively with memory and memorialisation: 'Visibility ten miles eighteen years' (Monk, 1990, p. 21). Forgetting someone is injurious, a kind of banishment:

one invisible field negating features
to exile
and half remembrance —
faces corroded with gauze and sepia

(Monk, 1982, p. 14)

Monk's work has come to seem a project to recover and restore the (neglected or suppressed) forgotten. As she puts it: 'I want the physicality of words to hook around the lurking ghosts and drag them from their petrified corners' (Monk, 2003c).

Hooks are associated, via the name for a now-unusual mode of dress fastening, with eyes, in *La Quinta del Sordo*: 'And here more hooks more eyes and this | fleshless wet bandaging of loneliness with black marrow gape' (Monk, 2003, p. 22). The sequence is based on a suite of enigmatic and grotesque etchings by Goya known as 'Disparates'.[3] To the 'sordo' (deaf one) the silent speech of fellow beings is a gaping mockery, and visual sensations—especially for an artist—are magnified painfully. In both poems and prints, all of this is extrapolated into an interior realm tormented with contradictions of repressions and exposures, needs and repulsions. In Monk's original publication (Monk, 1980) each poem was keyed to a particular print, and the covers were illustrated with magnified details from two of them. The 'black marrow gape' is that of the figure on the front (see Sànchez et al, 1995, p. 182)[4] whose eye sock-

---

[3] Translated as follies, riddles, fantasias (Sànchez et al, 1995, p. 176).

[4] In subsequent books the poems of *La Quinta del Sordo* have not been referred to their individual prints, and we should of course beware of confusing information about a poet's intention or methodology with the production of meaning. Such information can however reasonably suggest interpretative possibilities, and the acquisition of extraneous knowledge is a legitimate benefit of reading poetry.

ets seem as slack and empty as his/her jaw ' (See p. 139 for a reproduction of this image). On the back, with eyes and fists clenched shut, is a
bald figure from the print traditionally known as 'Lealtad' ('Loyalty') (see
Sànchez et al, 1995, p. 192), where she sits isolated among a group of
apparently far-from-loyal mockers:

> [...] now you are the queen who'll
> never be seen you're   one on your own

> (Monk, 2003, p. 23)

This prefigures by twenty years Monk's project on Mary Queen of Scots,
who was kept prisoner for many years in Sheffield (the poet's home city
since 1984).[5] Incarcerated, like the subjects of 'Interregnum', Mary is
invisible: Monk proposes her to view. The mode of *Mary Through the
Looking Glass* at its simplest is dramatico-lyric monologue, in the tradition of the book of characters, *Walks in a Daisy Chain* and much of
Interregnum, but also ascribes a new level of reflexivity to the subject's
own 'nooky-aye' (Monk, 2002, [p. 3]). Punning hard, the highly
abstracted, compact and quick-changing language that heightens in
Monk's sequences from the later 1990s here alludes to aspects of Mary's
life, her predicament and its frustrations and occurrences (mainly meals
and sleep), her appearance in the mirror, her breath (foreboding) upon
it, its associations with water:

> it's a tear before bed every neet
> terse up-river through yr
> veer o soot-sheen
> gat a cool clear.

> (Monk, 2002, [p. 3])

By no means is the majority of the writing straightforwardly readable
out of the popularly-known details of Mary's biography. The reader is
obliged to surrender to the language and engage with its 'Woos and
ogles', and thus may come to empathise with the intelligent, sensuous
prisoner who could sometimes be diverted by pleasure in the intervals
between servings of gruel (Monk, 2002, [p. 14]), even if, finally, 'Escape is
fraught. | Appearances bleed to edginess' (Monk, 2002, [p. 15]).

---

5 The project came into print shortly after this essay was written: *Escafeld Hangings*
(Sheffield: West House Books, 2005), is a book about Sheffield concentrating
mainly on the figure of Mary Queen of Scots. It includes a revised and extended
version of *Mary Through the Looking Glass*.

The Transparent Ones is a more personal work of preservation, written 'In memory of and thanks to all the patients I worked with [. . .] as Creative Writer in a hospice' (Monk, 2003, p. 235). The implications of the title are to conjure with, but it should not be forgotten that transparency is a type of appearance. Though the absence of the now-dead is re-populated above all through voice, an acutely synaesthetic sensibility is at work. Speech is 'turquoise' or 'odd coloured', landscape shines 'with a gabbling of | green' (Monk, 2003, pp. 197-98); meaning itself is coloured, in one reading of the following:

> your ancestral dig
> into colourful
> meaning
> deeply
> shady crooks
> and songbirds
>
> (Monk, 2003, p. 203)[6]

'Then One Morning' commemorates an especially heightened encounter with a jaundiced patient who 'seers' an intimate secret, as if it were the poet who were transparent:

> 'Marry him'
> she yellows
> [. . .]
> eyewhites gone daffodil
> sheshines and
> hurls her voice ceilingward
> Upperstraight.
> See through.
> Oracular.
> ! Do it !
>
> (Monk, 2003, pp. 209–10)

Like witness, prophecy involves seeing and speaking: the eye (oculus) is literally (*not* etymologically) involved in the oracle. The organ of seeing is also that which expresses human sympathy—'weeping' is a recurrent item in Monk's vocabulary, and *The Transparent Ones* starts and ends with it, as how could it not?

---

6 However, on double-take, 'colourful' modulates to 'deeply shady', these demotic euphemisms functioning, remarkably, as pastoral invocations, so the 'crooks' (minor criminals) recalled by the subject, pertain simultaneously to shepherds in the Derbyshire dales.

So weep. So weep
       with me
           all of you.

                (Monk, 2003, p. 198, p. 211)

III.i

the spatial canvas of the page
            (Monk, 2003a)

The visual appearance of poetry is commonly held to be its minimum indicator: a recent major study of 'the written poem' confirms: 'The graphic line has been identified as the basic sign of poetic discourse since at least the fourteenth century' (Huisman, 1998, p. 70). This line-based norm is implicit in, and enables the formulation of, contrary approaches like 'poèmes en prose' and the sentence-based poetics of some American 'language' writing. The development of conventions such as lineation, indentation and grouping of lines into stanzas originally served to clarify the sound patterning inscribed in metrics founded on recitative mnemonics: 'memory itself was the primal need that verse came to answer' (Barker, 2001, p. 2).

Not that Geraldine Monk's work falls into the regular patterns of conventional prosody; indeed there is barely an example of regular or iterative patterning, either of sounds, words, syllables or lines, anywhere in her work. It is characteristic of avant-garde free verse as it developed during the twentieth century, that 'one-time-only events tend to be as important as repetitive events in the poem's structure' (Wesling, 1993, p. 426). Out with measure and chime often went standard sentence formation and its associated punctuation; replaced by a new awareness of the page as a field of expressive spatial possibilities, and also of the text as object. These ideas, referring in part to the work of Ezra Pound and William Carlos Williams, were formulated influentially by Charles Olson in his essay on 'Projective Verse', (Olson, 1966, p. 15–30).[7] One of Olson's conceptual breakthroughs was to notice the specific influence of writing technology. The typewriter provided the means for a new kind of poetry. Olson's own work became progressively more innovative in its typography, with lines, words and letters sometimes departing from the

---

[7] The essay was first published in 1950 but had wide circulation after 1960, when it was reprinted in an anthology (also issued in England), Donald M. Allen, ed. *The New American Poetry*. New York: Grove Press and London: Evergreen.

horizontal and slanting, twisting or scattering over the page.[8] Coming to the fore contemporaneously with Olson was the international concrete poetry movement, one tendency of which was to develop the typescript as a visual medium. Among the *virtuosi* were Henri Chopin, dom sylvester houédard and Jiří Kolář.[9] The basis of projective verse and open form however was not the visual word but 'content' and 'the breath.' The subordination of typography to utterance had been strongly maintained in the Anglo-American poetic traditions; thus Louis Zukofsky wrote in 1932: 'Typography—certainly—if print and the arrangement of it will help to tell how the voice should sound' (McGann, 1993, p. 83). Today it can be alleged that 'a pervasive phonocentrism [. . .] dominates contemporary poetics' (Davidson, 1997, p. 196).

Geraldine Monk is well-known as a performer of her own work, with a highly developed vocal style drawing on a wide range of intonation and pronunciation, including (but not confined to) the typical sounds and verbal traits of her native Lancashire working-class idiom. Her poetry importantly embraces the 'presence' of voice: an overall analysis and evaluation of Monk's work would explore this, in relation to the range of modes and effects available to contemporary poetry (as Chris Goode does in this volume). There is perhaps a link to be made between poetic diction and typography, under the heading of rules and conventions; here however we can only register the insertion of speech elements specific to regional or social circumstances orthographically into the poems constructed on the page, alongside the gamut of usages from the banal to the arcane, archaic, highly Romantic and neologistic. In *Interregnum*, intolerance of linguistic difference emerges thematically as key to the catastrophe:

> A could ave pushed iz supper up
> for't grief and sufferin e set in motion
> and time trapped eternity,
> [. . .]
> talkin do-dah-lah-di like
> talking do-dah-lah-di

(Monk, 2003, p. 156)

---

[8] For examples see Olson, 1966 and Fraser, 1998.

[9] Examples are to be found in the concrete poetry anthologies, one of whose editors put forward in her introduction a view of the similarities and distinctions between concrete generally and Olson's poetics (Solt, 1968, pp. 47–48). Riddell, 1975, is a specialist anthology of 'typewriter art.'

Despite the importance of 'speech' in her work however, the vocal does not take precedence in Monk's compositional process:

> I once experimented with writing by using a Dictaphone—and it didn't work. I need the spatial canvas of the page, where I can push around the verbal daubings, if you like. [. . .] I want the words to work both on the page and [. . .] in the vocal arena as well.

(Monk, 2003a)

The painterly metaphor leaves no doubt that Monk's poetry, preoccupied as it often is with an optical thematic, is also inherently visual in its first realisation. The commitment to design declared itself strongly in her earliest mature work. 'Beacon Hill', the first piece in *Long Wake* (Monk, 2003, p. 3) is arrayed across the whole width of the page on an implicit three-column grid, with a central figure constructed of place names in upper case (see p. 128). In the terms put forward by a recent classification of visuality in verse, this page exploits several different 'semiotics': repeated elements suggest invocation or call-and-response, making this a ritual or magic text governing utterance ('the semiotic of the body'); mimesis and diagram are both activated in the central figure which resembles the form of a hill as well as a map ('the semiotic of art'); while at head and foot more abstract elements operate solely within 'the semiotic of language' (Huisman, 1998, Part One *passim*). Monk's work has continued to work in all three modes, though the last predominates.[10]

Long Wake was originally co-published by the Pirate Press, founded by Monk's friend the poet Bill Griffiths, and Writers Forum, of which the proprietor was Bob Cobbing (see Griffiths' remarks on it in this volume). Cobbing was a major British exponent of the concrete poetry movement in the 1960s and '70s. It is not only the formal example of concrete poetry in the classic period, but also the movement's empowering sense of being an avant-garde really in the ascendent, that arguably renders its influence robust and useful beyond its historical moment for poets like Geraldine Monk, whose work would never quite come under its banner. Cobbing was a hero and mentor to generations of younger poets; he himself did not remain set in concrete, so to speak, but throughout his long career pursued a relentlessly experimental course in visual and sound poetry, as well as improvisational music and performance, and would undoubtedly

---

10 Contrast 'Beacon Hill' with the similar but more abstract 'Pendle' in *Interregnum* (Monk, 2003, p. 99) . See p. 33.

BEACON HILL - The Coming of the Night

Settlement   Settling

            instinctive navigations
            to the final procession

Flicking days off   Picking words from
our lives like   between our teeth ——
cornflies   sweet spiky apples
                             like   Hograh

            HOGRAH   SILPHO
              STUDFAST HILL
         JUGGER HOW   SCALING DAM
                 LASKILL
              S A   A S
           K T   T K
         L I   I L
       L   A   D   K   I   L

            This is night

Ma-ni-na-le-ha-no   Let it fly —— the arrow
Ma-ni-na-le-ha-no   Let it fly —— the arrow

Hin-khu lush-ka-le   Let me loose I cry
Hin-khu lush-ka-le   Let me loose I cry

'The hooded hawk'   my little cock sparrow   'The hooded hawk'

            This is night

Original typography and layout of Long Wake [p. 1] (Writers Forum, 1979).

have encouraged Geraldine Monk's dual emphasis on vision and voi
Writers Forum often published in large formats, closer to the statio:
ordinarily used by writers and thus liable to preserve the layout of their
final drafts. The effect of 'Beacon Hill', and the three other pieces in the
same style in *Long Wake* on the generously proportioned 10-by-8 inch page
often favoured by Writers Forum, cannot but be slightly diminished in
the 21.5 × 13.5 cm. trade format of the *Selected Poems*. The same press
published four further books of Monk's in similar size (or A4), and one
(*Animal Crackers*) in a trimmed A5 landscape format. The influence of the
small presses on the writing they published is a subject for a thesis, but
some mention of it is crucial here. Though traditional methods of
production were not unknown, their proliferation was based on the wide-
spread availability of office duplicating (later photocopying) equipment,
making 'amateur' publishing convenient and affordable. Composition
and typesetting converged in the poet's typewriter, potentially dissolving
the alienation of intellectual from mechanical work; for many authors,
the traditional thrill of seeing their texts mysteriously transubstantiated
'in print' would be superseded by that of extending their creative intention into its final appearance. Self-publishing was no longer 'vanity
publishing' but an answer to 'the difficulty of the aesthetic object in capitalist society of escaping its commodity status' (Davidson, 1997, p. 63). A
left-wing political stance, though not obligatory, was undoubtedly
fostered in the social formations that arose from the needs for resource
and skill sharing, and especially for distribution networks. Cobbing and
Griffiths were both closely associated with the Association of Little Presses
(co-founded by Cobbing),[12] and in 1979–80 Monk also published several
books herself under the imprint of Siren, 'an outlet for the writing of
Geraldine Monk and the occasional graphic work of painter Robert Clark'

[11]   Classic anthologies such as Bann (1967), Williams (1967) and Solt (1968) show that
a considerable variety of poetic practices, in fact, came for a while under the
rubric of concrete poetry. Bob Cobbing and Peter Mayer in their *Concerning Concrete
Poetry* point to Khlebnikov's remark, 'We have begun to attach meaning to words
according to their graphic and phonic characteristics' as 'a definition of concrete
poetry in one sentence' (Cobbing, 1978, p. 16). Cobbing in turn offers the following definition: 'Concrete poetry, for me, is a return to an emphasis on the physical
substance of language—the sign made by the voice, and the symbol for that sign
made on paper or in other material and visible form' (Cobbing, 1978, p. 43).

[12]   For further information on British small press poetry publishing see Wolfgang
Görtschacher's two-volume study: *Little Magazine Profiles: the Little Magazines in
Great Britain 1939–1993* and *Contemporary Views on the Little Magazine Scene*,
Salzburg: University of Salzburg Press, 1993, 2000.

(ALP, 1979). These were produced in a variety of formats and with quite high production standards, for the most part typeset rather than type-written, and printed. The illustrated *Rotations* (Monk, 1979) moved towards the style of the artist-press or private-press, with original woodcuts by Clark, printed on Japanese tissue paper. (see Bill Griffiths' account of it in this volume.)

Long Wake as a whole is structured as deliberately as any sonnet sequence. Alternating with those following the visual style of 'Beacon Hill' are six 'Dream' poems, in two distinct forms. Those in the 'Corridor' group are fully justified on a narrow gauge (like a newspaper column); they evoke a claustrophobic physical or psychological interior. The other set run in prose-length lines whose words are interspersed with punctuation marks: first slashes (/) and then ellipses (...). These can represent a landscape with horizon, or, given the semantic content, a sea-scape, or/and a shoreline, where,

> The fish are / dead / lying open / mouthed [...]
> Above ... .lemon ... .skyjuice ... .swings ... .silently ... .
>
> (Monk, 2003, p. 6)

The three formal modes enable a reading in which a personal and cere-monial elegy for 'my grandmother? | [...] lying amongst candles and flowers' (Monk, 2003, p. 5) is ambitiously interfolded with, on one level, elemental intimations amid the North Yorkshire Moors—where 'Spirits submerged form frantic quivers' (Monk, 2003, p. 7)—and on another, premonitions of the social and environmental effects of modern unleashed energies:

> precision / polaris / missiles leaping / bring / ing
> storm / cloudcreep / ing horizon /
>
> (Monk, 2003, p. 4)

The problematic of 'precision'—compare 'how deranged | this | preci-sion' (Monk, 2003, p. 80); 'straight as in die' (Monk, 1990, p. 13)—surely informs both the multivalent use of language and the refusal of measure in Monk's verse. Counter-values are rife, and readers seeking an approach to her work might follow a trajectory of 'diversion', drunken-ness, dangerous driving (as dramatised in the zig-zag layout of *Dream Drover* (Monk, 2001, pp. 57–60)), 'rambling' and everything 'erratically intact' (Monk, 2002d). In one of the prefatory poems to *Interregnum*, eponymous 'Hikers' emblematise an ends-related approach to experience, emphasising destination and knowledge constituted reductively as a repertoire of terminology:

> [we] warble out our
> naming of the
> parts
>   of nature's
> rambling
>   incoherence
>   Fol di raa

(Monk, 2003, p. 101)

However, while her poetry might sometimes appear to 'ramble' intuitively over the page, Monk's form is really typified by something we might call a liberated constructivism.

III.ii

> liquid b / linking
> off-side thinker

(Monk, 2003, p. 77)

Though Monk's highly organised structures, and her avoidance of regularity, are visible on the page, multifarious ad hoc effects may be more conspicuous to the reader. The usual gravitational inequality of left and right margins is often countered; sometimes the holding force is centripetal. Though the central axis has little to do with textual traditions (and was tedious to achieve prior to automated text processing), it is a natural compositional principle in art. Three of the poems in *La Quinta del Sordo* employ centring. In two of these cases, the originary images depicting two figures in intense and conflicted inter-relation (See Pèrèz Sànchez et al, 1995: p. 182, p. 185): a woman being abducted, flung backward in peril astride a bucking horse; a man and a woman attached together back-to-back, literally or figuratively victims of their 'twinning | this Siamese disease' (Monk, 2003, p. 22). The poems then are cyclones, whipped up by dialectic, with an intensity that has led them to be read in terms of love desire (Tuma, 1998, p. 232). The last poem in the sequence is also centred, but its symmetry is disrupted by the capitalisation of the words nearest the middle of the lines. In the print, a band of soldiers is dwarfed by, and fleeing from, a looming, cowled and robed giant—but a bare-branched tree nearby suggests that the ghoul may be no more than another tree, draped in parasitic over-growth perhaps (Pèrèz Sànchez et al, 1995, p. 178). The poem's visual crooked spine responds directly to the irregular verticals of both objects, and more indeterminately to the folly of fear, taken to be the picture's subject, 'crumpling at the slightest shade' (Monk, 2003, p 24). Among recent analogues for these strongly emotional centred poems in England were many of Barry MacSweeney's 'Odes' (MacSweeney, 1978), but in the modern Anglo-American poetic tradition the form is most closely associated with the American Michael McClure, who, like Monk, talks of 'painting' with visual form, and who also proposes an organic potential for the poem on the page, centred, 'so that the poem would be bilaterally symmetrical, as all evolutionary beings are' (McClure, 2002), validating a 'semiotic of the body' beyond that of breath.

As well as a grid and a vortex, the text can be multi-columnar (with the panels readable in any order). Monk's second ecphrastic piece (i.e. poem about a work of art) matched the triptych format of its model, Max Beckmann's 'Departure'; which, like the Goya etchings, inhabits dark psychological territory. The poem seems both to shrink from and seek some deeply personal knowledge: 'blind | folding on blind | [. . .] trying to | remember' (Monk, 1990, p. 30). 'Van Roll in Sussex' (Monk, 1980a, [p. 16]) was an earlier experiment, its central text, traumatised by the accident, almost overpowered by two side panels set in capitals. The margins of poems, and the spaces between them, have increasingly become active sites in Geraldine Monk's work. *Herein Lie Tales of Two Inner Cities* made striking use of 'catch-words'—the old printer's knack of adding the first word of a page below the previous page's text, to aid correct sequencing. They may have been genuinely useful in collating this book, as they replaced the accumulative, abstract order of page numbers with a poetic, multivalent parallel text: 'GLASS || WITHIN || AVAILABILITY || STREETS || RING' (Monk, 1986a, [pp. 16–21])—and like-wise countering the other ordering principle of this book, which is binary, the poems numbered '1' or '2' and printed accordingly on either yellow or green paper. 'Transgression | of | Hemispheres' (Monk, 1986a, [p. 18]; 2003, p. 82)!

Herein Lie Tales of Two Inner Cities was completely reconceived for the format of *Selected Poems*, with the catch-words replaced by a semi-autonomous sequence of (different) words in the right margin (Monk, 2003, pp. 76–82). The marginal summary or commentary is another archaic bibliographic feature experimentally revived by Monk. In *The Transparent Ones* the margin might be read as a corridor of memory

outside life and death/text, where the irrepressible lost continue (in italics) to whisper and flicker across the more conclusive poems (in normal
Roman type), memorial / marmoreal:

    And that is
    that?
            Pup-a-love—
            that is that

                                  (Monk, 2003, p. 202)

In *Absent Friends* by contrast, the marginal prose texts are as substantial
as the short verses and are the realm of the fixed and factual. Some
resemble the side-notes of scholarly tradition, containing researched
information; others provide the narrative context: an overnight stay at
Coleridge's cottage in Nether Stowey, Somerset, now maintained as a
museum to the poet. Whilst there, Monk 'saw' an exhibit which, the
next day, did not exist. In the original pamphlet publication (Monk,
2002a) the two types of text are ranged against the opposite margins—
like display cases?—and the poem's closing allusion to *The Rime of the
Ancient Mariner*: 'Never a breeze up-blew' (Monk, 2003, p. 233) suddenly
reinforces the relevance of the format by reminding us of the marginal
glosses Coleridge added to that poem, and to its Preface, which acknowledged the existence of 'invisible beings', yet advised maintaining the
distinction between certainties and uncertainties (Coleridge, 1817,
[p. 2]).

In *Walks in a Daisy Chain*, the links from one poem to the next are,
strictly, invisible, having been incorporated into the main text; however
they are germane to the present theme, and provide us too with a useful
transition. Each poem opens with the closing word/s of the previous
one, with the last in the book linking back to the first. This device
dramatises the characters, often to humorous effect, through exempli-
fying the pragmatic multivalency of almost any utterance; it is also
readable as symbolising social degrees of separation. This wider import
perhaps led Monk to want to draw special attention to it, not only in the
book's title but also in a note: 'These transitions are an integral component of the series' (Monk, 1991, [p. 7]). It is arguable that the page as such
has cultural valency: 'Centre' and 'margins' are socio-political and
cultural categories also. Matters of practical poetics, such as prosody,
typography and visual arrangement, can be held to imply and even to
activate these categories. On one level it is entirely plausible that, in
France,

during most of the nineteenth century, the number of identical phonemes in a poet's average rhyme (like the length of his lines) is a fairly accurate guide to voting intentions.

(Robb, 1996, p. 8)

More ambitiously we may consider the implications of:

Symmetry and asymmetry are themselves psychological functions, since stability is historically associated with symmetry and centrification.

(Mottram, 1977, p. 32)

Yet visual symmetry in text is unusual and *de*stabilising; or considered naively decorative, by association with commercial graphic conventions in e.g. greeting card inscriptions, along with script-style type fonts. Monk's work is robustly immune to snobberies and programmes in this as in other respects (for instance her incorporation of working class and domestic dictions and her loyalty to poetic Romanticism). This essay opened with Monk explaining that the deprivation of her background fortuitously saved her from 'staid' literature teaching, but the poetry hints often at the real blight of poverty and ignorance upon liberty of being and thought. 'The Concise History of Historical Forces' sequence in *Quaquaversals* suggests how young women, without status or opportunity, come to a bewildered scepticism, 'to see | [. . .] That chaos that order were twin opposites of | deception'; and how, eventually, 'We turned our backs in | disbelief' alike on 'disintegration' *and* on 'the underlying | permanence' (Monk, 1990, p. 32, p. 35). The material forms also of Monk's work are free, or excluded, from fixed orientations.

III.iii

Encountering poetry through Dada, Surrealism and Futurism must have had a huge effect on my poetry with regards to spatial and typographic possibilities.

(Monk, 2002c, p. 177)

From her studies and affiliations in the visual arts Geraldine Monk learned about the wave of European modernist movements at the beginning of the twentieth century in which, as Johanna Drucker has shown in an essential study (Drucker, 1994), poetic typography was considered 'an art practice' in its own right. The canonical figures include the

French poet Guillaume Apollinaire for his semi-pictorial 'calligrammes', the Italian Futurist artist and polemicist F.T. Marinetti, who championed 'parole in libertà' ('words in freedom') and often quite simplistic typographic expressivity: 'italic face for a series of similar and rapid sensations, boldface for violent onomatopoeia, etc.' (1913, quoted in Drucker, 1994, p. 114), and the Russian Futurists who in their own ways also pushed language beyond sense into a mode they called 'zaum', recombining affixes and phonemes into suggestive neologisms and nonsense, sometimes set in wildly miscellaneous type, or reproduced in the author's holograph (Janacek, 1996 is a substantial account).

As well as the larger architecture of text on the page, Monk treats details at the level of word, letter or punctuation mark with a similar freedom from regular conventions, sometimes with a literalism and humour also found in the early-Modernist forbears. For example:

(((warm runny thing   cold unmoving tarmac)))

(Monk, 2003, p. 105)

—this line (revised from the original single parentheses (Monk, 1993, [p. 16]) suggests the cartoon judder of impact and aftershock, as an animal is hit by a car.

Another (likewise from *Interregnum*):

dangling
ont end
of
s
t
r
i
n
g
s
of
root
twisted
FIBS

(Monk, 2003, p. 134)

Effects of this kind are sometimes trivial, but here the simplistic transposition of the metaphor encodes the bewildered rage of those manipulated (like puppets, as we say) to their destruction, not by any great wit but by the testimony of children, and by lethal ignorance.

Geraldine Monk has often made free use of the slash, a mark like a blade, somewhat violent (even in its usual name—contrast the alternative terms, 'oblique' or 'virgule') especially when inserted within a word. Wedged between words, it Siamese-twins them together; and it is a switch, as in the poem 'Glass Snake Electric Eel':

> mirror voltage/watery
>   sh/ock manically
>   gathering face
>   muscles /freeze
>   in sp/l/it
>   Eternity

> (Monk, 2003, p. 46)

Here the first slash insulates electricity from water; or is the membrane between reflection and the depths; the second dramatises electric shock, or any instinctive shock of encounter, with its momentary delayed reaction; the third emphasises an interior command ('freeze!'); the word 'split' is split to spit as the ('glass') lizard's tail snaps off.

It has been suggested that Geraldine Monk's liberated typography owes more to the graphic design of mass culture ephemera than to these art traditions (Tuma, 1998, p. 32) but this is to underestimate the leap of originality it takes for one discourse to open to another in this way. From the Dadaists in particular, poets learned to appropriate commercial-graphic features such as display fonts, discontinuous phrasing and exclamatory imperatives, as Drucker points out:

> Between 1916 and 1920, [Tristan] Tzara's language was selected from the [. . .] discourse of the newspaper, advertisement, published train schedule etc. [. . .] And [. . .] [these borrowings] bear the material traces of their original sites in their typographic form.

> (Drucker, 1994, p. 114)

If visual experimentation in poetry is held in low esteem, mistrust of these associations is one, understandable, reason. The historian of 'the visible word' also charts 'the demise of typographic experiment' (Drucker, 1994, pp. 223–47), pointing out that basically the movement was re-appropriated: 'the avant garde poets of the 1910s became the graphic designers [. . .] of the 1920s and 1930s', their 'utopian agenda of intervention through [. . .] mass production print media [. . .] codified into a system [. . .] enabling corporate style' (Drucker, 1994, pp. 238–39).

Monk is not naïve about the challenge to poetry of advertising and gutter-journalist language: her 'Sub-Editor' in *Walks in a Daisy Chain*, 'obscure[s] the word':

> I even make alliteration
>   swear
>   to God I am a poet —
>   Oh Modernism!
>   I salute you.

(Monk, 1991, p. 49)

On behalf of the poem she asserts,

> I am not an advertisement. I am myself.
> I am words enjoying being.

(Monk, 1990, p. 44)

Many poets find a kind of grim glee in commercial and propagandist language and typography. In 'Prague Spring' Monk coins 'ColaMacAmericanA', a portmanteau term for a new invasion of the former so-called Eastern bloc of Europe by the global bad-food conglomerates (Monk, 2003, p. 177). The several type fonts suggest indiscriminate vulgarity and disconnectedness in commercial graphics (in other printings the heterogeneous letters also jiggle loosely above the baseline as if animated (Monk, 2001, p. 34)), but they also reveal that at some point in the late 1990s, the poet too succumbed to the hidden persuaders and acquired a word processor. The work from *Noctivagations* onward gradually includes new features, especially italic and bold styles, some variation in font size, and occasionally indulges the novelty 'Symbol' font (e.g. playing card suits, in 'Insubstantial Thoughts on the Transubstantiation of the Text' in Monk, 2003, p. 215).

IV

(I
my (self)-per-por-trait-(or)

(Monk 1982, p. 16)

Many of Geraldine Monk's books conspicuously bear images of the poet, or rather perhaps we should say, of 'the poet': some are recognisable photographic portraits, others graphic or treated images that we cannot but read as her emanations,[13] including those which definitely do not depict Monk: the woman in the sensuous 1940s movie still on *Banquet* (Monk, 1980b) whose lover pulls down the shoulder of her dress from behind to graze on her neck; Theda Bara, the Vamp, looking like Gustave Moreau's decadent Salome (a role she did play) but perhaps costumed for Cleopatra, on *Tiger Lilies* (Monk, 1982); and even the Xerox-enlarged Goya grotesque on the front of *La Quinta del Sordo* (Monk, 1980), who bears a remarkable similarity to Monk as depicted on *Long Wake*, *Rotations*, and *Quaquaversals*, in trance or performance transport, with mouth open—and *eyes closed,* reminding us that there is no comfortable settling for unitary readings, for instance of the 'blind' theme developed earlier in this essay. The apogee of Monk's up-front cover '(self)' though is perhaps the open-eyed and sultry-starlet version on *The Sway of Precious Demons,* her first 'selected' volume (Monk, 1992). Monk is photographed semi-recumbent (on the back seat of a car?) in strong chiaroscuro, one bare white arm upraised, a tawny tint of lipstick and a hint of red hair breaking through the otherwise sepia print. If the impressionistic textural atmosphere is reminiscent of the early art photography of Alvin Langdon Coburn or even Julia Margaret Cameron's mid-19th-century fancy-dress portraits, the sharp abstract values derive from classic fashion photographs by Irving Penn or Bill Brandt: a mirror set beside the subject, redoubling and making strange the already cropped figure. But her gaze is drawn neither to the viewer's nor to the mirror.

It is yet open to women in general to betray whatever feminism achieved by using sex appeal for self-promotion. This is one of a range of

---

[13] The swirling expressionistic drawings on *Rotations* and *Long Wake,* as well as on the early repudiated book *Invasion,* were by the artist Robert Clark. *Spreading the Cards,* also a Siren book, has an unattributed photograph. The cover image, in red and black, on *Quaquaversals,* is a two-colour Xerox treatment of a photograph of Monk in performance, made by the publisher, Bob Cobbing. The photograph was taken by Lauper Annalou. The photograph on the cover of *The Sway of Precious Demons* is unattributed, the book was designed by Peterjon Skelt.

GERALDINE MONK

THE SWAY OF PRECIOUS DEMONS

SELECTED POEMS

Avatars of the poet: some of Monk's book covers. See footnote 13 for credits.

strategies available to writers and artists who are women. Failing (or rejecting) that, if they aspire to make work that is engaged, they do well to easily please in other ways, adhering to certain normative modes, thought of as relevant and accessible. The dilemma experienced by many, between representation and expressivity, and explicitly female thematics as against formal experiment, is now an established topic of critical discussion: especially relevant here is Kathleen Fraser's essay (1998) addressing the masculinism historically inherent in visual poetics, and the work of some American women poets (see also Frances Presley's essay in this volume). Part of Geraldine Monk's importance at the start of the twenty-first century is as a (British) exemplar who confounds this dualism. Her writing is formally and linguistically experimental, including as we have seen its visual design; it is disjunctive and collagist, but its inclusions of traditional poetic diction and regional vernacular, and of evident emotional responses to human situations and to landscape and nature, tend to render it warm in effect, rather than the cool or complex distancing thought more typical of classic modernist poetry. While her poems can rarely be adequately read as coherent closed expressions of a stable consciousness, she is unafraid of personae, dramatic or lyric.

Monk's self-presentation as 'poet', especially in performance but also, as we see here, in her printed images, has no truck with the fastidiousness that equates self-display or even flamboyance with vulgarity;[14] however it is by no means merely spontaneous. As regards performance, Monk has discussed it in the third ('Voca-visu') section of her verse essay on types of poetic reading, 'Insubstantial Thoughts on the Transubstantiation of the Text': 'To perform is to *in habit* space' (Monk, 2003, p. 222)—thus (for instance) costume is a profound necessity:

---

[14] For a discussion among poets on the subject of publicity photographs, poetry marketing that emphasises the author's personality, and poets' self-presentation, occasioned by an evasive picture of J.H. Prynne in the catalogue of Bloodaxe Books to advertise his *Collected Poems*, see the open archives of the British and Irish Poets email list, 14–18 November 2000 (subjects 'Bloodaxe' and 'Bludaxe'). Geraldine Monk contributed a posting (16 Nov 2000 18:14):

> I cannot see what is so terribly wrong with poets having faces and personalities, I mean they do have them. [. . .] Is this some kind of weird Puritanism: denial of the poet as body, flesh, blood. [. . .] I have stunning photos of poets (Stein, Marianne Moore, Sitwell, Djuna Barnes, Nancy Cunard—a regular rogues' gallery of the good, the bad and the crazy). Plus shelves full of biographies of poets. I love them. But they are there because of their poetry.

Bloss. Webbings.
Blue plastic mac. Feather boa.
Redriding hooded habit.
Dietrich slink—

(Monk, 2003, p. 222)

The *Precious Demons* cover was counterbalanced by a full-page black-and-white portrait photograph at the end of the same book, this one apparently as natural and spontaneous as the first was carefully composed, costumed, propped and lit. Attention has visibly been paid to hair (partly coiled and braided, in a folksy rather than glamorous manner) and maquillage (flares of eyeshadow) but the mouth is open, in mid-conversation or recital (a note on the same page refers to the 'expressive intensity' of her performances) and the picture is not particularly flattering. A selection of poems; a selection of selves.

Since then, the portraits on Monk's books have been confined, more conventionally, to back-cover thumbnails, but these too are carefully considered: on *Interregnum* a moment in performance has her cloaked and hooded with the usual closed eyes in front of large letters written on a wall behind, suggesting the trance and ritual of witchcraft, perhaps the garb of execution, and possibly the handwritten banners of political protest. On *Selected Poems* she wears a snood or coif-style headdress referring to the era of Mary Queen of Scots (one 'poor traitor'?); the association is confirmed by a hand-painted Elizabethan wall from a pub in Southwell visible as a backdrop in a less-cropped (and colour) version of this picture sometimes used by Monk (Monk, 2003c).

Monk's empathy with women (and others) condemned by role and varieties of repression to be oppressively surveilled, or confined out of sight, or both, is based in personal experience:

Working class, Roman Catholic, girl. It didn't get much worse than that in the 1950s and early '60s industrial north of England.

(Monk, 2002c, p. 176)

Without exaggerating the centrality to Monk's work of her experimental self-representations, it can be argued that they are not incidental but constitute an aspect of her exploration, in person and in print, of the 'scope of the possible' for (especially women) poets. It is certainly relevant to note analogues in the visual arts, most notably the life's work of the American photographic artist Cindy Sherman, Monk's near contemporary.

V

Sky Scrapers

The 'high rise of convoluted domes' in *Sky Scrapers* (Monk, 2003, p. 70) is that of clouds, not of buildings. The central motif of the sequence is the visual similarity between cigarette smoke and rain clouds: a common-place—as we say 'clouds of smoke'—which here effects vertiginous conflations or switchings between the personal and the meteorological scales of existence, and between that which is seen or otherwise regis-tered as an external phenomenon, and subjective sensations. But it is not such a simple duality. Clouds are real, albeit vague, objects; they have position and formation, and are subject to scientific classification on that basis, thus ten of the poems are designated by their abbrevia-tions, 'CI' (Cirrus), 'AS' (Altostratus), and so on. There is more to them than description, but they do refer recognisably to appearances, albeit not scientifically or with pre-Raphaelitish precision, but flamboyantly and employing a range of linguistic registers. For instance:

Cirrocumulus [. . .]
mackerel glints   ripply

Cirrostratus [. . .]
kinda whitish rimmed
haloes

Cumulonimbus [. . .]
tainted expanses
sickly pink

(Monk, 2003, p. 56, p. 58, p. 72)

The sky, however is different: the plane we 'see' behind the clouds is nowhere and has no real properties, it is an optical effect. This doesn't make it purely subjective of course. Alternating with the ten 'cloud' poems Monk inserts a parallel series of untitled 'sky' poems, each begin-ning the same way:

Today
sky provocative   skittish

Today
sky vanity charged   muscular

Today
sky nerve crested   fragile

(Monk, 2003, p. 57, p. 61, p. 71)

— and so on. The subjectivity of these epithets, being non- (or barely) visual, is conspicuous, they 'tend to imbue the natural world with human feeling', according to the definition of the trope known as the 'pathetic fallacy' (Burris, 1993). At best this was usually considered a manifestation of (the poet's) powerful or disturbed emotion; by the late twentieth century it would be an archaism, inadmissable, if played 'straight', in any kind of serious poetry. If, without being comic or ironic, Monk in *Sky Scrapers* successfully rehabilitates the pathetic fallacy, it is on several accounts. The object is not turned into a pseudo-person even for a moment, but remains (what the sky is) a projected screen, suffused with a succession of associations by vocabulary unforeseeable but not arbitrary. (The noticeable predominance of the letters 'v' and/or 'u' in the 'sky' epithets, structuring sound patterns, show another aspect of the poet's care for word choice.)[15] The effect is disruptive of narrative or descriptive continuities:

thinking how a giant
gestural skid mark of
cerulean blue or
jigger of red rum would
break it nicely
              how a jiggle and a zig-zag cockles
              innocence to treachery
              sends old familiar
              stampeding

sinister how weather determines mood

(Monk, 2003, p. 62)

---

[15] The complete account: 'vital   frenetic', 'provocative   skittish', 'vacant   prosaic', 'vanity charged   muscular', 'rheumy   congealed,' 'puzzled   lumpy', 'uncomfortable   hunched condition', 'overturned   annoyed', 'nerve crested   fragile', 'brutal   arctic' (Monk, 2003, pp. 53–73). Other sonic repetitions will easily be discerned.

This quotation describes a hypothetical visual effect, enacts its impact typographically, and in that slippage exposes an emotional trauma. The inner left margin is used on several occasions in this sequence, as an enclosure for what might be particularly personal material, including a passage of insomnia in 'NS': 'when all who loveyou | youlove sleep (Monk, 2003, p. 68)—and a more ambiguous 'memory siege' in 'CB' [Cumulonimbus]:

> attraction/
> repulsion accepting a
> kiss or
> withdrawing

> (Monk, 2003, p. 72)

Elsewhere all the spheres of reference are jumbled, or simultaneous, as clouds and thoughts meld and morph, as

> rolling memories / cigarettes / clouds
> which may / may not
>
> be merged

> (Monk, 2003, p. 60)

When first published as a book (Monk, 1986), the cover of *Sky Scrapers* deliberately led the reader to expect the more usual meaning of the phrase: wrapped right around it, a striking photograph printed in blue depicted a city at night, high-rises ablaze with electric light towering over a mixture of other buildings, modern and old (neo-Gothic?). The title lettering glows red, like—as the reader might come to imagine—cigarette tips. Prior to the text came a frontispiece, a fairly unusual luxury in a book of poems. Reproduced from a drawing or perhaps an etching this is another version of townscape, this time in a naïve, stylised manner obscuring straightforward representation, but elements of older industrial structures are discernible: a viaduct and a smoking mill or factory chimney, cranes (shipyard?) as well as motor vehicles and a possible modern multi-storey building. In the distance seems either open country or the sea, and a blinding whiteness presumably of low sunlight.[16]

---

[16] Geraldine Monk has divulged that the places depicted are Middlesbrough and London respectively.

The visual paratexts strongly counter any impression that this suite of poems 'about' clouds consists of Wordsworthian lonely wanderings in natural landscapes. Romantic though the poems are in their exploration of emotion, sense-impression and memory, the book places them clearly in the social, urban world inhabited by most of England's population—whose activities began to depend less upon the weather, and affect it more, with the industrial revolution. This is the subject of *Sky Scrapers*. From smog to global warming—the year before the sequence was first published, an article in *Nature* had informed the public at large about the hole in the ozone layer (Farman, 1985), while the atomic mushroom cloud, once seen, iconised humanity's new capacity for total destruction by cataclysm and contamination. Within the poems, the term 'energy' recurs, and other small verbal elements are applicable, *inter alia*, to anxieties, resurgent in the early 1980s, with the siting of American nuclear missiles at airbases in England, about all aspects of nuclear power. 'Elemental grains | merge to separate', together with 'rallying of body swerves' (Monk, 2003, p. 56) clearly alludes (*inter alia*) to the atomic physics of Lucretius, but can also suggest the internal process, as well as the consequences in many senses, of the thermonuclear bomb. Monk had certainly engaged territory like this before (as in *Long Wake*'s dream of missiles). A revision for *Selected Poems* provides further evidence. In 'CB', cumulonimbus, high piled thunder clouds, are associated with poison, sickness, hazy sexual repulsion, excessive sudden force. One line occurs twice in the poem, and in the *Selected* version Monk has revised both occurrences, introducing, in the first instance, word spacing:

slow   creep   of   megatons

(Monk, 2003, p. 72)

The words are paced across the page as clouds might cross your field of vision, or be depicted. In the second instance, line breaks are introduced:

slow
creep
of
megatons

(Monk, 2003, p. 72)

Here, in terms of representation, the same words descending vertically are coming towards you, especially as in this case the last word is the largest, like the nearest object in perspective. The megaton measures explosiveness. A slow creep contracts to a scrape, sore, injurious. *Sky Scrapers* is a Romantic poem for the nuclear age, meditating on contemporary relations between people and nature, and this couplet in revision figures its two axes.

VI

in my end is   my beginning

(Monk, 2002b)

The online poetics magazine *Pores* conducted a survey of writers' responses to the destruction of the World Trade Center by terrorists in 2001, asking among other things, 'Has your commitment as a writer changed since September 11th?' Geraldine Monk recalled a series of formative traumas in her lifetime, both personal and public, including a domestic eruption during the Cuban Missile Crisis of 1962, when she was ten: the television on during a meal, 'the sibling flicking of peas', and suddenly the father, listening to the news, shouting at them to shut up, 'fired a range of full stops' (Monk, 2002d). For the future poet, a formative complex of explosion and fear associated with punctuation marks. Even on paper full stops can be full of horror: 'sign on the dotted line to be a victim [. . .] sign where it says | *collateral* | *damage*' (Monk, 2002d).

This might be thought abnormally sensitive, 'a kind of eccentricity' when surely 'inconspicuousness is what punctuation lives by' (Adorno, 1991, p. 96). But no less than other graphic signs punctuation marks are real affective objects, carriers of meaning;[17] as with all aspects of language, if the writer does not engage with them intentionally, she is half-way to becoming their victim. As the philosopher and social critic Theodor Adorno declared:

> When syntax and punctuation relinquish the right to articulate and shape the facts, to critique them, language is getting ready to capitulate to what merely exists, even before thought has time to perform this capitulation.

(Adorno, 1991, p. 95)

---

[17] Compare Ciaran Carson, another poet hypersensitive to punctuation: 'this hyphenated line, a burst of rapid fire . . . ' [etc] ('Belfast Confetti').

Monk says, with heavy irony, 'You know it makes sense, to mince words till they bleed' (Monk, 2002d). The deformations, dislocations and inventions in her own work are a serious part of the poet's 'commitment as a writer', when the ownership of sense is a matter of life and death. Readers unused to poetry that avails itself of visual semiotics may be initially resistant to such effects, and reviewers often do little more than register them generically as 'exuberant' or 'playful' (one exception is Frances Presley (2003), discussing Monk's layout, type and punctuation marks). Neither do all poets take much interest in the potential of their material means. But what are the limits of poetry, the art that brings language to its sen*ses*?

Another fundamental, related, question: Where is the poem? Is it reasonable (sometimes?) to extend the reading of poetry, as I have attempted here, to the material aspects of the books in which it is published? If so, is a reprint, by different means, in a different typeface, format and binding, a species of translation, in which something essential is inevitably lost (and other potentials opened)?

Less controversial is to ask to what extent, for a given poet, do the writing technologies available to him or her, and specific conditions of publication, feed back into and influence her creative sensibility. This is at least implicit in Olson's formulation, 'that verse which print bred', as what was 'NON-projective' (Olson, 1966, p. 15). It is clear that Geraldine Monk benefited greatly from the existence of a small-press publishing context that accommodated and encouraged perspectives on form and practice derived from the visual arts. The non-continuance of Siren Press can doubtless be ascribed to a combination of personal and economic factors; however the centrality of the material text to her creative life has found a new outlet at the turn of the century, when she began issuing tiny pamphlets of new work as 'Gargoyle Editions', printed directly by a computer laser printer, sometimes with coloured titles or an image, and in various formats. The exquisite *Marian Hangings* for example (Monk, 2002b) consists of a single folio of blue paper pasted into a cover of thin, pale grey, textured card bearing a coloured image of an embroidery worked by Mary Queen of Scots herself and featuring her phoenix emblem (currently kept at Oxburgh Hall in Norfolk). The small texts are arranged characteristically as a double-columned grid but with two centred, crossing the centrefold. Inside and out, titles are all printed in blue. The format is tall and narrow, and turns out to be not an 'A' size sheet, standard in Britain today, but the old 10 × 8 inch of *Long Wake*.

As quoted earlier, Monk has stated flatly that, 'I do not work with visuals per se.' That definitive iambic pentameter sounded a challenge, to which one might riposte: *Oh yes you do.* Of course I know what she means; and it is also true that Monk's work on the page is—unlike her performances—not essentially spectacular: there are many more radical exemplars of visual poetics this side of full-blown 'visual poetry' today.[18] But that is what makes her work most useful and potentially influential in raising the visual stakes for poetry on the page, when there is generally a way to go towards maturity and the establishment of standards in poetic practice, publishing, and criticism. The impact of word processing on Monk's work is ongoing but she will ever resist the pre-set: the special characters in *The Scottish Queen's Cypher Alphabet* (Monk 2003b) are handwritten.[19]

References

Adorno, T. W. 1956. 'Punctuation Marks' in Tiedemann, R. ed., 1991. *Notes to Literature*, trans. Shierry Weber Nicholson. Columbia: Columbia University Press, pp. 91–97

ALP (Association of Little Presses). 1979. Catalogue.

Bann, Stephen, ed., 1968. *Concrete Poetry: An International Anthology.* London: London Magazine Editions

Barker, N. *Things Not Reveal'd: The Mutual Impact of Idea and Form in the Transmission of Verse 2000BC–AD1500.* [Privately printed]. The three Panizzi lectures, delivered at the British Library, London, November-December, 2001. A book is forthcoming, based on these and the Rosenbach Lectures in Bibliography delivered at the University of Pennsylvania, April 2002, in which Nicolas Barker discussed the same theme, covering poetry from 1500 to the present day.

Burris, S. 1993. 'Pathetic Fallacy' in Preminger, A. and Brogan, T.V.F. eds., *The New Princeton Encyclopedia of Poetry and Poetics.* Princeton: Princeton University Press. pp. 888–89

Cobbing, B. and Mayer, P. eds., 1978. *Concerning Concrete Poetry.* London: Writers Forum

---

[18] Examples could include Susan Howe's rotated and inverted lines and the Australian internet-based poet Mez's 'mezangelle' dialect, that certainly minces words with obsessive multiplication of parentheses.

[19] *The Scottish Queen's Cypher Alphabet* is republished in *Escafeld Hangings*, p. 76.

Coleridge, S. T. 1817. *Sibylline Leaves: A Collection of Poems*. London: Rest Fenner. The 1817 text of 'The Rime of the Ancient Mariner', including an English translation of the preface, is available online at the University of Virginia Electronic Text Center, edited by Marjorie A. Tiefert: http://etext.lib.virginia.edu/stc/Coleridge/stc.html

Davidson, M. 1997. *Ghostlier Demarcations: Modern Poetry and the Material Word*. Berkeley: University of California Press

Drucker, J. 1994. *The Visible Word: Experimental Typography and Modern Art, 1909–1923*. Chicago: University of Chicago Press

Farman, J. C., Gardiner, B. G. and Shanklin, J. D. 1985. 'Large losses of total ozone in Antarctica reveal seasonal ClOx/NOx interaction'. *Nature* 315, 207–210

Fraser, Kathleen. 1998. 'Translating the Unspeakable: Visual Poetics, as Projected Through Olson's "Field" Into Current Female Writing Practice' in Sloan, M. M. ed., *Moving Borders: Three Decades of Innovative Writing by Women*. Jersey City: Talisman House, pp. 642–54. (I am grateful to Peter Jaeger for drawing my attention to this essay.)

Huisman, R. 1998. *The Written Poem: Semiotic Conventions From Old to Modern English*. London and New York: Cassell

Janacek, G. 1996. *Zaum: The Transrational Language of Russian Futurism*. San Diego: San Diego State University Press

MacSweeney, B. 1978. *Odes: 1971–1978*. London: Trigram

McClure, M. 2002. 'Michael McClure on Projective Verse—Part One' [radio interview with Jack Foley]. Transcribed: *Alsop Review*, 2002. Viewable at:
http://www.alsopreview.com/columns/foley/jfMcClure2.html

McGann, J. 1993. *Black Riders: The Visible Language of Modernism*. Princeton: Princeton University Press

Monk, G. 1979. *Rotations*. Staithes: Siren Press
———— 1979a. *Long Wake*. London: Writers Forum and Pirate Press
———— 1980. *La Quinta del Sordo*. London: Writers Forum
———— 1980a. *Spreading the Cards*. Staithes: Siren Press
———— 1980b. *Banquet*. Staithes: Siren Press
———— 1982. *Tiger Lilies*. Bradford: Rivelin
———— 1984. *Animal Crackers*. London: Writers Forum
———— 1986. *Sky Scrapers*. Newcastle-upon-Tyne: Galloping Dog Press
———— 1986a. *Herein Lie Tales of Two Inner Cities*. London: Writers Forum
———— 1990. *Quaquaversals*. London: Writers Forum

———— 1991. *Walks in a Daisy Chain*. Hebden Bridge: Magenta

———— 1992. *The Sway of Precious Demons*. Twickenham and Wakefield: North and South

———— 1993. *Interregnum*. London: Creation Books

———— 2001. *Noctivagations*. Sheffield: West House Books

———— 2002. *Mary Through the Looking Glass*. Sheffield: Gargoyle Edition. (This is the version considered here. The sequence is revised and extended in Monk, 2005.)

———— 2002a. *Absent Friends*. Sheffield: Gargoyle Edition

———— 2002b. *Marian Hangings*. Sheffield: Gargoyle Edition

———— 2002c. Interview with Martin Corless-Smith. *Colorado Review,* Vol. XXIX, no. 3 (Winter 2002), 175–181

———— 2002d. Survey response. 'Has my commitment as a writer changed since September 11th?' *Pores*, no. 2 (2002). http://www.pores.bbk.ac.uk/

———— 2003. *Selected Poems*. Cambridge: Salt Publishing

———— 2003a. Interview with Elizabeth James. Broadcast on radio: 'Clear Spot' (co-presented with Caroline Bergvall), Resonance 104.4 FM, 22 January

———— 2003b. *The Scottish Queen's Cypher Alphabet*. Sheffield: Gargoyle Edition

———— 2003c. 'Geraldine Monk' Author page, British Electronic Poetry Centre, http://www.soton.ac.uk/~bepc/poets/monk.htm.

———— 2005. *Escafeld Hangings*. Sheffield: West House Books

Mottram, E. 1977. *Towards Design in Poetry*. London: Writers Forum

Olson, C. 1966. *Selected Writings*. New York: New Directions. (Later editions of this book are available.)

Pèrèz Sànchez, A. E. and Gàllego, J. eds., 1995. *Goya: The Complete Etchings and Lithographs*. Munich: Prestel. The 'Disparates' are discussed in general on p. 176, and those referred to in *La Quinta del Sordo* are on p. 185, p. 179, p. 182, p. 192 and p. 178 respectively.

Presley, F. 2003. 'Metablethers of Getha' [review of *Noctivagations*]. *How2,* Vol. 2, no. 1 (Spring 2003). Viewable at: http://www.departments. bucknell.edu/stadler_center/how2/current/alerts/presley.shtm

Riddell, A. ed., 1975. *Typewriter Art*. London: London Magazine Editions

Robb, G. 1996. *Unlocking Mallarmé*. New Haven: Yale University Press

Solt, M. E. ed., 1968. *Concrete Poetry: A World View*. Bloomington: Indiana University Press

Tuma, K. 1998. *Fishing by Obstinate Isles: Modern and Postmodern British Poetry and American Readers.* Evanston: Northwestern University Press

Wesling, D. and Bollobaś, E. 1993. 'Free Verse' in *The New Princeton Encyclopedia of Poetry and Poetics* (as Burris, above) pp. 425–27. This article is a very brief but useful introduction to aspects of free verse.

Williams, E. ed., 1967. *An Anthology of Concrete Poetry.* New York: Something Else Press

Author's Note

I am deeply indebted to Harry Gilonis, for support, information, and much practical assistance. Thanks to Geraldine Monk, for answering enquiries and supplying publications.

Speak and spell: Geraldine Monk's voiceprint
CHRIS GOODE

There was a newspaper cartoon a while ago in which a character specu-
lated on what would happen if he searched for 'Google' on Google.
Would the resultant feedback loop make the internet explode? A similar
thought crossed my mind when I started researching this piece.
Geraldine Monk is herself something of a search engine. Would
Googling her plunge me catastrophically into some kind of *mise en
abîme*, and into what mirror-written wonderland would I emerge? I'm
still not quite sure what happened, but among the information thrown
up by the process was a fact of which I had previously been unaware. On
16 April 1964 (birthday of such fellow-travellers as Wilbur Wright, Dusty
Springfield and St Bernadette), Geraldine Monk 'became the first
woman to complete a solo round-the-world flight' (Camelot Village).
There are those who, in the face of all contrary evidence—not least the
postscript to *Noctivagations* (Monk, 2001, p. 118)—will insist that this
pioneering aviatrix was 'the other Geraldine Monk.' Of course this
particular formulation merely compounds their silliness. Anyone who
has read, or heard, Monk, or seen her in performance, will readily agree
that Geraldine is *herself* 'the other Geraldine Monk.'

It's apt, though, that her ineluctable otherness should find its expression at bird's-eye height. (Monk would possibly conjure the word
'alt(er)itude' to encapsulate this; I wouldn't dare.) In introducing a radio
reading from *She Kept Birds*, Ian McMillan describes Monk as

> a poet who loves the sound of words, and takes risks with what a poet can
> do; and who opens up all sorts of areas for discussion about the work *on
> the page* and the work *in the air*, as it were.

(McMillan, 2004)

McMillan's typically unhistrionic (if slightly fudging) characterisation of Monk's activity is ultimately far more acute and provocative than the sort of addled caricaturing that frequently infects the discussion—and, tellingly, the promotion—of her work. A recent reading as part of the fortieth anniversary celebrations for Morden Tower, for example, was trailed thus:

> When you hear the words 'Woman Poet', you think of some exceptional magical creature weaving wondrous spells [. . .] and when you hear Geraldine Monk you know you were right.

(Morden Tower, 2004)

Even Frances Presley, who has rightly deplored the overemphasis on Monk's 'wildness' at the expense of a more meticulous appreciation of 'her capacity for a deep attachment to the people she works with, and her essential humanism' has recourse to the same language when she remarks that Monk 'wants her work to cast as wide a spell as possible' (Presley, 2003).

I've no idea whether Monk herself feels, as I do, that an unadventurous elision of animism and eco-feminism, seasoned with the nearly-tacit invocation of certain depleted tropes regarding women poets (not least the subsuming of the 'experimental' by the 'esoteric'), underpins much of the various discourse around her, with the effect that the intellectual commitments of her poetry become obscured: magic, after all, is even less like work than poetry is. But the thematic content and immediate sources of her work have not, for the most part, encouraged such a limited—and, arguably, distorting—appraisal. (The obvious exception is *Interregnum*: though even here, Monk mostly uses the idea of witchcraft circumstantially, as a passport: just as the feuding families of Pendle did in 1612.) So where does this language of magic and occult wildness—in talking *around* this work—come from?

Well, partly from Monk herself, of course. I omit, a bit naughtily, from the Morden Tower advertising copy above, its embedded (mis)-quotation from her own statement of intent:

> I build atmospheric narratives gleaned from the coincidences of circumstance and the emotional geography of place. I want the physicality of words to hook around the lurking ghosts and drag them from their petrified corners.

(Monk, 2003a)

This partial manifesto appears to abut and uphold Geraldine's decision, on being invited to give an extended reading at the first Total Writing event (at Camden People's Theatre, London), drawing not only on her own work but also on other writing that had had some influence on her development as a poet, to bill it as a 'séance.' (Nate Dorward's generally enthusiastic *Paris Transatlantic* review of that reading describes Monk's work as 'haunted' (Dorward, 2003).)

In reaching for the languages of spiritualism and the supernatural, Monk seems principally to be attempting to indicate in and beneath her work an assured belief that the ultimate categorical distinction we face is not the binary *alive : dead* but the continuum *living—deathly*. I have an email from her in which she uses the word 'magic' in just this way:

> I have to say at this junkchewer Chris if I knew exactly what I did why I was doing and how I did it, it would lose its edge and magic.

> (Monk, 2004)

Magic, then, as opposed to a stultified (and neurotic) academic response in which the currents and momentary crises of creative writing are so unrelentingly analysed *after the event* that the human vestiges of live composition are, so to speak, backed into 'petrified corners.' In this respect, the vocabulary of magic and the spirit is employed to protect from prosaic scrutiny the operations of instinct and contingency: operations which, given Monk's reputation as an almost peerless reader and performer of her own work in front of audiences, can come to seem dauntingly vulnerable to the constraining influence of overdeveloped 'self-consciousness.'

This, though, does nothing to explain, or even approach, the 'otherness' which many reviewers and critics (to say nothing of readers and fans) have sought to describe. So, to rephrase the question: why is this line from Peter Manson's *Adjunct: an Undigest* funny?

> Fire in same guesthouse Geraldine Monk once stayed in kills tourist.

> (Manson, 2005, p. 5)

There is a sort of satirical halo around this statement which attaches at two points. Firstly, it pokes fun at a blue-plaque culture in which 'heritage' value accretes to places where famous historical figures have lived or passed through or merely slept, and in doing so deftly turns a table on Monk's propensity for twocking celeb identities (from Mary Queen of Scots to Jeremy Paxman) for her own loaded vent acts. But secondly, Manson's report is gorgeously tinted with the presumably unsupportable implication that Monk is in some way remotely culpable for the fire; drawing on the dynamic operations of the 'coincidences of circumstance' that Monk herself invokes, it channels a welter of critical prejudice and promotional guff and below-stairs anecdote into a single item of gossip, concentrated into an improbable headline. But what's the story? Did she put a curse on reception as she checked out? Did she leave a not-quite-sleeping dog-end lying in a lounge bar ashtray? It's hard to imagine a more succinct deconstruction of the impediments to a closely engaged critical assessment of Geraldine Monk *en page*.

The problem with this is that any survey of the various facets of Monk's practice will have to attend not only to what's on the page but also, as McMillan says, what's in the air: in which region 'the physicality of words' is of a different *order* of physicality, and promotes quite different registers of legibility, to the physicality of the material text.

I want to suggest in this piece that it is above all the idea(s) of voice which can be taken to carry through Geraldine Monk's project, on paper and in (live and recorded) performance; that the outward movement of the voice, starting within and emanating from the body and travelling through the air and finally out of range, models, both in its procedural complexity and social import, the activity of her poetry. Furthermore, I would argue that it is the particularity of Monk's acute and unstinting fidelity to the production of voice, and the challenges that this commitment proposes to the conventional constructions of authority, that has confounded some critics to the extent that they have allowed themselves recourse to a finally inadequate language of 'magic' and 'spells' which it is hard to imagine them visiting, at least, on any male poet of Monk's stature.

~

I feel sorry for those who have not heard Monk's voice: her rhythmic energy, her timing, and unmistakably, her Lancashire accent.

(Presley, 2000)

Geraldine Monk gave an over-dramatic and mannered reading which obscured verse that otherwise sounded interesting and provocative.

(Milloy, 2004)

Many people (though evidently not everyone) would agree with Frances Presley that hearing Monk perform her work, ideally live, is—precisely— a *vital* component in appreciating her poetic practice, and acutely suggestive of routes and approaches for one's own private reading of the poems on the page. Admirers will attest to the ways in which texts which may initially appear dense or disorienting on paper, before an attentive audience reveal fluid constructs whose slipperiness is meticulously controlled and whose interior mobility and surface valency is boundlessly attractive in its gregariousness.

It is interesting, however, to see Presley elide voice and performance. It is only really in poetry, and perhaps in music (especially, though not exclusively, composed music), that such qualities of performance as 'timing' or 'rhythm' can be considered as elements of voice, categorically similar to a regional accent. That this is, arguably, not illogical can be traced to a fundamental set of questions about how a poet's 'voice' is constituted and where (and when) it is produced. In some contexts, voice may be contiguous with style, in two different but overlapping ways: as a network of characteristic or typical writing behaviours which become identifiable and eventually recognizable markers inside a text, such that a poet's 'voice' becomes familiar to her readers in the same way that a bird's distinctive call will allow an ornithologist to identify it by its voiceprint alone; but also as an intratextual rendering of the poet's speaking (or reading-aloud) voice, from which a fully 'authorized' vocal reading might be remotely inferred almost as a reconstruction of the poet's original intent. In referring towards Browning's phrase 'the printed voice', David Kennedy describes

> a double nature in printed poetry [. . .]—a text of hints at voicing, whose centre in utterance lies outside itself, and also an achieved pattern on the page, salvaged from the evanescence of the voice in air.
>
> (Kennedy, 2002).

It is in the intersection between these two constructions of the poet's 'voice' that an inherited attribute such as an accent can meet a stylistic trait such as an idiosyncratically developed sense of timing. But if this constellation of voice elements can be encoded into 'an achieved pattern on the page' and finally drawn out by the reader, why then should hearing Monk's own voice, her own renditions, be so apparently fundamental to a full understanding of her project? If Monk's 'printed voice' really offers private readers 'a text of hints at voicing', why should the above-mentioned 'suggestiveness' of her own public readings be so critically important?

The nearest answer is, of course, that this construal of 'the poet's voice' is so partial as to be, taken on its own, quite false. I have proposed that it depends upon an understanding of 'voice' which is more or less unique to composition in sound. But outside of that construction, many other, less obviously sophisticated, pressures may prevail. 'Finding one's voice' may be a proper concern for the young poet; but the fear of 'losing one's voice'—in the middle of a reading, say—is an anxiety that is neither equal nor exactly opposite.

In the great adventure of the voice within the corpus of modernist writing, the physiology of the voice, the production of vocal utterance within the body, has drawn both close attention and wilful inattention. For Charles Olson, it was imperative that the importance of breath within poetry was restored: because 'breath allows *all* the speech-force of language back in', returning the poem to 'its producer and its reproducer, the voice' (Olson, 1950, p. 44). (Interestingly, Tim Allen's reading of *Noctivagations* outsources this breath function to a kind of free-range gremlin or rodent within the fabric of the poems: '"Something" is moving, we can hear it in the sounds and feel its weight in the heavy breaths between them' (Allen, 2002).)

The prior achievement of modernist poetry, however, had been to express—or rather, perhaps, to mimic—a dissociation of voice and body: an irreversible uncoupling which was redolent of the 'unreal city' while at the same time describing a particular, widely replicated, domestic disconnection. T.S. Eliot's selection of a phrase from *Our Mutual Friend* for his original title for *The Waste Land*:

> 'For I ain't, you must know,' said Betty, 'much of a hand at reading writing-hand, though I can read my Bible and most print. And I do love a newspaper. You mightn't think it, but Sloppy is a beautiful reader of a newspaper. He do the Police in different voices.'
>
> (Dickens, 1998, p. 198)

seems to allude not just to the polyphonic fracturing of urban narrative in the newspaper and the home (as well as in the city itself), but, by extension, to the ventriloquist gramophone in the corner of the typist's room (Eliot, 1974, p. 62).

Anyone who has ever been startled to hear playback, say from tape, of their own voice will know that the complex of anxieties surrounding the mechanical reproduction of speech did not simply dissipate, once and for all, through acquaintance (and eventual familiarity) with the technology. As Geraldine wrote to me, the problem with hearing yourself in this way is that

> it sounds alien, slightly disturbing because you're disembodied from your *you* are not going through your usual kinesthetic channels of vibrating larynx, labyrinthine skull tunnels, membranes and mucus etc.

> (Monk, 2004; her emphasis/ syntax)

For Monk, the body is not (or is not principally) an idea in space or some kind of cultural test-site: it is a thing of 'membranes and mucus' and the voice it produces is not only generated and shaped by physiology but is *itself* a palpably physical disturbance 'in the air, as it were'; in other words, the poet's voice is substantially and meaningfully—and specifically—embodied, before and below any conversation that may ensue regarding the stylistic or ideological locus of that voice and its attributes.

Perhaps paradoxically, it is exactly the physicality of the sound wave which carries the spoken voice that permits some of the most fanciful speculations around the disembodied voice, particularly in crosstalk with the visionary edge of technological development. Gavin Bryars has recounted, in notes to accompany his piece *The Sinking of the Titanic*, how Marconi, the prime mover behind wireless telegraphy, towards the end of his life became obsessed with the idea that:

> Sounds once generated never die, they simply become fainter and fainter until we can no longer perceive them. [. . .] To hear these past, faint sounds we need, according to Marconi, to develop sufficiently sensitive equipment, and one supposes filters, to pick up these sounds. Ultimately he hoped to be able to hear Christ delivering the Sermon on the Mount.

> (Bryars, 1993)

Wireless commentator Paul Golding succinctly summarises the reaction of witnesses to Marconi's early successes with telegraphy:

> Some spectators were so in awe of this effect that they convinced themselves it had a supernatural significance. Some were even convinced that radio had potential for communicating with the dead.

> (Golding, 2005)

Thomas Edison, in fact, went so far as to follow up his invention of the phonograph with a device referred to as a 'spirit catcher' and intended for just that purpose: to communicate, through sound, with the spirits of the deceased. Nor was this considered to be cranky: the project won an approving lead editorial in *Scientific American* (22 December 1877), appearing as it did to be little more than an advance and refinement of what the phonograph made possible (Kahn, 1999, p. 217).

In this light, Tim Allen's description of Geraldine Monk as 'a materialist lexicographer utilising the paraphernalia of spirit' (Allen, 2002) seems to fall in to place. Allen's reference to 'the paraphernalia of spirit' points not (so much) to the topical content of Monk's poetry, nor to some of the language that she and her commentators like to use in proximity to the work, but to the furthest conceivable tendencies of disembodied vocalisation—or perhaps, more accurately, *post*-embodied vocalisation, given that the voice remains characterised by, and a carrier of information concerning, the body within which it originated. I'll discuss later some of the ways in which these tendencies manifest themselves within the material of Monk's poetry; for now, it is enough to return, in this light, to Geraldine's Total Writing 'séance.' In response to a question about the other (stylistic) voices that may have informed her own, Monk writes:

> Certainly hearing the recording of Gertrude Stein's '[If I Told Him: A Completed] Portrait of Picasso' when I was 17 had a profound effect on me and on what I thought constituted poetry. I think hearing this was probably the most influential moment in my poetic life—in fact I know it is.

> (Monk, 2004a)

And now I am listening to, and deeply affected by, a recording of Monk's own reading of 'If I Told Him', as part of that Camden 'séance.' In this respect the technology of voice storage encompasses a number of implicit questions about the nature of the voices with which it brings audiences into proximity. Above all, I wonder how many voices I am listening to. Do I hear Stein *through*, or *behind*, Monk? The content doesn't sound like Monk's voice but the performance does, *mutatis mutandis*. In other words, a dialogue emerges—perhaps a conversation, if I am included in the scenario—in which I listen to Monk 'listening' to Stein, searching out in the instant of performance a way to reconcile their voices: which requires that Monk embodies (as a host; which is to say that she does not *re*-embody; she produces but she does not *re*-produce) the printed voice of Stein. This, then, is Monk not just as lexicographer, *pace* Allen, but as, herself, literally, phonograph; the body as voice-writer, as itself a technology for the recording and playback of the spoken word. And as such, it becomes possible for the body to come into a new relation with the disembodied, or post-embodied, or once-embodied, voice.

To start to describe the terms and conditions of that relation, we have first to return to our earlier pairing of 'finding one's voice' and its not-quite-antithesis, 'losing one's voice.' These notions seem to find a peculiar but accommodating synthesis in the action of 'freeing the voice': a phrase which might readily invoke any number of drama school voice classes or new age workshops. ('Freeing the voice can lead to increased health, emotional joy, and spiritual ecstasy,' threatens healer Jill Purce in the online blurb for what she describes, tantalisingly, as a 'glorious foliage weekend' (Purce, 2004).)

Instead, I'm referring to 'Freeing the Voice', a 1975 performance at the Studenski Kulturni Centar, Belgrade (and subsequently elsewhere), by Marina Abramovic. The artist's description of the content of the performance is typically succinct: 'I screamed until I lost my voice and could not produce any more sound' (Abramovic, 1976). Bart Rutten quotes Abramovic and adds his own observation:

> 'When you are screaming in this way, without interruption, at first you recognize your own voice, but later, when you are pushing against your own limits, the voice turns into a sound object.' The voice seems to be breaking free from the body and to fill the space independently.
>
> (Rutten, n.d.)

Watching documentation of this piece at the ICA's 'Video Acts' exhibition in 2003, I found it upsetting not so much because of the relentless screaming, and not particularly because of Abramovic's wilful prosecution of her voice-loss—which though extreme in its conception and in the single-minded diligence of its execution does not itself ramify much more than, say, the spoiling of a ballot paper. What was most disturbing was the corollary implication of the title: that the voice *within* the body (in other words not just the produced voice but also the not-yet-produced, the pre-vocal) is constrained *by* the body, by its own embodiment. The predicament invoked but not explored by Abramovic's piece is that the 'freed' voice is already 'lost' not just to the injured apparatus of voice-production within the body, but spatially lost, radically disoriented and already 'out there' in the no-place of the Sermon on the

Mount. In this respect it matters greatly that Abramovic *screams* towards silence, rather than shouting text for example: so the printed voice is also disavowed.

In what ways, then, can the body be said to constrain the voice? In approaching this question, many of the different constructions and locations of voice that we have noted so far begin to collapse into each other: the physiological and ideological meet for Abramovic just as I want to suggest they do for Monk: and they meet within the person, though not entirely within the body.

In 'Freeing the Voice', Abramovic both loses and 'finds' her voice: though that found voice, too, is rejected, expelled: and that rejection occurs on as many levels as the contrary grateful acceptance which is many poets' objective. At a superficial level, for a poet to find her voice is very close to the process of identifying (and subsequently perhaps isolating and exaggerating) what used to be called a 'unique selling point' and would now be referred to as a 'differentiator' in the crowded market-place of literary brands. A distinct voice is an advantage in the way that a widely recognized mark or logo or jingle can be exploited for competitive advantage.

Only slightly less superficially, to find one's (own, distinctive and sustainable) voice is taken to connote a coming into maturity, a sense of integrity in which the influences of other writers become 'digested' or fully 'absorbed', to use the endorsing terms most often thrown up in this connexion by a critical language which sees the body not as crucially and vividly implicated in the production and negotiation of voice but rather (ideally at least) as the steadfast unit container for authority. The 'uniqueness' of this voice is praised and respected for its adaptation to a capitalist microeconomy in which the production of cultural meaning is tethered to an incentive scheme predicated on artificial scarcity and the ultimate prestige notion of 'individual genius.'

For both of these models of 'own'(ed) voice, neither Marina Abramovic nor Geraldine Monk appear to have much patience. Where they diverge is at the next level down.

There is a profound, and for some poets a devotional, significance to the individuation of that 'voice' which is not discovered or 'found', exactly, or come into, but which is (or can be taken to be) immanent. This notion of inherent singularity expressed through voice would certainly have been recognised by Christopher Smart (like Stein, one of Monk's *amis de séance*), whose massive *Jubilate Agno* is formed and propelled by beliefs of this kind; while Scotus's thirteenth century formulations of *natura communis* and *haecceitas* (the universal and the precisely individuated) closely informed another of Monk's poetic influences, Gerard Manley Hopkins: as in these frequently quoted lines from 'As kingfishers catch fire':

> Each mortal thing does one thing and the same:
> Deals out that being indoors each one dwells;
> Selves—goes itself; *myself* it speaks and spells,
> Crying *What I do is me: for that I came.*

(Hopkins, 1970, p. 90)

As someone trying to handle with extreme caution the idea of 'magic' in Monk's work, I may be unwise to draw too much out from the word 'spells.' On the other hand, Hopkins may be allowing just such resonances to carry some weight here, despite the religiosity of the context; 'spell' with the meaning of 'charm' or 'incantation' is hypothesized to share with his primary meaning here the Proto-Germanic root *spellan*, 'to tell' (*OnED*).

The notion of 'telling' seems currently to reverberate with overtones of 'testifying' or 'witnessing', of not just speaking but speaking *out*, and it is this dimension of voicing—'Crying', here—which appears to link Hopkins's conviction that the individuation of creatures bears witness to their Creator, to a contemporary (and humanistic) treatment of the same perception such as the refrain introduced by Tom Spanbauer into his novel *In the City of Shy Hunters*: 'It is the responsibility of the survivor to tell the story' (Spanbauer, 2001, p. 460).

In this light, it's funny that Tim Allen (or an over-zealous subeditor), perhaps unwittingly, 'corrects' one of Monk's titles: 'There are also what she calls "Three Short Stories"' (Allen, 2002). No down-the-line story-teller, Monk's testimony advances itself, both in her 'Three Short Sorties' *(sic)* and elsewhere, through narratives—and linguistic imitations—of journeying, travel, expeditions; through restless motion.

That movement is a defining feature of her voice both literally (in the projection of sound) and stylistically, on the page as much as in performance, is, I think, a response to the same crisis which Marina Abramovic tackles through the extrovert self-denial (and mild self-harm) of 'Freeing the Voice.' Such strong identification of, and with, an individuated voice necessarily invokes numerous concentric constructions of alterity. The 'found', embodied voice is constrained precisely by its originary discreteness within an individual body and its expression of the cultural and sociopolitical location of that body; it follows that what it signals, inevitably, is contradistinction. It can only assert the otherness of other voices. Perhaps for Abramovic this position is so unwelcome that to perform its disabling, the temporary dismantling of this primary technology of identity, is a compulsory reaction.

Geraldine Monk's solicitous care over the work to which the voice can be put is an altogether more discriminating response to the same dilemma. In her most extendedly explicit published engagement with the questions of voice, *Insubstantial Thoughts on the Transubstantiation of the Text*, she can be observed thinking through a number of oppositions and, often, disclosing or deducing a continuity between them: most saliently, the intersection of vocalised/unvocalised and private/public, but also the functions of dis/embodiment (and, as the title suggests, the word 'made flesh' (Monk, 2003, p. 215 and *passim*), and their various destabilisations of authorial singularity. The journey of the voice through these pieces, from privacy to 'interaction' (Monk, 2003, p. 224) corresponds interestingly to some early observations in Steven Connor's *Dumbstruck: A Cultural History of Ventriloquism*:

> My voice is not something that I merely have, or even something that I, if only in part, am. Rather, it is something that I do. A voice is not a condition, nor yet an attribute, but an event. [. . .] This is to say that the voice always requires and requisitions space, the distance that allows my voice to go from and return to myself.

> (Connor, 2000, pp. 4–5)

Compare: 'To speak is to perform work' (Connor, 2000, p. 3) and 'To perform is to *in habit* space' (Monk, 2003, p. 222). (It is worth noting, in passing, the smart, slightly self-lampooning, teasing out of the 'habit' in 'inhabit': our attention is rightly drawn to the place of habitual or sustained behaviours in manufacturing individual voice; and the value of the manoeuvre is doubled precisely because such word-splitting is one of the most recognizable characteristics of Monk's printed—and performing—voice.)

Needless to say, the space requisitioned by the voice and occupied by performance is a turbulent zone in which the tensions identified by Monk within her own voice may be momentarily reconciled individually only to come into a new communal interrelation. I want to suggest that this zone has much in common with the space described by *Angel High Wires*, her first CD collaboration with electroacoustic composer

Martin Archer: which in the light of these discussions could be seen as something approaching a laboratory examination of the contingencies alive within even the recorded, post-embodied voice, and of the fault-lines traversed in any communal space when an individual voice travels between producer and listener, or between 'self' and 'other.'

∼

As Archer's sleeve-notes attest, the *Angel High Wires* project begins with him and Monk, aptly, in communion with—in fact, confronting on a grand scale—disembodied voices: those of Schubert and his interpreters as they listen through, (incredibly) in one sitting, to the *Lieder* on CD: or, rather, on twenty one CDs. From this outset, the two of them are tuning in to voice: necessarily, in this context, voice as a survivor, a courier of information from the past; but also, more interrogatively, the vulnerability, the fragility of the voice outside the body, its evanescence, its eventual and unprotectable tendency away from fidelity through its physical susceptibility to distortion and interference, and the fatal promiscuity that leads to its co-option by enterprises over which it can have no control. Archer refers to 'a world where music has become less forgiving' (Archer, 2001) and it is this uneasy relationship between the voice and the sometimes hostile environments—not just in a social or cultural sense but actually within the soundworld with which the voice is in most ways continuous—that host it, which sets the tone for the collection. It is a tone that expresses itself even within the title of the album, taken from one of Monk's texts (printed in *Noctivagations* as 'Songings', in a different order to the recorded tracks and with two poems not used by Archer):

> enwrap feet
> with angel-high-wires
> mandrake cumber
> world
> turn-turtle

(Monk, 2001, p. 46)

Particularly in isolation, the phrase 'Angel High Wires' seems to speak not just to the lonely precariousness of the funambulist, who in this case with one wrong step becomes, I suppose, a fallen angel; but also reaches down, perhaps, to one of the half-hidden meanings of 'angel' as a radar echo, whose cause might be clouds or lightning or 'atmospheric inhomogeneities' (IEEE, 1997), or bird migration (Wolff, 1996): so it seems that she who keeps birds also keeps, by reflection, angels. Monk emphasizes in an email the importance of echo:

> Before the very recent [. . .] technology of audio-recording the only means of hearing one's own disembodied voice was through naturally occurring echo with all its fragmented distortions. Little wonder the echo was imbued with much myth and magic. [. . .] The fear of our own disembodied voice [. . .] strikes at the root—the body.

> (Monk, 2004b)

Perhaps, then, in 'Songings', Monk is trying somehow to get past audio technology to tune into the authentic unmediated echo of Goethe, Schiller and all those poets whose 'sentiments and longings' (Archer, 2001) were set by Schubert: understanding nonetheless that, particularly in translation, their 'printed voices' may not be sufficient to the task and that, like Marconi attempting to tune into Christ broadcasting live from Kfar Nahum, she may, paradoxically, be greatly assisted by some quite sophisticated technology.

Which brings us, then, to the disc itself. Into a conceptual zone already characterised by distance and disembodiment, Archer introduces first a sparse field of splintered, semi-pitched noise, and then, close miked and surprisingly intimate, the first of the four voices that we'll hear: Steve Roden—better known as a 'lower-case' sound artist acutely concerned with the activity and philosophy of listening—singing 'Stoop rich fruit through nothingness' (Monk, 2001, p. 43) in falsetto. What is immediately striking is the unresolvable compound *otherness* of Roden's voice: compound because it patiently reveals its otherness in stages. For the first few seconds, the voice is not immediately traceable back to a body, it seems to transcend (or perhaps to exceed) both categorical gender and, by extension, a physical identity prior to its disembodiment; yet it is, right from the start, recognizably organic (as opposed to synthetic). It may not take long to locate it *as* falsetto (countertenor is not quite the right word for the tonal quality Roden produces) and therefore as the production of a male body: but this step does nothing to neutralise its otherness: falsetto is inescapably *the other male voice*, and its otherness may yield meanings of frangibility and insecurity, or emasculation or a queer(ed) a-corporeality, or a sense of the *unheimlich* perhaps generated in its discomfiting (and patently 'false') adult mime of the 'innocence' and 'purity' of the prepubertal boy treble; or simply the kind of transgressive weirdness associated with Tiny Tim or Justin Hawkins, or Mickey Mouse. All of these readings depend on the same assumption: that the falsetto voice is temperamentally divorced from the immanent voice; not only is it self-evidently affected but it cannot be easily reconciled with the 'true' voice which inheres in the body.

The careful closeness with which this irretrievably 'other' voice is recorded creates a tension from which one clear inference can be drawn: placed so near to what is so remote, we as listeners are immediately corralled into a contiguous position of radical difference. We have, as it were, crossed to the far side of the performance space right at the start, and our task in accompanying the recording with our attention is not, therefore, passively to experience a titillating excursion into Monk and Archer's requisitioned space, but to work cartographically within the sound field, to orient ourselves and find a way home.

In Roden's vocal register, however, is none of the histrionic self-regard or neurotic triviality we might associate with male falsetto in contemporary culture (think simply of the Bee Gees' sensationally absurd 'Tragedy'). His voice is plaintive, and curiously cautious: the entire compass of the melodic line he sings is no more than a minor 6th, and the word in the poem most pointed by its placing at the top end of that range is 'fear' ('Some fear to lose the day' (Monk, 2001, p. 43)). Could it be that this voice is, *pace* Abramovic, somehow constrained by its inability to signal its occupancy of, or origin within, a specific body, a body identified as 'self' rather than 'other'?

We have seen how split words *in habit* Monk's performance space, further evidenced by 'a-bout' and 'a-parts' and the abrupt termination of 'daffo' in the second song. For the third, 'Breakers rave her | dis tresses' (Monk, 2001, p. 45), this is pursued to a new level. (Perhaps not *totally* new to those who have heard Monk read.) The vocalist here is Julie Tippetts, to whom the atomization and disordering of language and vocal utterance is second nature: and suddenly the possibilities for transformation within the social life of the song suite are sheerly—one might almost say dauntingly—multiplied.

The first we hear of Tippetts's voice, ironically, after a flutter of electronics and heavily processed prepared piano, is a long 'sssshh.' Does she mean to silence or console? Or is she interjecting a patch of white noise into this busy and convulsive sounding-space? Before we can attempt to read it in any of these ways, the sound is ended, and immediately followed by one of quite different character, a long, high, tremulous cry, with a steep upturn right at the end. A more 'singerly' vocalisation breaks down into what briefly sounds like laughter before coming to resemble a bird or animal call. Each of these sounds in turn is at once abstract ('pure' sound) and locatable (within highly abbreviated mimetic narratives or snapshots of people and animals); yet at the same time, we might surmise that it is the words of Monk's tiny poem that are the maddening 'breakers', and what we are left with are the jarring fractions of language in a vortex of self-destruction: are we in fact hearing the 'sssshh' of 'banished', or, in that extended cry, a distressed and bitterly sardonic mimicking of the 'aahh' at the heart of 'hearts'?

The next incident is perhaps the most crucially momentous of the album. Archer introduces a second track of Tippetts's voice, running in parallel to the first. The effect of this doubletracking, in the context of what has so far established itself to be a set of recordings with a deep investigative interest in the *placing* of the voice, is a startling defamiliarisation that for the first time locates us quite explicitly inside the recording studio. Apprehending the disc so far as an account of a single linear experience unfolding in time, we are for the first time confronted with an impossible situation—one singer, two simultaneous voices. And so we are sharply reminded that while the voice itself is, as Steven Connor says, an event, what we are hearing is Archer's composition *after* the event, and his curation and choreography of the piece is, at least in part, a critical response to, and reflection on, the questions which Geraldine Monk asks of the voice: of the voice as a category and a cultural production, and her own voice within that matrix. Indeed, reading Archer's own 'composition notes', it becomes clear to what extent this recording is a fiction, compiled in the studio and only existing there and in the rendered output; it seems, for example, that Archer and Roden may not even have met during the recording process. There is an element of virtuality about this which is quite at odds with the traditional ethos of improvised music; but Archer's harnessing of the permissions and fluidities of the studio is unassailably faithful to the ethical commitments of Monk's voice work. By so assiduously and dramatically compelling the listener's attention to the instrumental qualities of the studio, he draws remarkably close to Monk's word-splitting disclosures. Maybe those 'breakers' are not, after all, words themselves but the technologies through which words are processed by readers: including the readings taken by samplers, breaking the voice down into perhaps 48,000 digital images per second.

Moreover, this doubletracking or multitracking of the singing voice transmitting the poem is indicative of an inventive fidelity to Monk's printed voice and the lone reader's encounter with these 'Songings' on the page. Our experience of reading poetry is not like reading a novel or a newspaper article (even if one is reading it out in different voices): all of 'Breakers rave her' is visible at one time, it can be held *in toto* within the gaze, and reading it may be more like reading a painting: we read in several directions, we form conceptual or sensual relations between words, the end of the poem may send us back to the start. Doubling Tippetts's voice allows us to hear the lines 'dis tresses | round | scattered ruins | ruined' (Monk, 2001, p. 45) in a way that more closely approximates how we read, with 'ruins . . . ruined . . . ruins . . . ruined' superimposed on the repeated 'dis tresses': the sibillance of which bleeds into the sound-world of the remainder of Tippetts's performance just as it informs the rest of the poem. Similarly, addressing the phrase 'the knave | of darts . . . darts . . . ' (Monk, 2001, p. 45), the word 'darts' is, aptly, thrown multiply all around the stereo field, spatially translating the polysemy and paronomasia bundled up in that word. This all points to a strategic approach which is faithful to the conditional qualities and layers (and the tumbling gameplay) of Monk's voice while rejecting the inert monophony of a single 'authorized' reading.

Along with the dialoguing voices of Rachel McCarron and Sedayne—first heard on the second song ('Be still my | float-a-bout | soul' (Monk, 2001, p. 47)—Roden's falsetto and the densely intricate (and more extended) improvisations by one or more instances of Julie Tippetts rotate through the rest of the twelve songs that make up the suite. In each case we hear a parallel movement in the direction of heightened complexity, widened intervalic compass and a greater dependence on the proliferation of surface and incidence promoted by the pressures of simultaneity within the field.

In the penultimate piece in the suite, 'Setting bird' (Monk, 2001, p. 47; the final poem in the book version of 'Songings') the voices of Sedayne and McCarron are set in what seems like a cherished antagonism with each other. Sedayne first sings the verse alone, accompanied by the drone of his crwth (a Celtic lyre developed towards the start of the seventh century and not widely played since the early 1800s) and embedded within a field of fluttering electronic wings and bat-squeaks: and the extreme constraint of (what it seems *de trop* to call) the melodic range—the tonic, matching the crwth pedal, and the semitone above it—could almost be read as a satirical caricature of the cautiousness of

Roden's first song. The verse begins again with McCarron winding a teasing countermelody around and to either side of Sedayne's narrow line; to this, Sedayne responds in the third and fourth verses by pitching words above his established ground. Except 'pitching' isn't quite right; though these odd words are indeed at a higher pitch, they are more spoken than sung. It is the first time, in the hour or so since the start of the album, that Monk's words have been so obviously spoken rather than sung, and in that respect, it is curious and surely significant that Sedayne's speech should figure as a kind of escape from the constraints of the singing voice. Furthermore, when Julie Tippetts enters the final song, 'Deepest abyss' (Monk, 2001, p. 43), picking up from an extended instrumental solo by Mick Beck's awesome bassoon, the first voice track has her *reading* Monk's poem through from beginning to end. The tone is a low semi-whisper and the words are precisely placed within the register, but this is definitely speech rather than the speech-singing which Tippetts has used from time to time on previous tracks.

We might see the journey of the human voice in *Angel High Wires* as a movement from the constraints of diatonic song systems to the infinitely microtonal chromaticism of the speaking voice: rather like a heavily pixellated picture, so blocky as to be barely legible, gradually gaining in resolution until its definition matches the unassailably high fidelity of 20/20 vision. Initially coupled to the compound alterity of Roden's opening phrases, we have found our way back to the speaking and the spelling of self: from falsetto to intimate truthfulness; from artifice to authentic utterance; from voice lost to voice found. It stands to reason that, on their next collaborative project, the immensely successful *Fluvium*, Monk's own vocal performances (alongside those of Julie Tippetts) should inhabit the turbulent zones of Martin Archer's no less distinctive studio voice.

Ah, and lest anyone should doubt the schema of my reading of *Angel High Wires*, I should probably point out that Geraldine's agenda was adumbrated in the very first track, wherein Roden sings her exquisite lines: 'The lioness maymove | o'er her prey' (Monk, 2001, p. 43) Some readers will perhaps recognize this as an elliptic sample—with tape drop-outs—from a late medieval lyric of unknown authorship: the original lines are: 'The lioness, you may move her | To give o'er her pray'; and the refrain? 'Love will find out the way.'

～

Finally, then, it is the currents of human love (in the most compendious sense) and affinity to which Monk's poetic voice cleaves, and the movement of that voice between located physical bodies, that causes it not just to 'speak itself' but, in Chris Emery's spot-on phrase, to venture 'a kind of saying the world into existence' (Emery, 2003). The self is carried out into that world, propelled by the urgency of its testimony. Discussing Beckett's Winnie, among the most freighted voices in dramatic literature, Elaine Scarry proposes that:

> The voice becomes a final source of self-extension; so long as one is speaking, the self extends out beyond the boundaries of the body, occupies a space much larger than the body. [. . .] Only in silence do the edges of the self become coterminous with the edges of the body it will die with.

> (Scarry, 1985, p. 33)

(A further endorsement of Spanbauer's insistence that the survivor must speak on behalf of the dead.) This notion of the extension of the voice beyond the body obtains to some extent, as we have seen, in relation to all poetry, in its imprint on the page: Browning's 'printed voice.' But we have also observed the particular importance to Monk of the voice signal's physical journey beyond the body, and also the peculiar disturbances of the textual surface and the integrity of words that occur when a voice as singular and powerful as Monk's irrupts into print. One perspective on this might be gained from the relation of late modernist and postmodernist dance to traditional notions of the extent of the body frame. The *kinesphere* was choreographer Rudolf Laban's conception of the more-or-less spherical space which surrounds the body and whose perimeter can be defined by the distance that can be reached by the individual without their taking a step (Schofield, 2004). Outside the kinesphere lies 'the rest of space', and when the body moves into that new space the kinesphere travels with it; in other words, the kinesphere is always in a fixed relationship to the body (Baudoin & Gilpin, n.d.). But Laban's kinesphere takes balance to be a fundamental corollary of reach; Patricia Baudoin and Heidi Gilpin suggest William Forsythe as a contemporary choreographer who has been interested in re-imagining the predicates of body-space and the space outside the body:

> Forsythe [. . .] searches precisely for those superkinespheric moments when the limits are transgressed, when falling is imminent: he offers the failure to maintain balance as an essential project.

> (Baudoin & Gilpin, n.d.)

Could the projection of the voice, its extension beyond the body, then be seen as a similarly 'extrakinespheric' movement, tending inevitably towards disequilibrium? That this is plausible is perhaps more clearly demonstrated in the presentation of the *printed* voice, rather than in what can be deduced about the post-embodied voice in a performance space. It is apt that *Insubstantial Thoughts* offers some of Monk's most far-reaching experiments in the textual equivalent of what 'avant-garde' instrumentalists would call 'extended technique.'

Just as the human voice has access to a range of expression far wider than the scope of linguistic utterance (and, needless to say, has recourse to extra-linguistic vocalisation for many of the most profound human experiences, in the face of which language fails), so the range of text symbols available to any user of, say, Microsoft Word is vastly wider than the conventional repertoire of alphanumeric characters (in any number of world alphabets and, of course, typefaces) and punctuation. During his time as art director of the magazine *Raygun*, David Carson notoriously (and brilliantly) set an entire spread—an interview with Bryan Ferry—in Zapf Dingbats (Blackwell, 2004, p. 153); legibility is no longer a stable *sine qua non* of paper communications, but a facet of tone of voice and a secondary marker of tribal relations.

Interestingly, it is in the first section of *Insubstantial Thoughts*, headed 'Unvocalised (private)', that the typographical inventiveness is at its busiest, suggesting a double-edged identification relating to the dispersal of the printed voice: that one's individual cognitive (or instinctual) productions, occurring perhaps at the threshold of language operations, are most likely to require non-alphabetic signs for their accurate rendering (if the permission to do so is assumed); and that sending that individual language out in to the world may require some reconciliation with the *lingua franca* of public broadcasting. This set of conditions could be said to extend the liveness of performance back to the moment *before* the poem begins to be written: in other words, it may matter how you pronounce the punning graphic bundled within 'dis♥embodied' (Monk, 2003, p. 215), but it doesn't matter *yet*. Nor might there be a single answer to the question when it does, eventually, pertain. In Monk's reading of 'The Unspeakable Softness of Flesh' (from *The Transparent Ones*, Monk, 2001, p. 21) at Total Writing, the tilde symbols in 'ridd~~led' were pronounced as extra d's, the effect a bit like a CD sticking; but the tildes *outside* words were not pronounced. Instead, if I remember correctly, the tildes after 'furl' were performed (though not emphatically) as hand movements; at the time this struck me as feeling like improvisation, or even as a less-than-fully conscious physical movement in sympathy with the poem, rather than a rehearsed or exemplary instance of extra-textual writing. This is an obvious consequence of the approach to the poem *in* performance as a score *for* performance, with all the contingencies that implies: and this approach in turn requires a score that addresses itself to the imperatives of performance, which can barely be approximated without some extension of the textual battery that may be employed. Referring to the scoring technologies developed by Laban around his conception of the kinesphere, Baudoin & Gilpin note that William Forsythe is

> adamant about the fact that his choreographies, unlike classical ballets, cannot be recorded using Labanotation. A Labanotation expert has confirmed that the operations performed on movement could be recorded generally, but that sequences of movements themselves were impossible to notate.

> (Baudoin & Gilpin, n.d.)

The full range of typographical conceits (and their related stylings in lineation and word disorder) that Monk employs across the printed body of her work might be said to show her using the page in much the same way that her collaborator Martin Archer uses the recording studio: the available technologies make possible within the printed voice things that wouldn't be possible in the (untreated) spoken voice, or otherwise divulge the arguments within words that, in a reading, can only be spoken once. The vocal extensions Monk enjoys most are those which help to excavate or illuminate the simultaneities which language embodies but does not normally give (printed) voice to; the pun, for example, one of Monk's signature manoeuvres, in which a single, normally visually inert, word or part-word signals two or more competing meanings or references which adamantly refuse to yield primacy. Does punning resemble the studio multitracking of Julie Tippetts's voice, or the shifting electronic harmonizations of Steve Roden's? Is a pun a type of drone, in which the interferent cross-reverberation of two meanings creates a kind of beating effect? It is in such moments that the 'gorgeously polyphonic' quality to which Emery (2002) refers is seeded.

Monk's intrepid problematizing of the assumed accord between sign and sound is just one of the unbalancing moves she habitually throws to ensure and protect the 'liveness' of her work as it transfers from the page to the performance; there are always momentary decisions to be made about the reading of her work, and which fundamentally cannot be made prior to that reading. Naturally enough, this gives rise to a quality in her poetic voice which can only be described as difficulty, though it has nothing to do with the approachability or accessibility of her work or the intellectual positions behind it (see David Kennedy and Christine Kennedy's essay in this volume). Difficulty in *those* respects, I think, she would find self-defeating and inimical to her project: which is why she tends to reject labels such as 'experimental' and, certainly, 'avant-garde', while continuing to present her readers with work that offers challenges equal to or greater than those posed by other contemporary modernist practices which exclude any attempt to engage with the practical contingencies of live reception.

Geraldine herself is acutely aware of these difficulties and by no means militant in her own approach to them: 'Some pieces I have never read aloud/performed. They just don't seem to flow in open spaces' (Monk, 2004a). I'm quite sure she would sympathise, as would many of her readers, with Scott Thurston's account of attempting his own 'Vocalised (private)' engagement with *Noctivagations*:

> While no stranger to Monk's impressive presence in the performance of her work, my attempts to vocalise the texts constantly led to trip-ups, indicating something of the sonic complexity of these pieces.

> (Thurston, 2002)

Such 'trip-ups' are by no means the exclusive preserve of the cover artist. Among my early researches for this essay was a (rather ungallant) catalogue of the discrepancies between the printed texts of the pieces of her own that Monk read at Total Writing, and the recordings of the live readings. These discrepancies—they were, it is fair to say, numerous, if mostly negligible—are not mistakes in any meaningful sense, of course: rather, they are the inevitable failures of voice and language to tessellate: which, as we have seen, is one of the substantial concerns of Monk's poetic. That the poem is altered as it is read—*when* it is read, and *because* it is read—is a reliable and entirely consonant indication that it does not function as a closed system. 'What is paramount to both [the architect Daniel] Libeskind and Forsythe is, in Libeskind's words, that "as language falls and falters the open is opened"' (Baudoin & Gilpin, n.d.).

It is exactly this openness that allows Monk's work to signify politically beyond its content and immediate topical activity. The field Monk describes, populated (in her own terms) by 'lurking ghosts', remains acutely and determinedly responsive to the post-embodied voice by redrawing the limits of the text so as to include and amplify such traces: a gesture of benign reappropriation which effectively collapses the distinction between past and present while evading the ethically vacuous levelling of contextual detail promoted within postmodernism. Such an important evasion is only possible because of Monk's fierce commitment to the realisation of a fully distinguished voice, however, and it is in the negotiation of individuation and collaboration that her work achieves its primary overarching value.

Introducing her Total Writing reading from *The Transparent Ones* with the words 'I'm starting with dead friends' (Monk, 2003), Monk reminded me of the opening chapter of Stephen Greenblatt's extraordinary *Shakespearean Negotiations*:

> I began with the desire to speak with the dead. [. . .] If I never believed that the dead could hear me, and if I knew that the dead could not speak, I was nonetheless certain that I could re-create a conversation with them. Even when I came to understand that in my most intense moments of straining to listen all I could hear was my own voice, even then I did not abandon my desire. It was true that I could hear only my own voice, but my own voice was the voice of the dead, for the dead had contrived to leave textual traces of themselves, and those traces make themselves heard in the voices of the living.

(Greenblatt, 1988, p. 1)

This is not magic, not spiritualism, not even (*pace* Monk) a séance; it is the movement of voice between the individual and the collective, framed by a profound understanding of the social and political exigencies of both. As Monk wrote to me, in the context of a discussion of *Interregnum* and her recent work on Mary Queen of Scots:

> All the characters I write fascinate me for sure but the purpose is to probe the nightmare of wrongful or unjust imprisonment. [. . .] So it's my voice because it's my morbid fascination, fear, anger and hopelessness which binds peasants and queens.

(Monk, 2004)

A willing acceptance *inside* poetry, and *through* performance, of the vocal bond between self and the self which stands opposite self: this is the project of 'the other Geraldine Monk', as she circumnavigates the globe at sky-high alt(er)itude, flying solo, landing always among friends. For that she came. It seems not inappropriate to summarise the exhilarating political saliency of such writing 'in the air' by ending with a deplorable pun: the opening lines of Lawrence Ferlinghetti's 'A History of the Airplane':

> And the Wright brothers said they thought they had invented
> something that could make peace on earth
> (if the wrong brothers didn't get hold of it) . . .

References

Abramovic, M. 1976. 'Freeing the Body (compilation version).' Netherlands Media Art Institute Catalogue. Viewable at: http://cyclope.montevideo.nl/art.php?id=728

Allen, T. 2002. 'A Droll Philology to Set Us Free'. *Terrible Work*. Viewable at: http://terriblework.co.uk/a_droll_philology_to_set_us_free.htm

Archer, M. 2001. Sleeve notes to Archer & Monk

———, & Monk, G. 2001. *Angel High Wires*. La Cooka Ratcha LCVP149CD

Baudoin, P. & Gilpin, H. (n.d.) 'Proliferation and Perfect Disorder: William Forsythe and the Architecture of Disappearance'. No longer at the Ballett Frankfurt website.

Blackwell, L. ed., 2004. *20th Century Type*. London: Lawrence King Publishers

Bryars, G. 1993. 'The Sinking of the Titanic at Xebec'. Viewable at: http://www.gavinbryars.com/Pages/titanic_xebec.html

Camelot Village website. 'April'. http://www.camelotintl.com/365_days/april.html

Connor, S. 2000. *Dumbstruck: A Cultural History of Ventriloquism*. Oxford: Oxford University Press

Dickens, C. 1998. *Our Mutual Friend*. Oxford: Oxford Paperbacks

Dorward, N. 2003. 'Camden People's Theatre Total Writing London, 27–29 June'. *Paris Transatlantic*. Viewable at: http://www.paristransatlantic.com/magazine/monthly2003/09sep_text.html

Eliot, T.S. 1974. *Collected Poems*. London: Faber and Faber

Emery, C. 2003. 'Circles of art' *Jacket* 21 (February 2003). Viewable at: http://jacketmagazine.com/21/emery-monk.html

Ferlinghetti, L. 2001. 'History of the Airplane'. *City Lights*. Viewable at: http://www.citylights.com/beat/LF/CLLFhstair.html

Golding, P. 2005. 'Mobile spiritualism . . . '. Web log entry 17/2/2005 at: http://wirelesswonders.blogspot.com/2005/02/mobile-spiritualism.html

Greenblatt, S. 1988. *Shakespearean Negotiations: The Circulation of Social Energy in Renaissance England*. Oxford: Clarendon Press

Hopkins, G.M. 1970. *The Poems of Gerard Manley Hopkins*, ed. W.H. Gardner and N.H. MacKenzie. Oxford: Oxford University Press

IEEE (The Institute of Electrical and Electronics Engineers). 1997. 'Standard Definitions of Terms for Radio Wave Propagation'. Venik's Aviation website. Viewable at: http://aeronautics.ru/archive/research_literature/aviation_articles/IEEE/topics/plasma_em_wave_interactions/

Kennedy, D. 2002. 'Voiceprints—Poetry on CD and cassette (Part I)'. *Cortland Review*. Viewable at: http://www.cortlandreview.com/features/02/04/kennedy.html?home

Khan, D. 1999. *Noise, Water, Meat: a history of sound in the arts*. Cambridge, Mass: Massachusetts Institute of Technology

Manson, P. 2005. *Adjunct: an Undigest*. Edinburgh: Edinburgh Review

McMillan, I. 2004. Spoken introduction to Geraldine Monk for *The Verb*, BBC Radio 3, broadcast 17/7/2004

Milloy, A. 2004. '3 Poets from Sheffield—12 March, 2004'. *Poetry Leicester*. Viewable at: http://www.poetryleicester.co.uk/June%202004.htm#Poets%20from%20Sheffield

Monk, G. 2001. *Noctivagations*. Sheffield: West House Books

——— 2002. *Insubstantial Thoughts on the Transubstantiation of the Text*. Sheffield: West House Books and The Paper

——— 2003. Reading at Total Writing London, Camden People's Theatre, 29/6/03. Unpublished DAT recording by Tim Fletcher.

——— 2003a. 'Geraldine Monk' Author page, British Electronic Poetry Centre, http://www.soton.ac.uk/~bepc/poets/monk.htm

——— 2004. Personal email to the author, 28/2/2004.

——— 2004a. Personal email to the author, 3/3/2004.

Morden Tower web site. 'Modern Modernists 40 Years On'. Viewable at: http://www.mordentower.com/2004.html#

Olson, C. 1967. 'Projective Verse' in *A Charles Olson Reader*, ed. Ralph Maud. Manchester: Carcanet, pp. 39–49

OnED: Online Etymology Dictionary. http://www.etymonline.com/

Presley, F. 2000. 'Geraldine Monk's *Dream Drover*'. *How2*, Vol. 1, no. 3 (February 2000). Viewable at: http://www.scc.rutgers.edu/however/v1_3_2000/current/alerts/presley.html

———— 2003. 'Metablethers of Getha' [review of *Noctivagations*]. *How2*, Vol. 2, no. 1 (Spring 2003). Viewable at: http://www.departments. bucknell.edu/stadler_center/how2/current/alerts/presley.shtm

Purce, J. 2004. 'The Healing Voice'. The Rowe Center. Viewable at: http:// www.rowecenter.org/schedule/2004/20041001_JillPurce.html

Rutten, B. n.d. 'Freeing the Voice'. Netherlands Media Art Institute Catalogue. Viewable at: http://catalogue.montevideo.nl/art.php?id=4457

Scarry, E. 1985. *The Body in Pain*. New York and Oxford: Oxford University Press

Schofield, A. 2004. 'Body Language in Mediation Including Recuperation Patterns during Work Cycles for Mediators'. *Mediate.com*. Viewable at: http://www.mediate.com/articles/schofieldA2.cfm

Spanbauer, T. 2001. *In the City of Shy Hunters*. London: Atlantic Books

Thurston, S. 2002. 'Substantial Thoughts' [review of *Noctivagations*]. *Stride Magazine*. Viewable at: http://www.stridemagazine.co.uk/

Wolff, C. 1996. 'Weather radar clutter'. Radar Basics website. Viewable at http://www.itnu.de/radargrundlagen/wetter/wx25-en.html

Author's Note

I should like to express my grateful thanks to Tim Fletcher and Rob Holloway for making available a substantial extract from Tim's digital recording of Geraldine's reading at Total Writing London in June 2003; to John Lennard, who first alerted me to the work of Stephen Greenblatt; to my colleague Theron Schmidt, whose patient and intrepid collaboration has provided an alternative forum in which to explore ideas about the production or incitement of voice constellations beyond the individual kinesphere; and especially to Geraldine Monk herself, who kindly consented to an email interview early on, and whose responses were self-searching, candid, and characteristically good-humoured.

Editor's Note

A longer version of this essay, which includes a more detailed musicological analysis of the rest of *Angel High Wires* is viewable at: http://beescope.blogspot.com/

Collaborations with the Dead
Geraldine Monk

The potential infinities of poetry are impossible in one poet alone.

no(wo)(man)(is)(an)(is)land

Our minds are the embedded journalists of our bodies. We can't see everything but everything we do see is edited by the determination of our own psychological make-up. There may be trivial or profound reasons why we prefer or obsess about a certain colour, sound, word or perfume or there may be no reason at all except a physiological prefer- ence given at birth: to luxuriate in the word, colour, texture and roman- tic provenance of 'olive' but to abhor the taste creates an unavoidable ambivalence. The 'olive' becomes the 'curate's egg'—good in parts but the curate's egg can be subjective.

Together we produce x-trillion variegated preferences whereas indi- vidually our variations are miniscule but it's what makes you not me. These are the necessary limitations on the unlimited mind. No matter how much we try to second guess or out-wit our own leanings, learnings and obsessions we can never convincingly escape our own embedded psychological and physiological states.

But we are human so we try.

Artists of all disciplines try even harder. We try every subterfuge we can muster to undermine or overstep our given social, temporal, geographic and individual entrenchments by experimenting with form and content. We experimented to the point of abstraction via chance and random elements. From the psychic dabblings of the ouija board or planchette to found texts/objects, from surrealism to super realism,

from the nonsense rhymes of pre-speak to the disruptive devices of
tion and obliteration. The ultimate form is the attempted obliterati_
self or identity by forays into persona or pseudonym.

But no matter what subterfuge we employ if we work alone we always
have the last word. Such an effective self-policing of the mind can only
be truly disrupted by the invasive undermining or enhancement of an
other. This other is 'collaboration.' But collaboration can sometimes
lead to a very negative loss of control over one's work. It is a double-
edged sword which may add another voice that isn't necessarily going
where we want it to go. Even if we're not sure where that place is we
know if we are going in the wrong direction. It can be fraught and end
in tears before bedtime.

So I collaborate with the dead.

My first significant collaboration was with Gerard Manley Hopkins in
my long work *Interregnum* (Creation Books 1994). *Interregnum* is centred
around Pendle Hill in the north of England. Hopkins was stationed at
the Jesuit teaching college of Stonyhurst in the shadow of Pendle where
just under 3 centuries earlier the unhappy drama of the Pendle witches
had unfolded. They were eventually hanged in Lancaster in 1612 for
witchcraft. I was born in a neighbouring town and grew up with the
myth of the witches but not, alas, with the realisation that Hopkins had
lived so close by.

When researching the witches I came across one of their spells and it
seemed remarkably similar to some of Hopkins' poetry written during
his time at Stonyhurst. As it has always been my belief that the women,
whilst indulging in the usual spells and incantations of rural folk, were
practicing Roman Catholics under a king who had narrowly escaped
being assassinated in the Gunpowder Plot. The convergence of people,
place and religious belief was irresistible. The witches would speak
Hopkins in the section Chantcasters. Here are a couple of excerpts:

Wild air,
world-mothering air,
nestling me everywhere
that's fairly mixed
with riddles
and is rife
in every least things life
and nursing element

or

> What we have lighthanded left
> will have waked
> and have waxed
> and have walked
> with the wind.
> This side,
> that side hurling
> while we slumbered

or

> Three biters bitten:
> Earth's eye. Earth's tongue. Earth's heart.
> Our counterparts cleaved. Wreathed. Cloven.

Making extensive use of his poems written at Stonyhurst without alteration except editing down my only interjection is to slip in one of the witches' own spells (as in the above) which only a Hopkins scholar would be able to identify. It posits the question: if Hopkins had written what he did in the seventeenth century would he have been hanged? If the witches had written in the nineteenth century would we hail them as poets? How much does the balance of a life hang on its placement in time, social position and gender? My collaboration with Hopkins allowed me to expand and collapse many social, political and historical myths. Using my own words in this section, no matter how brilliant they may have been, could never have made the same impact as these chance collisions of words and worlds.

My next collaboration was with the Roman poets. A very short series of short poems with none of the words my own. The sequence was called 'Roman Rumourals.' Here's a couple:

> Lest heat flash from eyes
> surge burst the breast
> as if from grape
> bear my sour words
> find the names!
> [. . .]
> Raving past control so bright
> that darkles end I hate
> huge blocks unfixed
> trembling as for life
> markle me

Unlike Hopkins whose poems introduced a dichotomy of social and political injustice my Roman Rumourals were a total appropriation of poems by men but reworked and signed by a woman. I liked the fact that they may have disapproved of such a heresy. A form of retribution and redressing from the future but a retribution that is intended to be complimentary towards the work.

My latest work *Escafeld Hangings* (West House Books 2005) is similar in structure to *Interregnum* but here I have the stout, sometimes foolish, never dull and hopelessly romantic figure of Mary Stuart, Queen of the Scots as my main collaborator. Here I return to my enduring or preferred theme of wrongful or circumstantial imprisonment. Geographical place (Sheffield, England) and historical occurrence (Mary's 14 years imprisonment in Sheffield) galvanised by my own emotional attachment to the place (I live in Sheffield). I make such extensive use of Mary's letters and poems I am no longer sure which are her words and which are mine. Here is an excerpt from one of the letters to Queen Elizabeth I which we both wrote:

The stone walls steer a distraction then stare back. Can a mind pass my life by and leave a body wholesome? The meat is bad with rancid fat as I grow gauche and stringy and a monody of crashworthy ermines sways from the rafters and furthermore sways to a chanson some stocking-woman sang as a chit.

This is what a mind does mid mindless onrush.

At first glance the words gave up a system shock on reading 'several hands' as 'severed heads'—it speaks a maybe sleight of eye or worried mind or both conspiring on the side of darker plurals.

Collaboration with the dead is collaboration without permission. I've always felt comfortable with the dead and feel no qualms in what I am doing. I always acknowledged my sources and last year I took the whole thing a step further by 'inviting' John Donne into a collaboration with me and signing his name as joint author. I wouldn't do this to a living author because I have the option of asking them but with no such option available I take the consequences of my own actions and if there is an afterlife my requisitioned collaborators will have all eternity to wreak their anger upon my celestial being.

Here is what Monk and Donne did:

A Nocturnall Upon S. Lucies Day
Being The Shortest Day

Geraldine Monk & John Donne

Tis the yeares midnight,
                    it is the dayes, Lucies,
who scarce seaven
                    hours
herself unmaskes.

So place Iraq
ever-so-gently
into a state of
pending
wrap it fast in
swaddling clothes
tie a tinsel tag
around
its sore and sorry toe —
                    let it go
for the worlds all
sap is sunke:

> The generall balme
> th'hydroptique earth
> hath drunk,
> whither, as to
> the beds-feet,
> life is shrunke,
> dead and enterr'd;

laugh at

          we their

              Epitaph

bee spring thing
new alchimie
expresse
nothingness
emptiness
re-begot
                    not
                are not
            which are not
        things which are not
you me s/he re-begot
                        not
again
            of absence
dearth   of
                    things
            not
no
        things
                    not

lovers
        be
lovers
        be
next
        be
dead
        be
next

every dead thing
dull privations
leane
      on meanboned
beauty be bountyfling
ruin'd
       art
expressed
a quintessence even
from
no
things which are *not*
which are *not*
are *not*
things
no
      thingness
no
      thingness

no rest to wrest
rest to wrest
to wrest
wrest
-est
-st
-t

       Lucie   Loves   *Lucifer*
Darkkinglux   Hates   Queenblindlight
      lights fight to the death
          of life
       which light will win
         the dish
       brimming with eyes

before

            drawn-out-dawn

four candles play the vigil
on a precipice of hair

white-big big-frocked
     red
    sash't
   saffron buns
abreast all the sons
    yu-e-ss
     go
    the
   Star Boys
pointy hats erect

The lesser sun shines
     goat-runne-fetch
       new-lust

the body must
     be
here body
     be
must
   be
here
   be
body must
    be
the body must
      be

       as shadow

  if we an ordinary
    nothing
were

an echo caught
    in looped
      light

        prepare towards
       the yeares dayes deep
        midnight

        is

Editor's Note:

This article and poem were first published on the web at *Fascicle*, no. 2 (Winter 2005–2006):
1http://www.fascicle.com/issue02/main/contents02.htm.

Bibliography
GERALDINE MONK

BOOKS

Scarlet Opening (Staithes: Siren Press, 1974)

Invasion (Staithes: Siren Press, 1976)

Long Wake (London: Writers Forum/Pirate Press, 1979)

Rotations (Staithes: Siren Press, 1979)

Banquet (Staithes: Siren Press, 1980)

Spreading the Cards (Staithes: Siren Press, 1980)

La Quinta del Sordo (London: Writers Forum, 1980)

Tiger Lilies (Bradford: Rivelin Press, 1982)

Animal Crackers (London: Writers Forum, 1984)

Herein Lie Tales of Two Inner Cities (London: Writers Forum, 1986)

Sky Scrapers (Newcastle-upon-Tyne: Galloping Dog Press, 1985)

Quaquaversals (London: Writers Forum, 1990)

Walks in a Daisy Chain (Heptonstall: Magenta, 1991)

The Sway of Precious Demons: Selected Poems (Twickenham and Wakefield: North and South, 1992)

Interregnum (London: Creation Books, 1994)

Dream Drover (Cheltenham: Gratton Street Irregulars, 1999)

Trilogy (Sheffield: Gargoyle Editions, 2000) (includes versions of 'Prague Spring' 'Prelude V' and 'La Tormenta')

Noctivagations (Sheffield: West House Books, 2001)

Insubstantial Thoughts on the Transubstantiation of the Text (Sheffield: West House Books/The Paper, 2002)

Marian Hangings (Sheffield: Gargoyle Editions, 2002)

Mary Through the Looking Glass (Sheffield: Gargoyle Editions, 2002)

Absent Friends (Sheffield: Gargoyle Editions, 2002)

She Kept Birds (Somerville, MA: Slack Buddha Press, 2004)

A Nocturnall Upon S. Lucies Day Being The Shortest Day (Sheffield: Gargoyle Editions, 2004)

Escafeld Hangings (Sheffield: West House Books, 2005) (includes CD *Mary Through the Looking Glass* with Ligia Roque)

MISCELLANEOUS PROSE

'Move Over Darlings', Geraldine Monk and Maggie O'Sullivan, *City Limits*, July 13–19 (1984)

Survey response. 'Has my commitment as a writer changed since September 11th?' *Pores*, no. 2 (2002). Viewable at: http://www.pores.bbk.ac.uk/

'Working Note' and text of poem 'Opus Anglicanum', *How2*, vol. 2, no. 2 (Spring 2004). Viewable at: http://www.asu.edu/pipercwcenter/how2journal/archive/ online_archive/v2_2_2004/current/new_writing/monk.htm

ANTHOLOGIES

The New British Poetry: 1968–88. Eds. Gillian Allnutt, Fred D'Aguiar, Eric Mottram and Ken Edwards. (London: Paladin, 1988)

High on the Walls: An Anthology Celebrating Twenty-Five Years of Poetry Readings at Morden Tower. Ed. Gordon Brown. (Newcastle upon Tyne: Morden Tower/Bloodaxe Books, 1990)

Verbi Visi Voco: A Performance of Poetry. Eds. Bob Cobbing and Bill Griffiths. (London: Writers Forum, 1992)

Dust: A Creation Books Reader. Ed. Jack Hunter. London: (London: Creation Books, 1995)

Conductors of Chaos: A Poetry Anthology. Ed. Iain Sinclair. (London: Picador, 1996)

Out of Everywhere: Linguistically Innovative Poetry by Women in North America & the UK. Ed. Maggie O'Sullivan. (London: Reality Street Editions, 1996)

The Virago Book of Love Poetry. Ed. Wendy Mulford. (London: Virago, 1998)

OTHER: British and Irish Poetry since 1970. Eds. Richard Caddel and Peter Quartermain, (Hanover, New England and London: Wesleyan University Press, 1999)

Anthology of Twentieth-Century British and Irish Poetry. Ed. Keith Tuma. (New York: Oxford University Press, 2001)

Ahadada Reader 1. Ed. Jesse Glass. (Tokyo/Toronto: Ahadada Books, 2004)

RECORDINGS

Hidden Cities (London: Audio Arts Magazine, vol. 16, no. 1, 1996)

Hexentexts: A Creation Book Sampler (CD) (Hove: Codex, 1999) (with James Havoc, Alan Moore, Mick Norman, Jeremy Reed, Aaron Williamson)

Angel High Wires. Martin Archer and Geraldine Monk. (Tyne and Wear: La Cooka Ratcha/Voiceprint, 2001) LCVP149CD (Monk contributes texts but not voice on this recording)

Fluvium. Martin Archer, Geraldine Monk and Julie Tippetts (Sheffield: Discus Records, 2002) Discus14CD (Monk contributes texts and voice to this recording)

A twenty-four minute recording of Monk reading in 2004 is downloadable at the Pennsound website at: http://www.writing.upenn.edu/pennsound/x/XCP.html

Mary Through the Looking Glass. Geraldine Monk and Ligia Roque. (Sheffield: West House, 2005)

COMMISSIONS

A Brief in Inquisition for Sheffield Readers & Writers Festival, 1989

Reworking the Title for Sheffield City Art Galleries, 1990

Hidden Cities for Ruskin School of Fine Art, Oxford University, 1995

SECONDARY MATERIAL

Allen, T. Review of *Noctivagations*, published as 'A Droll Philology to Set Us Free', *Terrible Work* (2002). Viewable at: http://www.terriblework.co.uk/a_droll_philology_to_set_us_free. htm

Annwn, D. 'Her Pulse Their Pace, Women Poets and Basil Bunting' in *The Star You Steer By*, ed. by J. McGonigal and R. Price (Amsterdam & Atlanta: Rodopi Editions, 2000), pp. 123–48

Annwn, D. Review of *Noctivagations*, *The David Jones Journal* (Winter 2002 / Spring 2003), 133–136

Baker, T. Review of *Tiger Lilies*, *Reality Studios*, no. 5 (1983), 87–88

Bonney, S. Review of *Noctivagations*, in *Poetry Salzburg Review*, no. 3 (Autumn 2002), 58–61

Broom, S. *Contemporary British and Irish Poetry* (Basingstoke/New York: Palgrave Macmillan, 2006), pp. 241–245

Clay, J. Review of *Insubstantial Thoughts on the Transubstantiation of the Text*. *Readings* (2005). Viewable at: http://www.bbk.ac.uk/readings/r2/jon.html

Corless-Smith, M. Interview with Geraldine Monk, *Colorado Review*, vol. XXIX, no. 3 (Winter 2002), 175–181

Dorward, N. Review of *Noctivagations*, *The Gig*, no. 12 (November 2002), 58–60

Dorward, N. Review of *Fluvium*. *Paris Transatlantic* (April 2003). Viewable at: http://www.paristransatlantic.com/magazine/monthly2003/04apr_text.html

Dorward, N. Review of 'Camden People's Theatre Total Writing London, 27–29 June'. *Paris Transatlantic* (September 2003). Viewable at: http://www.paristransatlantic.com/magazine/monthly2003/09sep_text.html

Dorward, N. 'Latitudes: Geraldine Monk's Sequences', *The Paper*, no. 8 (September 2004), 49-58. A revised version now available on-line at: http://www.ndorward.com/poetry/articles_etc/monk_ latitudes.htm

Flores-Bórquez, M. '"A Nocturnall": Donne, Monk, Josipovici', *Intercapillary Space* (2006). Viewable at: http://intercapillaryspace.blogspot.com/2006/04/nocturnall-donne-monk-josipovici.html

Goodland, G. Review of *Escafeld Hangings*, Stride Website (2005). Viewable at: http://www.stridemagazine.co.uk//2005/Oct%202005/monk.goodland.htm

Hamilton-Emery, C. Review of *Noctivagations, Jacket*, no. 21 (February 2003). Viewable at: http://jacketmagazine.com/21/emery-monk.html

Hunt, I. Review of *Hidden Cities* tour, published as 'Babylon by Bus', *Art Monthly*, no. 191 (November 1995), 18–19

James, E. Interview with Geraldine Monk, broadcast on radio: 'Clear Spot' (co-presented with Caroline Bergvall), Resonance 104.4 FM, 22 January 2003

Kennedy, D. Review of *Noctivagations*, published as 'Writing Larks', *PN Review* 147 (September-October 2002) vol. 29, no. 1, 78–79

Kidd, H. 'The paper city: women, writing, and experience' in *New British Poetries: The Scope of the Possible*, ed. by Peter Barry and Robert Hampson (Manchester and New York: Manchester University Press: 1993), pp. 156–180 (pp. 176–177).

Kinnahan, L. A. 'Experimental poetics and the lyric in British women's poetry: Geraldine Monk, Wendy Mulford, and Denise Riley', *Contemporary Literature*, vol. 37, no. 4 (1996), 620–670. Reprinted as 'Theory and the Lyric 'I': Feminist Experimentalism in Britain', in Linda A. Kinnahan, *Lyric Interventions: Feminism, Experimental Poetry and Contemporary Discourse* (Iowa City: University of Iowa Press, 2004), pp. 180–221. See pp. 190–198 ('Positioning the 'I': Lyrical Practice and Geraldine Monk').

Nuttall, J. Review of *Invasion, Aquarius*, no. 9 (1977), 65

Peverett, M. Review of *Ahadada Reader 1*, first published in *Stride Magazine* 2005. Viewable at:
http://www.geocities.com/mpeverett/selhist6.htm#ahadada2004

Peverett, M. 'Geraldine Monk: Embellishment', *Intercapillary Space* (2006). Viewable at:
http://intercapillaryspace.blogspot.com/2006/05/geraldine-monk-embellishment.html

Presley, F. Review of *Dream Drover*, *How2*, vol. 1, no. 3 (February 2000). Viewable at:
http://www.scc.rutgers.edu/however/v1_3_2000/current/alerts/presley.html

Presley, F. Review of *Noctivagations*, published as 'Metablethers of Getha', *How2*, vol. 2, no. 1 (Spring 2003). Viewable at:
http://www.departments.bucknell.edu/stadler_center/how2/current/alerts/presley.shtm

Selerie, G. 'Introduction' (to 'A Selection of Contemporary British Poetry'), *North Dakota Quarterly*, vol. 51, no. 4 (Fall 1983), 5–18 (11–12)

Steele, L. Reviews of *Marian Hangings, Mary Through the Looking Glass, Absent Friends*, published as 'En ma Fin gît mon Commencement', *Intercapillary Space* (2006). Viewable at:
http://intercapillaryspace.blogspot.com/2006/05/en-ma-fin-gt-mon-commencement.html

Thurston, S. review of *Noctivagations*, Stride Website (2002). Viewable at:
http://stridemagazine.co.uk/2002/august/substantial.htm

Tuma, K. *Fishing by Obstinate Isles: Modern and Post-modern British Poetry and American Readers* (Evanston, Illinois: Northwestern University Press, 1998), pp. 229–233

Tuma, K. ed., *Anthology of Twentieth-Century British and Irish Poetry* (New York: Oxford University Press, 2001), p. 821

FURTHER RESOURCES

Edmund Hardy's *Intercapillary Space* webzine currently hosts a Geraldine Monk Hyper-link Chrestomathy: a compendium of Monk material published on the world wide web. It is viewable at: http://intercapillaryspace.blogspot.com/2006/05/geraldine-monk-hyper-link-chrestomathy.html

Hardy's site also hosts a Geraldine Monk celebration at: http://intercapillaryspace.blogspot.com/2006/03/fleet-rooms-geraldine-monk.html

Monk's author page at West House Books comprises a lengthy article illustrated with images, recordings and poems which Monk describes as 'an incomplete mapping of my poetry with places where I have lived that have become infused in my writing.' Viewable at: http://www.westhousebooks.co.uk/gmonk.asp

Monk's author page at the British Electronic Poetry Centre: http://www.soton.ac.uk/~bepc/poets/monk.htm

Index

Printed in the United Kingdom
by Lightning Source UK Ltd.
122931UK00001B/325/A